Power, Knowledge,
and Politics

American Governance and Public Policy series

Series Editor: Barry Rabe, University of Michigan

Selected Titles

Power, Knowledge, and Politics

Policy Analysis in the States

JOHN A. HIRD

Georgetown University Press
Washington, D.C.

For my parents,
Doris and John,
again

Georgetown University Press, Washington, D.C.
©2005 by Georgetown University Press. All rights reserved.
Printed in the United States of America

10 9 8 7 6 5 4 3 2 1   2005

This book is printed on acid-free recycled paper meeting
the requirements of the American National Standard
for Permanence in Paper for Printed Library Materials and
the Green Press Initiative.

Library of Congress Cataloging-in-Publication Data

Hird, John A.
Power, knowledge, and politics : policy analysis in the states / John A. Hird.
    p. cm. – (American governance and public policy)
  Includes bibliographical references and index.
    ISBN 1-58901-048-5 (cloth : alk. paper) – ISBN 1-58901-049-3 (pbk. :
alk. paper)
  1. Policy sciences—Research—United States—States.   2. Legislators—
United States—States—Decision making.   3. Political planning—United
States—States.   4. Government consultants—United States.   5. Research
institutes—United States.   I. Title.   II. Series.

H97.H566   2005
320.6′dc22   2004023155

Contents

List of Figures

List of Tables

Preface

The public does not normally hold state legislators in high regard, as evidenced by a joke circulating in Albany: "What's the difference between a state legislator and a welfare recipient? At least the welfare recipient has a work requirement" (Kolbert 2003, 39). Nonetheless, states and state legislatures remain important policymakers and receive little attention compared with federal agencies and the U.S. Congress. States are particularly interesting methodologically because they offer the prospect of comparing different institutional environments across fifty states that share many common features, such as language and representative forms of government. This book is not, however, about states but about the relationship of knowledge to power, and states—and state legislatures in particular—provide excellent vehicles to explore this relationship.

When I was in graduate school in California in the 1980s, the state Legislative Analysts Office (LAO) had an outstanding reputation, and was known to be the state's equivalent of the Congressional Budget Office. Then as now, it hired exceptional analysts, commented broadly and thoughtfully on legislative proposals and citizen referenda, addressed controversial topics, and was—and continues to be—well regarded in the scholarly policy community. Upon moving to a teaching job in Massachusetts, I had expected that every state—at least relatively wealthy states with activist state governments, such as California and Massachusetts—would have an equivalent type of legislative agency. Massachusetts did have such an office,

called the Legislative Services Bureau (LSB), but it was completely
unlike the LAO. Although it provided basic services to Massachusetts legislators, the LSB did not conduct policy analysis. Most of its
functions consisted of helping legislators do their jobs (assistance on
how to organize their offices, how to record and respond to consti-
tuent communication, and so on), but very few of its functions
involved research or even information provision on matters of importance to the Commonwealth. The Speaker of the House eliminated its budget in 2001 and, tellingly, the LSB was insufficiently
useful to anyone for its demise to generate any public opposition.

As a result of what seemed to be an unusual pair of institutional
structures—two wealthy progressive states with professional legislatures, one of which had an outstanding nonpartisan policy research
organization (NPRO) and the other none at all—I wanted to learn
more about how other state legislatures organized their policy research. As it turned out, the nonpartisan policy analysis provided to
state legislatures varied tremendously from one state to the next,
even states with similar characteristics (e.g., Florida and Texas have
large offices, while New York and New Jersey have virtually none).
Some part-time legislatures in relatively poor states had much stronger policy analysis organizations than those in wealthy states with
professional legislatures. Furthermore, other expected predictors of
state analytical capacity—such as political culture, region, party affiliation, degree of legislative professionalism, and so on—did not
seem, at least on casual observation, to comport with the strength
of policy analysis capability.

A second and related puzzle was that there seemed to be little
concern among the full-time professional Massachusetts state senators and representatives for the dearth of nonpartisan policy analysis capacity in the legislature. One smart and powerful legislator told
me that he saw little need for such an office in the statehouse, yet
he was a frequent consumer of policy analysis from other sources. For
years, I had been interested in how policy analysis and research are
used by policymakers, but this pattern seemed unusual. Smart consumers of policy analysis did not demand that their legislatures provide nonpartisan policy analysis, while state legislatures in some

states had strong capacity and others had little or no nonpartisan policy analysis assistance.

Much of the extant research on how policy analysis is used in policymaking explores it as a one-way relationship, yet this book is as much about how power affects expertise as it is about how expertise affects power. Policy analysis shops in state legislatures have great potential to inform power and democratize decision making, but only a portion of that has been realized. They are, in some circumstances, seen as important influences over public policy, yet their influence has come at a price. Buffeted by partisanship and advocacy, both within the legislature and outside, NPROs have not been "politicized" (in the pejorative sense). Instead, they have become exceedingly neutral, providing relevant information in a timely manner, and yet devoid of the independence and creativity of the best of policy analysis. They have become such products of the legislature—politicized in another sense—that they are reactive, for the most part responding to inquiries rather than promoting new perspectives or generating analysis that challenges preexisting ideas or power relationships. Their relationship to power and expertise has allowed NPROs to become influential in some sense but only influential in ways congenial to legislative demands for neutrality. Their power, mostly as information providers, has come at the expense of independence—they provide useful knowledge and remain trusted advisers—but at the heavy cost of losing the ability to challenge prevailing norms and to bring new ideas, perspectives, and analysis to the legislative milieu. As a result, NPROs are unlikely to improve the policymaking discourse in ways that would redress the imbalance in many areas of expertise that favors moneyed interests over those lacking financial and expert resources.

As with any substantial effort, there are many people to thank for their contributions. My deepest gratitude is to the many hundreds of legislators and NPRO directors who responded to various written and telephone surveys and interviews. I could not have accomplished this work without their assistance, yet I was struck by how thoroughly respondents completed surveys and by the number and length of follow-up e-mail messages that I received that elaborated on their responses, provided additional examples, and commented thoughtfully on the relationship of knowledge and power in their legislatures; all are quoted anonymously in the text. It is my hope that some elements of this book will ring true with some legislators and that reforms will take shape that will strengthen the information base on which legislators rely for making decisions and learning about policy perspectives and possibilities. I would also like to extend thanks to the National Conference of State Legislatures (NCSL), and particularly to Brian Weberg, for survey assistance and for providing me with access to NCSL's electronic database of state legislators nationwide. Thanks also to Andrew Rich for providing me data on state think tanks, and to the Center for Public Policy and Administration and the College of Social and Behavior Sciences at the University of Massachusetts, Amherst, for financial support. Susan Etzel and Matthew Shilvock from the university's Master's Program in Public Policy and Administration provided superlative research assistance.

CHAPTER 1

The Development and Limitations of Policy Analysis

Policy analysis is conducted in nearly every university, every medium- to large-sized city in the United States, every state capital, every federal agency, and—copiously—for the U.S. Congress and White House. So-called "think tanks" have proliferated in the past thirty years, generating vast quantities of policy research and becoming so pervasive as to be considered by some as "virtually a new branch of the political system" (Ricci 1993). Graduate schools of public affairs—some 250 of them—train students in policy analysis and administration, sending off thousands of graduates each year, ostensibly to improve public policy and its administration. Policy experts fill high- and middle-brow television, such as *The NewsHour* (PBS) and *Crossfire* (CNN). As the profession dedicated to understanding and improving what governments do grows, the terms "public policy" and "policy expert" have entered the lexicon of the average citizen. In many respects, policy analysis has arrived.

Or has it? The proliferation of policy analysis and analysts has yet to be matched by an examination of whether the annual production of hundreds of thousands of memos, briefings, articles, reports, books, and sundry policy prognostications—informed and other-wise—is actually useful to policymakers. For all of the emphasis placed on policy research by both providers and prospective users, there has been little systematic research on the relationship between policy research and the research needs of policymakers.[1] Although policy researchers and analysts have a vague belief that their research must be useful in some sense—after all, why else would someone pay for it?—there is only limited empirical evidence linking policy research with its use. What we do know is not encouraging. "In public policy making, many suppliers and users of social science research are dissatisfied, the former because they are not listened to, the latter because they do not hear much they want to listen to" (Lindblom and Cohen 1979, 1). Contemporary studies rarely attempt to link policy reports and analyses with policy outcomes, partly for methodological reasons and partly because there is little past evidence that all of this policy analysis actually influences decisions. More recent studies seeking to identify whether policy analysis influences policymaking take an indirect path: If policy analysis is even mentioned in legislative committee reports, this is evidence of its use (Shulock 1999). Understanding different meanings of "use" has been an important contribution of the knowledge utilization literature and underscores how little "use" of a traditional means—influencing policy—has been found to take place.

This book engages these issues in different ways. Rather than studying individual policy reports or studies, or even focusing exclusively on written material, my focus is on *institutions* that policymakers create for the express purpose of providing them with germane policy information and analysis. I argue that past attempts to understand knowledge utilization are seeing only part of the influence of policy analysis. By concentrating most of their attention on written products, scholars have missed the potential for the substantial influence of individuals and organizations quite apart from their written products. That is, policy analysts qua professionals, who develop personal relationships, policy networks, and the trust of policymakers, may have greater influence than previous analyses of written products suggest. This volume examines the nature of the policy institutions that policymakers establish and sustain, representing a more complete reflection of what *policymakers* most want from policy analysts rather than what scholars surmise they want. Furthermore, rather than studying one organization, this volume examines institutions comparatively, tests theories of the use of policy analysis, and in so doing draws more generalized conclusions than can be drawn from single cases. Finally, this study examines nonpartisan policy research organizations (NPROs) operating in highly political environments: state legislatures. This provides a particularly rigorous test of whether and how nonpartisan policy research can survive in highly political environments. This book's principal contributions are to compare policy analysis institutions systematically across different political environments, to assess the use of policy analysis by examining institutions rather than individual studies, to evaluate comparatively the "success" of policy analysis with reference to policymakers' assessments, and to evaluate both the impact of policy analysis on policymaking and the reciprocal impact of politics on policy analysis institutions.

This chapter introduces the tensions between the values of science and democracy and describes the growth and practice of policy analysis in the United States. The book's motivation and purpose are explained in the context of providing expertise in democratic decision making. This book poses the following questions, which are subsequently addressed:

- Are policy analysis and research useful to policymakers?
- What types are useful and under what circumstances?
- Do political institutions shape the nature of policy analysis?
- What is the relationship of knowledge to power?
- Does the application of expertise promote democratic decision making, or does it vest power in an unelected and unaccountable elite?
- If knowledge is power, then what type of knowledge is powerful, and in which circumstances is it most likely to be used?

POLICY ANALYSIS EXPERTISE IN DEMOCRATIC DECISION MAKING

The tension between expertise and popular political participation in democratic decision making throughout the world is old, with manifestations ranging from the founders' disagreements over appropriate means of national government representation, to the role of scientific risk assessment in contemporary environmental decision making (e.g., deLeon 1997, Fischer 2000; Roy 2001). Duncan

MacRae notes that "science and democracy symbolise alternative modes of guiding society" (MacRae 1973, 228). Furthermore, he sees conflict between science and democracy in policy that applies to science and in the appropriate role of science in forming public policy (228). He cautions that "the risk of technocracy lies in the possibility of an uncontrolled power held by an elite and devoted to special values or interests rather than to the general welfare" (p. 233). The diverging values of science and democracy sustain this tension, yet previous work has provided conceptual space for a reformulated expertise and democracy to be mutually reinforcing (e.g., MacRae 1976). Similar issues and tensions arise in explaining the proper role of policy analysis in government decision making: Does policy expertise promote democratic decision making, vest power in an unelected and unaccountable elite, or become co-opted by political actors and exigencies? Or, is policy analysis, in practice, "more a tool of the democratic process than the problem-solving process," as one author suggests (Shulock 1999, 227) rather than antidemocratic?

Policy analysis institutions have proliferated at the national level, with growth in both the number and size of formal institutions, such as the General Accounting Office (GAO) and Congressional Budget Office (CBO), as well as think tanks, consulting firms, and others that provide information and analysis in support of policy-making (Abelson 2002; Whiteman 1995). Numerous studies have investigated the use of policy analysis in the U.S. Congress (e.g., Haveman 1976; Jones 1976; A. Rich 2001). Although the nature and degree of influence wielded by policy analysis is unclear, many commentators argue that policy analysis has only a modest influence over public policy debates, and its impacts—even when important—are largely indirect (Shulock 1999; Whiteman 1995). Even in Weiss's study involving interviews with numerous congressional committee staffers, which argues that there is a "trend . . . toward greater receptivity" (Weiss 1989, 422) to analysis, she concludes, "Congressional committee staff were clear that analysis doesn't have a chance of setting broad direction for public policy" (p. 428). Other studies focus on the use of policy analysis in individual agencies (e.g., Farrow 1991) or in specific policy domains (e.g., Haskins 1991). Regardless of the conclusions, studies of the use of policy analysis and research are notable for four characteristics: They treat policy analysis as an "independent variable" that may (or, most often, does not) influence policymaking; they are nearly always studies of U.S. federal agencies or policies; they frequently emphasize written policy research rather than examining the impacts of individuals or organizations; and they frequently study one agency or policy area rather than comparative research.[2]

Scholars and policymakers alike have an incomplete understanding of how and under which circumstances policy research and analysis are used in policymaking and, as importantly, know little about how politics influences the conduct of policy analysis. This stems from three problems. First, the traditional approach of tracing the path from written policy research to policymaking is problematic. As one observer said to a researcher, "One of the difficulties with your study [on the use of policy analysis] is that you are studying the effect of a microdose of information on a political system . . . so I would think that if you found any impact at all it would be a miracle" (Whiteman 1995, 155). Carol Weiss (1982) adds, "Inevitably, it is extraordinarily difficult to gauge the impact of a single input into the vast, complicated, and highly interactive processes of government action" (p. 13). Therefore, this approach is unlikely to yield strong conclusions because the independent influence of policy analysis on decision making is very difficult to isolate, particularly when studying any "microdose" of information, i.e., an individual study or report on a policy process where outcomes are indistinct. Second, most previous inquiries have been individual case studies of agencies (e.g., Bimber 1996) or policy domains (e.g., Szanton 1991) at the federal level. These excellent studies offer a rich understanding of individual circumstances, but provide little basis for generalization to other agencies and other institutional arrangements. As a result, the development of theory on policy expertise in democratic governance has been hindered by a limited set of methods and a relatively narrow scope of inquiry. Finally, studies of the use of policy analysis— based on an older analyst–client relationship—focus almost exclusively on trying to understand how individual studies or (occasionally) agencies affect policymaking. In social science terms, the dependent variable that knowledge utilization researchers have employed repeatedly—impact on policy—ignores the reverse possibility: that policymakers and institutions in turn affect policy analysis.

SOCIAL SCIENCE RESEARCH AND POLICY ANALYSIS

The belief that natural and behavioral sciences could consistently inform public policymaking is a recent phenomenon in the United States. Most of the growth in the use of policy analysis occurred after World War II, when the recognition that experts could assist government was married with growing budgets supporting research. During World War II itself, research and development (R&D) expenditures are estimated to have grown from $100 million to $1.5 billion, a fifteen-fold increase in the five-year period from 1940 to 1945 (Featherman and Vinovskis 2001a, 42).

After World War II, it was increasingly recognized that natural and social scientists could help inform policymaking by building on their wartime experience in both natural science (e.g., development of the atomic bomb, improvements in radar) and social sciences (e.g., economic planning, survey research). The scientific success during the war could, it was assumed, now be directed to improving the quality of life at home, and the boom in research funding continued through the 1960s. Overall, federal spending on R&D, as a percentage of total federal outlays, reached an all-time high of 11.7 percent in 1965, up from 2.4 percent in 1949 and compared with just under 5 percent today (see figure 1.1). As a percentage of gross domestic product (GDP), federal outlays on R&D rose from 0.3 percent in 1949 to 2.2 percent in 1964, and are today approximately 1.0 percent.[3] Federal spending on R&D reached its peak (as a percentage of outlays) in the mid-1960s; at the same time, social science began to be seen as an important contributor to policy formation and change. Basic and applied research spending in the Department of Health, Education, and Welfare (HEW) rose from $83 million in 1956 to more than $427 million in 1961 and more than $1 billion dollars by 1967.[4] As important, the development of civilian research meant both that basic research and federal funding became nearly inseparable. Federally funded research was now conducted not just in federal agencies, but also through newly established federal laboratories, think tanks, and universities. Consequently, federal funding of research permeated academia. Federal civilian employment similarly saw a marked increase in the post–World War II period and in the mid- to late 1960s, indicated by the line graph in figure 1.1. Increases in civilian employment generated new plateaus that continued through the 1980s, with a steady decline beginning in 1991 and continuing nearly unabated through 2001.

Arguably, social scientists have had a greater impact on policy-making through their employment in federal agencies and in prestigious roles in presidential administrations than through copious federal funding for the social sciences. There was early opposition in Congress to National Science Foundation funding for social

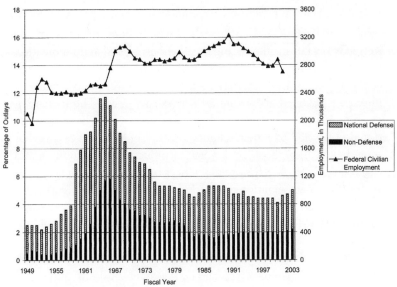

Summary of Outlays for the Conduct of Research and Development; 1949–2003
Source: U.S. Government Printing Office 2002, Table 9.7.

Federal Civilian Employment, 1949–2001.
Source: 1970–2001: U.S. Bureau of the Census 2002, Table No. 473, p.320; 1949–1969: U.S. Bureau of the Census 1975, p. 1102.

Figure 1.1   Research and Development Spending as a Percentage of Outlays, and Federal Civilian Employment, 1949–2003

science research; although funding continued to increase, the level of funding for social science research was (and remains) infinitesimal in comparison with that for medical, natural, and biological science research. Nonetheless, funding for social science research did increase but, more importantly, the prominence of social scientists in government expanded considerably, almost as if social scientists were judged to be more valuable qua individuals than qua researchers.

Although the social sciences grew in prestige and public recognition, economics attained the greatest level of social scientific prominence from World War II through the 1960s. President Truman signed the Full Employment Act of 1946, which not only charged the president with maintaining full employment and price stability, but also established a new Council of Economic Advisers to advise the president. Economists were recognized for their assistance in setting prices and allocating goods during the war, but they now had a formal institutional role in government not enjoyed by any of the other social sciences then or today.[5] The apparent success of the Kennedy tax cut in stimulating the economy served as an indication that the economy could truly be "fine-tuned" through new forms of economic analysis, ultimately with the widely repeated remark by President Nixon that "we are all Keynesians now." The increasing prominence of technically sophisticated researchers in setting national policy led to a new reliance on the social sciences. In what some have called their "golden age of influence" (Featherman and Vinovskis 2001a, 40), the social sciences became a focus of attention as the 1960s saw operations research, benefit-cost analysis, survey research, applied statistics, and other forms of social science research reach new levels of prominence in the Kennedy and Johnson administrations.

The belief that social science—and economics in particular—could guide policymakers was matched by an enthusiasm in the early 1960s that government could act decisively to improve public welfare. David Halberstam describes the exuberant feelings toward the new Kennedy administration:

> It was a glittering time. They literally swept into office, ready, moving, generating their style, their confidence—they were ready

to get America moving again. There was a sense that these were brilliant men, men of force, not cruel, not harsh, but men who acted rather than waited. There was no time to wait, history did not permit that luxury; if we waited it would all be past us. Everyone was going to Washington, and the word went out quickly around the Eastern seacoast, at the universities and in the political clubs, that the best men were going to Washington. Things were going to be done and it was going to be great fun; the challenge awaited and these men did not doubt their capacity to answer that challenge. . . . It seems long ago now, that excitement which swept through the country, or at least the intellectual reaches of it, that feeling that America was going to change, that the government had been handed down from the tired, flabby chamber-of-commerce mentality of the Eisenhower years to the best and brightest of a generation. (Halberstam 1983, 50)

The new Washingtonians were, in short, consummate policy analysts (other than the fact that most were male): smart, well-trained people of action trying to improve public life. Unlike previous advisers, the new breed earned their positions less by their experience than by their scholarly connections and aptitudes. About this there were mixed feelings: After Vice President Johnson reported excitedly of the brilliance of the new administration to Sam Rayburn, the latter replied, presciently, "Well, Lyndon, you may be right and they may be every bit as intelligent as you say, but I'd feel a whole lot better about them if just one of them had run for sheriff once" (Halberstam 1983, 53).

On the heels of the Kennedy tax cuts that were credited with stimulating the economy in the early 1960s, the belief in the power of social science to solve social problems escalated to the point where many believed that politics and policy were separable. Indeed, President Kennedy himself apparently believed many social problems were no longer political:

Most of us are conditioned for many years to have a political viewpoint, Republican or Democratic—liberal, conservative, moderate. The fact of the matter is that most of the problems, or at least many of them, that we now face are technical problems, are administrative problems. They are very sophisticated judgments, which do not lend themselves to the great sort of "passionate movements" which have stirred this country so often in the past. Now they deal with questions which are beyond the comprehension of most men, most governmental administrators, over which experts may differ, and yet we operate through our traditional political system. (Quoted in Aaron 1978, 167)

This emphasis on technique and analysis, coupled with federal and foundation funding, gave rise to the establishment of many new "think tanks" in Washington, DC, and elsewhere, as well as numerous presidential commissions studying education and welfare reforms. One study notes that nearly two-thirds of the Washington-based think tanks were established after 1970 (Smith 1991, 214). The expected achievements of scholars in policymaking reached the general public as well. In a series of articles in *Life* in 1967, Theodore White wrote of

> a new power system in American life . . . a new priesthood of action-intellectuals. . . . This brotherhood of scholars [had become] the most provocative and propelling influence on all American government and politics. Their ideas are the drivewheels of The Great Society: shaping our defenses, guiding our foreign policy, redesigning our cities, reorganizing our schools, deciding what our dollar is worth. . . . For such intellectuals now is the Golden Age, and America is the place. Never have ideas been sought more hungrily or tested against reality more quickly. From White House to city hall, scholars stalk the corridors of American power. (Quoted in Wood 1993, 33)

The belief that government functions could be rationalized led to President Johnson's Planning, Programming, and Budgeting System (PPBS), which was intended to bring analytical rigor to budgetary matters. Although PPBS was regarded ultimately as a failure, it led to many federal agencies developing their own in-house policy shops. These actions were preconditioned by the belief that social problems could be addressed as quickly and easily as technical ones.

The faith in government action, long embraced by reformers and spread to the mass of the population by the depression and war, achieved political expression in the 1960s. . . . The depression had lasted a decade, but it had been ended. Military victory in the Second World War had taken the United States less than four years to achieve. Eight years after President Kennedy announced a commitment to put a man on the moon, the promise was fulfilled. Perhaps the problems to which the War on Poverty and Great Society legislation were addressed were more difficult but, on the record, progress should have been perceptible and swift. (Aaron 1978, 151)

The heady days in the early 1960s—when operations research, benefit-cost analysis, and technical virtuosity were expected to *solve* social problems—soon vanished with the acknowledgment that the "best and the brightest" provided disastrous advice to the president on the war in Vietnam. The eroding confidence in social science was part of a much larger erosion of general faith in government. After the Vietnam War, Watergate, and a long, slow deterioration of the national economy suffering from both economic stagnation and inflation ("stagflation") of the 1970s, the belief that government would or could achieve important national goals abated, and, in turn, confidence that social science research could assist decision makers declined. Even Keynesian economists were humbled as attention turned from how to "fine tune" the economy to how to limit the upward spiral of *both* unemployment and inflation, a shocking turn of events to "Phillips Curve" predictions of a trade-off between inflation and unemployment. On its heels, confidence in government and public policy research eroded with the general public's perception that the "war on poverty" had been lost despite all the social science research, demonstration projects, and money poured into solving the poverty problem. Studies trying to establish linkages between social science research and policy decision making failed to find any evidence that social science and policy research was "speaking truth to power," at least in any positive sense, an ironic conclusion because the failings of social science were seen as partly responsible for policy failures. Prominent books—such as Moynihan's *Maximum Feasible Misunderstanding*—criticized education policy, urban renewal, and welfare policies as being not only ineffective, but downright harmful. Frustration mounted; as one scholar wrote, "If we can land a man on the moon, why can't we solve the problems of the ghetto? The question stands as a metaphor for a variety of complaints about the uneven performance of the American political economy" (Nelson 1977, 13). No one expected social science to choose social or economic goals, but increasingly people expected it to provide assistance in meeting identified goals. The belief that social science principles could help achieve commonly held goals (such as poverty alleviation) was questioned. This became "a crescendo of unrelenting attacks on the policies forged in the sixties and the academic research that underlay them" (Wood 1993, 113). The nearly limitless aspirations and hopes of social science to influence policy were replaced with deep skepticism and a neoconservative backlash. Policy analysis had been humbled.

TWO COMMUNITIES

The inevitable response to the vast expansion of R&D spending after World War II was a review of how scientific knowledge is used by decision makers and how it could be used more effectively. (The irony of how social science research could both be perceived as uninfluential and yet be blamed for social ills attracted little attention.) Explanations abound for why there is, as one scholar puts it, "So much social science, so little policy impact" (Danziger 2001). The inability of social science to make a clear, positive, and long-lasting impact on public policy has been traced to differences in the "two cultures" of science and policymaking (Snow 1961). C. P. Snow, before most others, was writing about the potential difficulties facing those who hoped to improve the connection between science and government. Snow pointed to two completely different cultures, and even personalities, drawn to scientific research on the one hand and policymaking on the other. Perceptively, he drew attention to a "common scientific temperament" that differed from that of administrators.

> A great many scientists have a trace of the obsessional. Many kinds of creative science, perhaps most, one could not do with-

out it. To be any good, in his youth at least, a scientist has to think of one thing, deeply and obsessively, for a long time. An administrator has to think of a great many things, widely, in their interconnections, for a short time. There is a sharp difference in the intellectual and moral temperaments. I believe . . . that persons of scientific education can make excellent administrators and provide an element without which we shall be groping: but I agree that scientists in their creative periods do not easily get interested in administrative problems and are not likely to be much good at them. (Snow 1961, 72)

Snow was not the only one to write about these differences between people of action and thought:

One sure mark of the man of action is to use intuitions in place of abstractions and this is true even in a society like ours, where skills are so generally explicit and "know-how" is so much discussed. The man of thought is very different; he will make a small cosmos out of the smallest experience. (Bryson 1951, 321)

As to solutions, Snow asks,

Is there any way, in this great underground domain of science and government, in which we can arrange to make choices a little more reasonably? . . . The whole problem is an intractable one, one of the most intractable that organised society has thrown up. It is partly the expression, in political and administrative terms, of the split between two cultures. (Snow 1961, 66–67)

Ultimately, Snow advocated for scientists to have a greater role in policymaking positions, although this extended mostly to the natural sciences (and not, to use his example, to engineers), who he believes possess what "our kind of existential society is desperately short of . . . foresight" (1961, 81).

A more recent explanation, which was once the most prominent explanation applied to social science research, is the "two-communities theory," based in principle on Snow's work and proposed by Nathan Caplan. Because scientists and policymakers have such different orientations, newer thinking indicated that social scientists—sometimes eager to mimic their natural science colleagues—could never expect to make an immediate impact on public policy, and that policymakers could not expect social science research to offer the kind of short-term, policy-relevant information and analysis they needed. Caplan contends that the community of scholars is, for a variety of reasons, unable to capture the attention or earn the trust of the community of policymakers[6] (Caplan 1979).

Why, according to this model, are there two communities? The reasons can be traced to the actions of both camps. Invoking the "ivory tower" image, the academic community of scholars writes for different audiences, and therefore sometimes produces analyses that are badly written, off target, poorly communicated, lacking in concrete policy recommendations, pedantic, ignorant of politics, or simplistic. James Wilson states, "Under most circumstances, social science research is not very useful for getting to any position. I am struck by the fact that, on any given topic that has become a crisis, the amount of extant, policy-relevant, well-done social science research is just about zero. Social scientists offer their advice to these commissions, but their advice is rarely the product of research" (Wilson 1978, 85). A related explanation is that policy analysts fail to engage the public in their analysis, preferring instead to "speak truth to power." Proponents of this view argue that analysts must change the forms of analysis used and engage broader constituencies if they hope to have more—and more appropriately democratic— influence (deLeon 1997; Fischer 1992).

Policymakers share some of the blame with scholars. They are often guilty of commissioning research efforts in order to delay a decision, to deflect criticism, to gain prestige, or to justify preconceived policy positions. Although scholars complain that their research is never used to make decisions, it is possible that it is not so used because it was never intended for that purpose. A variation on the demand side impediments is that policymakers do not need or care about analysis to make decisions; they reach decisions through other means, and use research to legitimize their positions rather than as an input to devising or choosing among alternatives (Lindblom 1986; Weiss and Bucuvalas 1980).

Somewhat ironically, around the same time that scholars and policymakers recognized that policy analysis's reach exceeded its grasp, policy analysis had been institutionalized in government agencies and a language of policy analysis—with its emphasis on marginalism, opportunity costs, decision trees, and so forth—began to permeate the discourse of policy debates. "At the turn of the twenty-first century, the notion that public policy should rest on social science was widely, though not universally, accepted by national governments and by the cosmopolitan elite of international finance and trade, international advocacy, and cooperation" (Anderson 2003, 81). Policy schools can, as a result, make a strong pitch to prospective students that to be effective in the policy world, one needs to understand the many perspectives that converge to form and change policy and its administration. These schools were, in effect, recognizing the belief that, "The resource in shortest supply in the development of good programs is not good research, but wise, farseeing, shrewd, and organizationally effective managers" (Wilson 1978, 92). Policy schools meant to train them.

THE GROWTH OF SCHOOLS OF PUBLIC POLICY

Theodore White argued that the potential success of the "action-intellectuals" was their ability to join government and ideas: "Between idea-producers and government stretches a gulf and across this gulf the action-intellectuals throw up a bridge" (quoted in Wood 1993, 33). Recognizing the need to train analysts who could bridge the two cultures of research and policymaking, major American universities began developing new schools of public policy (e.g., Berkeley's Graduate School of Public Policy) or augmenting existing programs with a new analytical focus (e.g., Harvard's Masters in Public Policy Program, which later became the Kennedy School of Government). Although to the public there is little distinction between public policy and public administration, the new faculty recruited to teach in public policy programs saw their positions as both newer and intellectually more elevated than their public administration counterparts. (Hierarchy knows no bounds in the academic world.)

The development of policy schools was strongly influenced by the belief that social science, and particularly quantitative, positivist social science, could have a profound impact on public policy—as the "whiz kids" did under Robert McNamara's defense department. The curricula of the new policy schools in the 1960s emphasized microeconomics, statistics, and mathematical approaches to policymaking, with the belief that better techniques would translate to better policymaking. It was thought that the intellectually moribund task of figuring out how to implement policies would be left to public administration specialists. Politics, management, budgeting, and traditional public administration courses were seen as "old school," and given short shrift in the new policy school curricula. Given the receptivity of national policymakers—including Presidents Kennedy and Johnson—to modern policy analysis, who could blame them? Their technique was scientific, as opposed to the old-style descriptive techniques of public administration. And their skills were in demand, as evidenced by the new emphasis on operations research, benefit-cost analysis, and program evaluation, all of which required analytical training not found in public administration faculty or curricula.

Policy schools were developed in the 1960s with similar attitudes: Public problems were essentially technical ones that could be resolved with modern techniques. Therefore, society needed more analysts trained in these technical fields, with little need for how to put together political coalitions, manage an agency, marshal resources to achieve collective ends, manage personnel, and undertake other traditional tasks left to the much-maligned public administration scholars. The academy's belief in the efficacy of method and technique was fully consistent with the more general belief that public policy could be crafted—indeed, *is* more effectively crafted—with as little reference to politics and public administration as possible.

Over time, more-enlightened views saw that both managerial and political skills were essential to success in the policy world. The reasons why well-intentioned policies were wrecked remained underappreciated until studies of implementation yielded the recognition that to implement meant to wield policymaking influence (Bardach 1977; Lipsky 1983; Pressman and Wildavsky 1984). To the common understanding of the analyst as *technician* (the "objective" and apolitical analyst) or *politician* (politically adept yet lacking analytical skills) was added a new category—the policy *entrepreneur*—that ideally spans both the analytical and political functions of the modern analyst (Meltsner 1976). Policy schools train analysts to be problem solvers in virtually any situation, whether it involves municipal refuse collection, managing a budget office, planning transportation systems, designing income transfer programs, or developing a new international nongovernmental organization (NGO). Students are taught a set of skills to enable them to solve all manner of problems, using the "eight-fold path" or some close variation.[7] The topics range from international affairs to local government, from the private to nonprofit to public sectors, and cross into every imaginable policy area. This, in effect, was the answer from the academic community to the "two cultures" problem: develop a third culture—policy analysts—that could span the political and research communities. This was also the primary justification for the development of new schools of public policy—that the "two communities" problem could be overcome by the introduction of a new cadre of policy analysts trained to operate effectively in both worlds to be effective consumers of scholarly research and apply relevant findings to public policymaking. Seldom was it recognized that they could serve the reverse role: to influence research based on policymakers' needs.

CRITICS OF POLICY ANALYSIS

Although policy schools were blossoming all over the country, ultimately offering doctoral degrees in public policy and forming their own association,[8] scholars began questioning whether policy analysis was even a useful tool to contribute to democratic deliberation, suggesting that its wanton application could create antidemocratic tendencies leading to elite control over policymaking.

Traditionalist Critiques

There is no doubt that policy analysis and applied research have proliferated over the past thirty years; nevertheless, their usefulness has been sharply questioned both theoretically and empirically. Some scholars, those more sympathetic to the application of policy analysis, place the problem in the political system where policy analysis operates. David Kirp makes the broad empirically based argument that changes in American political culture—including a focus on the greater personalization of politics, the emphasis on passion rather than reason, and over-promising by politicians—make the application of research to results all but impossible. He concludes, "Changes in American politics, policy, and the polity—changes that are abidingly hostile to the possibilities of analysis—are not ephemeral and reversible but deep, structural, and permanent" (Kirp 1992, 694). Therefore, Kirp's challenge for policy analysis is to conform to the new political reality or face political oblivion, if the latter can be avoided at all.

Other scholars adopt a modified "two communities" theory to explain differences between expert advice and policy outcomes. Economist Paul Krugman employs a simple model of politics to explain why contemptible economic ideas triumph over the deeper and more subtle thoughts of scholars. In *Peddling Prosperity*, Krugman argues that economic idea merchants are of two types: professors and policy entrepreneurs. The professors are scholars who think deeply about economic problems but, alas, are unable to provide answers to basic economic questions such as why income inequality is growing in the United States. Although some of the economics professors may be stereotypically stodgy and pedantic, others, like Krugman himself, write and speak directly and engagingly. The problem, according to Krugman (and Kirp), is not that the professors cannot speak to the public, but that there is no demand for their thoughts. Krugman argues that politicians want definite answers to difficult economic questions, but are frustrated that the professors sometimes acknowledge that they do not know the answers and that the answers they do provide are not always reducible to sound bites. This is where Krugman's policy entrepreneurs come into the picture, in an entirely demand-driven way. Because politicians crave short, simple answers to difficult, complex questions, and because the professors cannot (or will not) provide suitable responses to them, policy entrepreneurs are all too willing to bastardize the serious work of scholars into a simple and seemingly plausible story that politicians can sell to voters (Krugman 1995b).

Krugman believes that good analysis is frequently available but that hacks are constantly either ignoring or misinterpreting what economists know.[9] Underlying his account is the implicit belief that *ideas matter*; Krugman's gripe is that the wrong ideas hold excessive sway. Ideas can be important in subtle ways.

> Ideas matter because they establish the contexts within which policy debates are conducted, organizational activities are rendered coherent and meaningful, and people's actions are animated and directed. Ideas nominate particular people to do particular kinds of work and give them support for doing the indicated work. . . . The ideas define the conventional wisdom in the area, set out the questions for which evidence is necessary, suggest the alternative policies that are plausibly effective, and (most important), keep alternative formulations of the problem off the public agenda. (Moore 1990, 72)

Another demand-side limitation involves the nature of the institutions that would use social science and policy expertise. Bureaucratic obstacles, for example, can retard the use of policy analysis. One study reviewed the inner workings of numerous university-city partnerships to provide research and analysis. Using a comparative case method, this study concluded that even where such efforts are well-intentioned, successes are unlikely because of deep structural problems that preclude the application of knowledge to power (Szanton 1981). Szanton's conclusions, however, unlike Kirp's or Krugman's, do not stem from the belief that there is no demand for policy advice, but that bureaucratic and political obstacles make the realization of effective demand, met by available and willing supply, exceedingly rare, even when the best of motivations are at work.

Similarly, James Q. Wilson argues that policy analysis is rarely used because good social science research is rarely communicated to policymakers, as opposed to the opinions of famous social scientists who are wont to speculate beyond their professional competence (Wilson 1978). Like Szanton, Wilson believes that bureaucratic obstacles prevent effective use of policy analysis, because policy analysis rarely fits with the "maintenance and enhancement needs of bureaucratic organizations." Wilson argues,

> good social science will rarely be used by government agencies in a timely and effective manner. Most organizations change only when they must, which is to say, when time and money are in short supply. Therefore, most organizations will not do serious research and experimentation in advance. When they use social science at all, it will be on an ad hoc, improvised, quick-and-dirty basis. (Wilson 1978, 91–92)

Although traditionalists believe that policy analysis can influence policy for the better, at the margins and sometimes more, they doubt either that policy analysis is so influential as to create an elite policymaking apparatus, or that policy analysis methods are inappropriate for policymaking. David Weimer has asked rhetorically for examples where benefit-cost analysis has influenced public policymaking and led to a poor outcome; one is hard pressed to identify even one example. If so, at a minimum, policy analysts are meeting the Hippocratic Oath to do no harm, if only by being somewhat ineffectual in this conventional interpretation of what it means to use policy analysis. The question is whether they are doing any good and, if so, how and why?

In sum, the traditionalists believe that, although improvements must be made in policy analysis, many of the explanations for its lack of use are exogenous, such as the current political context or bureaucratic obstacles. This view does not necessarily promote greater reliance on policy analysis in making decisions, but neither does it recommend wholesale changes in it. An alternative view of policy analysis and decision making does.

Alternative Critiques

Other scholars ridicule the positivist orientation of policy analysis altogether, arguing that policy analysis should adopt a more participatory role in engaging policymakers and the public. They believe that conventional policy analysis—where "experts" advise powerful clients—is elitist and undemocratic, and that policy analysis should be fundamentally altered to serve multiple constituencies and democratic processes more generally. These scholars lament the pernicious effects of policy analysis, which, under the guise of objectivity, erode democratic impulses, invest excessive power in policy analysts who are far removed from the problems of the average citizen, and ultimately promote what Harold Lasswell calls a "policy science of tyranny" (deLeon 1997; see also Dryzek 1989; Durning 1993; Fischer 1992; 2000; Schneider and Ingram 1997; Stone 1997).

Where the above-cited authors believe that significant changes in policy analysis have the potential to make it more participatory, others argue that the entire enterprise is misdirected. These scholars argue that the problem with linking policy analysis with policymakers centers on policy analysis itself. At the theoretical level, one wide-ranging critique of the use of policy analysis insists that other forms of decision making are often preferable to policy analysis. For example, Lindblom and Cohen's contempt for the widespread use of policy analysis for decision making is undisguised: "Coin tossing is a frequently useful alternative to analysis" (Lindblom and Cohen 1979, 21). However, they make important contributions in broadening the perspective. Lindblom's subsequent work stresses the importance of "interactive problem solving" as an alternative to understanding and analyzing policy problems (Lindblom 1986, 1990). More despairingly, Edward Banfield argues that policy analysis is incapable of making important contributions to policymaking, referring to it as "metaphysical madness" (Banfield 1980).

Lindblom argues that analysts should drop the veneer of impartiality—no analyst or researcher, after all, can be truly impartial—and permit themselves to participate in partisan debates working in partisan organizations. According to Lindblom, the "public interest," the holy grail of policy analysis, should be satisfied through political rather than analytical means: "If there are genuinely *common* interests, they are the shared interests of *all* partisans, all of whom will consequently pursue them. . . . Partisans tend to develop alternative versions of the public interest, rather than ignore it. That is the best a society can do: acknowledge conflicting versions and work out—politically, not analytically—a resolution" (Lindblom 1986, 354; emphasis in the original). He also suggests that analysts stop training their analytical attention solely on government policy-makers and instead shift some of their focus to "you and me . . . millions of us, 'we the people'" (p. 354).

In a challenge to client-centered advice, advice that is usually directed to political leaders who can effect change, he asks, "By what argument has the research community come to fasten on leadership as its audience? By no argument at all. By thoughtless habit and the simple assumption that leaders are more worth talking to than the masses" (1986, 355). Lindblom argues,

> The great body of citizens in the democracies—to say nothing of less liberated citizens elsewhere—have hardly begun to explore the possibilities for solving their problems, thus for improving their prospects. The impairment, of course, afflicts our political leaders as well as the whole citizenry. But what is required to right it is not policy analysis directed largely to the special needs of political leadership, but analysis that constitutes an education and an enlightenment and liberation for leader and citizen alike. (Lindblom 1986, 359)

This is echoed by Deborah Stone's conception of causal stories, which are "ideas about causation" that "move situations intellectually from the realm of fate to the realm of human agency" (Stone 1989, 283). Other forms of problem solving may be preferred. Lindblom notes that ordinary knowledge, social learning, and trial and error may, under certain circumstances, be preferable to a rational problem-solving approach that uses information and expertise to arrive at social decisions (Lindblom 1990).

If we accept these critiques of the role of social science and policy research, what role, if any, remains for policy analysis? Lindblom provides an analogy:

> Regard life as a game. Social science helps in various ways: assists the game officials, and studies the rules of the game, how it might be improved, and how to take care of game injuries. Valuable as this help is, the players need more. They need to know how the game came to be structured as they find it, how they were induced to take for granted that they should play, whether any other game

exists, and how they might find and learn to play another game. This is what social science and research still might do for them. (Lindblom 1990, 279)

Like deLeon, Ingram, Stone, and many others who support a reformulated policy analysis, reformulated policy analysis that engages the public directly through interactive problem solving, Lindblom and Cohen argue that the entire enterprise of policy analysis needs to be reconstituted:

> One piece of evidence of misperception is the widespread identification of problem solving with problem understanding, to the exclusion of interaction. . . . We suspect that in one part of their minds many [professional policy analysts] take it for granted that the normal or necessary way to solve any problem is to understand it. They do not systematically conceive of problem solving as other than an intellectual or cognitive process, any more than they can conceive of rationality except by reference to intellectual or cognitive processes. Thus, in many of their systematic formulations of conceptions of problem solving, as well as in their choice of directions of research, they ignore the possibility of interactive problem solving. (Lindblom and Cohen 1979, 30)

Edward Banfield, author of *Unheavenly Cities*, a sharp neoconservative critique of urban renewal in the 1960s, argues, "[Policy scientists] have very little influence, certainly very little of a direct kind" (Banfield 1980, 180). He further notes that this is as it should be.

> It is a dangerous delusion to think that the policy scientist can supplant successfully the politician or statesman. Social problems are at bottom political; they arise from differences of opinion and interest and, except in trivial instances, are difficulties to be coped with (ignored, got around, put up with, exorcised by the arts of rhetoric, etc.) rather than puzzles to be solved . . . . What the political leader requires is not policy science but good judgment— or, better, the union of virtue and wisdom that the ancients called prudence. (Banfield 1980, 184)

These critics—from the political left and right—argue that policy analysis is so pernicious that it threatens effective democratic governance. "If the analytical techniques produced and propagated from the universities supersede the skills of the politician and (on the rare but all-important occasions when it is manifested) the wisdom of the statesman, the successful working of the political system will be gravely jeopardized" (Banfield 1980, 167). Like Wilson, Banfield argues that social science simply knows too little to inform policy effectively. "The persistent efforts of reformers to do away with politics and to put social science and other expertise in its place are not to be accounted for by the existence of a body of knowledge about how to solve social problems" (pp. 170–71).

Even Theodore White, who exulted over the newfound power of intellectuals in policymaking in the 1960s, nicely summarized the thoughts of skeptics regarding the potential influence of social scientists and policy analysts, what he termed action-intellectuals, over policymaking: "The action-intellectuals have no certain answers for tomorrow. . . . To measure something does not mean to understand it. . . . Their studies and surveys, however imperfect, are only road maps for the future showing the hazy contours of a new landscape. It is vital work—as long as the mapmakers do not confuse themselves as tour directors" (quoted in Wood 1993, 39).

The critics of policy analysis therefore view the problem—that policy analysis is infrequently used in public decision making—in decidedly different ways. The traditional critiques focus their attention on factors outside the realm of policy analysis, arguing that the political and bureaucratic context in which policy analysis tries to operate circumscribes its ability to have a profound impact. In contrast, alternative critiques argue that the problems are endogenous to the practice of policy analysis, and that policy analysis itself needs to be overhauled before it will be effective. Most pessimistically, some critics argue that it can never be useful and that evidence of its lack of use is all for the good.

ANALYSIS IS, AND WILL ALWAYS BE, POLITICAL

Despite the veneer of objectivity and scientific method, the application of policy analysis cannot be distinguished from politics and power. The fact that analysis is political is well understood, at least by most scholars of public policy and administration: "Decision-making, of course, is a euphemism for the allocation of resources—money, position, authority, etc. Thus to the extent that information is an instrument, basis, or excuse for changing power relationships within or among institutions, [it] is a political activity" (Rich and Goldsmith 1983, 101). To some extent, this recognition even manifests itself in the curricula of policy schools, which now routinely include courses on political analysis and integrate politics into the understanding of how policy is, and should be, made. Political analysis skills are fundamental to being a good policy analyst and leader (Meltsner 1976).

In keeping with the contemporary recognition that technique and method are insufficient to promote good policymaking and that modern policymaking is far less hierarchical and more diffuse than in the past, the curricula of schools of public policy and administration have, to a substantial degree, merged. Few if any schools of public policy now ignore the management of public agencies, the importance of politics and constitutionalism in policymaking, and other concerns normally associated with political science and public administration. Similarly, programs whose intellectual origins are in public administration now routinely include coursework in microeconomics and statistics to complement those in personnel relations, budgeting, and public administration. The tacit recognition that good public managers have to know analysis and that good analysts become public managers is nearly ubiquitous and embedded in contemporary curricula of schools of public policy and administration. Nonetheless, important criticisms remain that policy and administration schools need to "transcend the mechanical, scientist orientation," (Anderson 2003, 109) alter their excessive focus on "tools and skill sets," and more adequately recognize that "politics is a formative element of public policy" (p. 109).

Furthermore, policy analysts need in a sense to become more political if they expect to have influence, yet they also need to bear some responsibility for what they recommend:

> New ideas are to be welcomed and new paradigms embraced, but not if they are advanced untested and irresponsibly. The political

> arena is not a playpen, a sandbox, or a social laboratory for inter-
> esting ideas. . . . The expert advisers need to accept at least some
> of the responsibility for the consequences of the policy they have
> persuaded politicians and administrators to adopt and carry out.
> (Wood 1993, 176–77)

Despite this widespread recognition that policy analysis *is* political, there is virtually no research examining the impact of politics
on policy analysis institutions.[10] Much of the existing literature on
knowledge utilization and the use of information, at both the federal and state levels, speaks to a different set of concerns than this
book. The knowledge utilization literature (reviewed in chapter 2)
focuses mostly on federal institutions, largely on written studies and
reports, and is mostly case-study driven. The excellent studies of the
use of information in Congress (e.g., Whiteman 1995; Bimber 1991)
provide richly detailed examinations of specific issues (Whiteman)
or institutions (Bimber). They do not, however, compare the effects
of different political institutional forms on the execution and type
of policy analysis, nor the relationship between different types of
policy analysis organizations and measures of their effectiveness to
the clients they serve.

MOTIVATION AND APPROACHES

In this book I tackle some of the same issues researchers have studied before—How is research used? What information and analysis do
policymakers need? How does politics affect analysis? What is the
relationship between knowledge and power?—yet it approaches these
issues from a decidedly different angle. This project has both positive and normative dimensions, ones that are far better studied comparatively and that are not amenable to study only at the federal
level. This book offers several contributions.

The first contribution is to expand considerably the single-case
orientation of previous research and compare the use of policy analysis across multiple institutions. Rather than focus on one institution,
such as the U.S. Congress or a federal agency, I instead turn my attention to the fifty different structures for providing policy advice
in state legislatures. Furthermore, the importance of staff in legisla-

tive decision making suggests that a focus on staff organizations as-sisting policymaking represents a potentially important source of in-formation and analysis. Using the results of an original survey as well as follow-up interviews with directors of the approximately eighty nonpartisan policy analysis institutions now serving state legislatures, these new data provide a rich understanding of the nature and type of policy research institutions. This book tests political theories that seek to explain the variation in the sizes and types of policy analy-sis agencies established by U.S. state legislatures, a nearly ideal com-parative vehicle. The relationship between institutional form (the structure and functions of policy research organizations) and politi-cal and socioeconomic determinants is examined, and each plays a significant role in affecting the nature of policy analysis.

Through detailed semistructured interviews with research direc-tors of state policy analysis organizations, this work examines how these organizations function, their staffing, their work products, and their functional relationships with the legislatures they serve. Sur-prisingly little is known about what policy research organizations actually do and produce.[11] For example, are policy research organi-zations analytical problem solvers (as conceptualized by, e.g., Stokey and Zeckhauser 1978) or information providers to a broader political discourse (e.g., Shulock 1999)? This question also has substantive importance. Legislative policy analysis organizations were established as a means for legislatures to establish independence from the ana-lytical supremacy of the executive branch. Therefore, the effective-ness of policy analysis institutions has implications for the distribution of analytical power, not to mention the relative strength and independence of the legislatures themselves. In an era of added responsibilities shouldered by state governments, do they have the analytical capacities to help make good policy decisions?

The second contribution is a methodological reformulation of how scholars study so-called knowledge utilization. Some scholars have bemoaned the lack of political context that accompanies studies of knowledge utilization:

> Proponents and critics of the policy analysis paradigm have tended
> to view the world in which analysis is practiced as a homogeneous
> place in which factors affecting the relative influence of analysis,

the likelihood that analysis can replace more traditional politics, and the likely institutional alterations due to analysis will be constant. That is why generalizations drawn from specific instances of attempts to apply analysis, and why attempts to measure 'influence,' typically make no distinctions among kinds of policy environments. The implication is that the elements of the policy environment are unchanging or unimportant. This, I believe, has been a *fundamental roadblock* to progress in thinking about the potential and actual roles of analysis. (Jenkins-Smith 1990, 80; emphasis in the original)

Instead of trying to trace the impact of a single piece of research—or even written work more generally—or the work of a single agency to its policymaking conclusion, I focus on how and why legislatures create policy analysis institutions to serve their needs, and the degree to which these institutions are effective in serving their clients. In addition, by expanding the conception of utilization of policy research to the utilization of policy expertise more generally, this study conceptually broadens our understanding of what it means to use policy analysis. If policy analysis is what policy analysts do, then the findings of this volume suggest that policy analysis plays an important role in policymaking. In essence, part of this study treats policy analysis institutions as what social scientists refer to as a dependent variable—that which we seek to explain—rather than an independent variable, or that which explains. States provide an excellent natural experiment because their legislatures maintain noticeably different types of policy analysis agencies, even in states that are similar in many ways. Very little has been written about the range and type of policy analysis institutions at the state level and, therefore, about the analytical capacities of states to make informed decisions in the face of increasingly partisan and complex policy issues. Furthermore, there has been little comparative work devoted to policy analysis institutions,[12] and this book's focus on institutions permits the consideration of how policy analysis in all its forms—written and oral, short term and long term—affects and is affected by the world of public policy and administration.

Finally, this volume examines whether and how policy research affects different uses of policy analysis, such as the provision of information, and decision making, among others. Using an extensive original survey of more than 750 state legislators in nineteen states, this work examines legislative attitudes toward research generally, and legislators' assessments of the policy analysis organizations that putatively serve them. The survey results provide detailed information on the importance legislators place on information from various sources; their legislative role as trustee or delegate; the influence of various interests in state policymaking; the importance legislators place on policy analysis and information for decision making generally; legislators' evaluations of the policy research agency serving their legislature; their political-economic views; and demographic characteristics (e.g., education, age, gender, occupation). Multiple uses of policy analysis are examined, including its use as contributing directly to policymaking, use as enlightenment, use in providing information, use as rationalization, and tactical use. This study examines whether policymakers' various research needs are being met, and models the relationship between institutional form—the size and type of policy analysis institution—and performance as measured by client use.

In seeking to understand what policymakers need in terms of information and analysis, scholars have mostly neglected to study the institutions policymakers create to provide them with information and analysis, and accordingly have not analyzed how differences in those institutions vary across political and institutional structures. Furthermore, little effort has gone into examining the extent to which the legislators who create and sustain these institutions ultimately are satisfied with them and what they produce. Why study states? State legislative research organizations represent an excellent set of cases for assessing the use of policy analysis. First, there is sufficient variation across the fifty states, and sufficient numbers to perform multivariate estimates of variation. The states not only represent the entire population, but also allow a comparative analysis to replace the case-driven research most often identified with knowledge utilization studies. Although the unit of analysis normally is a report or study, in this volume institutions, states, and clients are the units of analysis.

Second, U.S. states retain several common features, such as common democratic systems; common legislative and gubernatorial

organizations; common political parties; common language; and so
on. Furthermore, states deal with similar levels of complexity in
policy issues such as health care, economic development, education
reform, environmental cleanup, and so on. Therefore, issue complexity should not influence significantly differential uses of analysis
across states.

Third, prior research on the use of policy research has questioned
whether "neutral" policy analysis can survive, much less thrive, in
openly political environments. Can neutral state NPROs survive in
a highly political environment? And if so, what form or forms do they
take in order to serve legislatures most effectively? Studying how
NPROs operate and how they vary can, therefore, can reveal much
about the interplay of politics and expertise, and begins to answer
whether neutral policy analysis can survive in overtly political
environments.

Finally, NPROs represent a useful object of analysis because they
permit methodological clarity concerning the direction of causality
in assessing the impact of policy analysis organizations over state
legislatures. The NPRO has a single client, the legislature, the only
client the office needs to satisfy. In other words, unlike contemporary analysts at many research and advocacy institutions whose work
has multiple clients, sometimes including the public at large, legislative policy analysis organizations typically serve only legislators.
Therefore, because NPROs are somewhat exceptional in that they
have a single institutional client, use can be examined directly based
on its utility to the legislators themselves without considering con-
founding factors (i.e., other prominent users of their policy analysis). Legislative policy analysis shops represent what legislators create,
not the information that bombards them from interest groups with
specific agendas. It is simply implausible to think that these organizations are anything but the expression of legislative intent, no matter how circuitous, rather than the other way around.

Legislative policy analysis organizations were established to foster
legislative independence from executive branch analytical supremacy. Therefore, in some instances, the degree to which policy
analysis shops are effective suggests the relative strength and independence of the legislature itself. The fact that states have absorbed

additional policymaking responsibilities makes it an important area of research. Whether one believes that devolution is something new or enduring, there is little doubt about the importance of states in developing, implementing, and enforcing public policy. What is less clear is whether states have the capacity to make informed decisions in light of the important responsibilities they maintain, and what institutional changes can improve state decision making. In addition, states have been labeled "laboratories of democracy," the source of government most likely to generate policy innovation. But can states innovate in the absence of sound, nonpartisan policy analysis?

OVERVIEW OF THE BOOK

This book investigates several dimensions of the political environment affecting the use of policy analysis and the influence of the political environment on policy analysis in state legislatures. How do institutions shape the nature of policy analysis? Is policy analysis useful? For what? At a minimum, policy analysis is supposed to provide decision makers with more information. What types of policy analysis are most valuable? Why do institutional forms of provision of policy analysis vary so considerably, even within U.S. states that share many characteristics?

Chapter 2 examines the theoretical underpinnings of expertise, different meanings of the term "knowledge utilization," and the existing empirical evidence of how policy analysis is used in policymaking.

Chapter 3 explores the nature of NPROs through the results of a survey of fifty state NPROs, as well as follow-up telephone interviews with agency directors. This chapter also investigates the strength of policy analysis organizations, measured in a variety of ways, including their independence from political influence, the number and type of analysts they employ, the level of analytical sophistication they have developed, and the scope of their policy coverage. The variation in the type and functions of these institutions is considerable, providing new descriptive information about them as well as forming the structural underpinnings for subsequent analyses.

Chapter 4 analyzes the determinants of varying institutional structures across states, i.e., why states choose such different institutional structures for providing legislative policy advice. The findings suggest that the political influence over institutional form is substantial, with political competition, state party organization, interest group influence, culture, and even state size playing substantial roles in explaining the size and type of NPROs established in state legislatures.

By reporting the results of a detailed survey of more than 750 state legislators, chapter 5 examines legislative attitudes toward research generally and legislators' views of the usefulness of the policy analysis organizations established to serve them. The analysis concludes that legislators value their NPROs highly, that Democrats do so more than Republicans, and, most importantly, that legislators value the basic functions of NPROs—gathering and reporting information—most of all. In fact, legislators value these basic functions over the more analytical functions that scholars tout and that dominate the curricula of schools of public policy and administration. Furthermore, chapter 5 finds that NPROs generally are not perceived to be influential in the policymaking process in relation to other political actors, despite their evident contributions to providing information and other forms of policy analysis to legislators.

Finally, putting several steps together, chapter 6 examines the relationship between the type and structure of policy analysis organizations and legislators' satisfaction with their performance. The chapter concludes that legislators in states with larger and more analytical NPROs assess them as more important providers of information than do legislators in states with smaller NPROs, and that larger and analytical NPROs achieve increased policymaking influence. Chapter 7 discusses conclusions, implications, and suggestions for future research.

NOTES

1. I deliberately conflate the terms "policy analysis" and "policy research" and use them interchangeably throughout. Although there are distinctions (see Weimer and Vining 1998), from a policymaker's perspective

they are all but inseparable. Furthermore, one distinction—the client orientation of policy analysis—is eroding as policy analysis speaks to multiple clients (Shulock 1999).

2. There are exceptions, such as Bimber's work (Bimber 1996) on an institution (such as the Office of Technology Assessment) or the comparative case study work on university-city partnerships (Szanton 1981) and an edited volume on policy analysis agencies in eight nations (Weaver and Stares 2001). Nonetheless, the overall conclusion regarding the considerable body of research holds.

3. U.S. Office of Management and Budget 2002.

4. National Science Foundation *Federal Funds Survey, Detailed Historical Tables, Fiscal Years 1951–99*, Table A, NSF-99-347. http://www.nsf.gov/sbe/srs/nsf99347/start.htm.

5. Accordingly, the Bank of Sweden Prize in Economic Sciences in Memory of Alfred Nobel, commonly referred to as the Nobel Prize in Economics, was awarded to economists beginning in 1969. No other social science is so recognized.

6. See the fictional and sometimes humorous account of a powerful White House adviser discussing domestic policy with a prominent academic over dinner in Georgetown (Lynn 1987). The adviser becomes increasingly exasperated with the professor's refusal to provide her with timely, politically sensitive, and usable information upon which to base policy decisions, and provides an illustration of how and why social science research results are routinely and sometimes understandably ignored by policymakers (Lynn 1987).

7. This has been renamed the "eight-step path," and is now available in book form (Bardach 2000 as well as on the Internet).

8. The Association for Public Policy Analysis and Management, or APPAM.

9. For example, in an invited article in the *Economist* on four "important" books on international trade, Krugman notes: "Although all four authors feel able to pronounce with authority on international trade, none of them is familiar with the contents of even the first two or three chapters in a standard undergraduate textbook on the subject. (I do not mean that they disagree with that textbook: I mean that they have no idea what it contains.) As a result, all four books are filled with conceptual and factual confusions that would be comical if so many people were not likely to take them seriously" (1995a, 99). He goes on to say, "It is a mark of the perplexity, if not necessarily the decline, of the West that such bad ideas can be taken so seriously" (p. 100).

10. An exception is Bimber 1996.
11. An exception is an edited volume by Weiss 1982; however, only one of the fifteen agencies portrayed is a state agency: California's Legislative Analyst's Office.
12. An exception is Weaver and Stares 2001.

Expertise and the Use
of Policy Analysis

As a subset of expertise applied to public problems, at its broadest level policy analysis is any form of expertise in service to public policymaking and administration. More narrowly, policy analysis can be called applied social science research. However, scholars generally understand *policy research* to be social science research with public policy programs, actors, or ideas employed as an independent or dependent variable. *Policy analysis* features two additional characteristics: a client orientation and a limited time frame in which the analysis is performed. (In contrast, policy research has neither an explicit client orientation nor externally imposed time constraints.) Because policy analysis requires the application of expertise to public problems, it is useful to study expertise more generally before delving into a review of how scholars have studied the utilization of policy expertise.

THE NATURE OF EXPERTISE

Studies of expertise occur at multiple levels. The simplest is expertise performed by individuals, where outcomes are easily observable. Examples, shown in the upper-left quadrant of the matrix depicted in table 2.1, include activities such as games (e.g., chess), tests of memory, and individual information processing (e.g., aptitude tests).[1] Evaluating this type of expertise is not straightforward, however. "A critical issue in the expertise approach is *how to identify standardized tasks* that will allow the real-life outstanding performance to be reproduced in the laboratory" (Ericsson and Smith 1991, 9; emphasis in original). Chess, for example, has been widely studied: "Because of its unique properties—particularly its rating scale and its method of recording games—chess offers cognitive psychologists an ideal task environment in which to study skilled performance" (Charness 1991, 39). Even though chess has sharply defined rules and clear outcomes, there is in general no unambiguous "best move" for each position of the pieces. Research has determined that experience—more than cognitive processes—separates the experts from weaker players. Chess masters and grand masters are no more able to recall the placement of randomly positioned pieces on the board than inexperienced players, but their ability to recall piece positions far outstrips those of weaker players when a game is stopped mid-play. Therefore, context is critical to the expert's superior recall (Ericsson and Smith 1991). In order to achieve a high level of play, chess players must possess a combination of game knowledge and search capabilities (Charness 1991).

Although the outcome of a game is easily observable and chess players are ranked explicitly according to scales based on these outcomes, it is still difficult to understand how certain players outperform others and why certain individuals have better memory recall and more efficient search processes than others. For example, when novices predict the outcome of a simple physical experiment (e.g., will a yo-yo balancing on a tabletop move left or right when the string is pulled to the left?), they rely on their own common sense instead of the physical principles relied on by experts (in this case, physicists) (Anzai 1991). In this case, expert knowledge of physical principles and the ability to apply them to observable situations help distinguish the predictions of experts from those of novices. This focus of research on expertise in individuals when outcomes are simple and observable is a far deeper study of expertise than that attainable for more complex or ambiguous outcomes.

A layer of complexity is added when groups of individuals attempt to generate collective expertise for outcomes that are readily observed, as in the upper-right quadrant of table 2.1. Examples include institutional stock market analyses, budget forecasts (e.g., by

make their assessments individually (lower left) or in groups (lower right). Not only is it difficult to assess the impact of specific policies, but understanding whether vague goals are being achieved, like improving educational performance or environmental quality, is decidedly ambiguous. Even when comparing expert performance in the case of medicine, "the depressing conclusion from these studies is that expert judgments in most clinical and medical domains are no more accurate than those of lightly trained novices" (Camerer and Johnson 1991, 203). Comparison of predictions by statistical models with those of experts underscores this point: "Sometimes experts are more accurate than novices (though not always), but they are rarely better than simple statistical models" (1991, p. 211). The paradox posed by these researchers is, "How can experts know so much and predict so badly?" In policy research, the theoretical base is not developed sufficiently even to observe whether models would outperform experience. In short, knowledge and experience matter, but it is not clear how or how much they matter.

In these situations, where policy analysts generally find themselves, the inability to observe outcomes—even under normal conditions, much less in controlled laboratory settings—makes the assessment of expertise problematic. In the absence of observable outcomes, how are we to recognize and interpret expertise? Policy analysts rarely make specific, testable predictions. In many cases, there is a notable absence of any precise outcome prediction upon which to assess expertise through direct observation. So what, exactly, separates the experts from others? In these situations, input measures frequently are used to evaluate expertise, e.g., licensing of barbers and physicians or graduate degrees from good programs in public policy and administration for policy analysts. However, there are no rating guidelines or certification systems akin to, for example, the bar exam for attorneys, for policy analysts. This presents a dual challenge: First, what constitutes expertise among practicing policy analysts? Second, how should graduate students be trained to be good policy analysts when we have only a loose understanding of what makes a good analyst? Some general ideas, gleaned by talking with individuals in the field, have produced a smorgasbord of courses, ranging from organizational management to advanced statistical techniques that are thought to be essential to training good policy analysts. In the absence of understanding what makes an expert in fields characterized by unobservable outcomes, these are little more than educated guesses that require ongoing evaluation and adjustment.

THE OBSERVATIONS OF INFORMED PARTICIPANTS

Few would disagree that ideas can have significant impact in public policy. Upton Sinclair's *The Jungle* exposed the dreadful condition of slaughterhouses, leading to the establishment of the Food and Drug Administration and substantial food safety laws and regulations. Michael Harrington's *The Other America* highlighted the pervasiveness of poverty in the United States, supporting the development of what would come to be called the war on poverty. Ralph Nader's *Unsafe at Any Speed* drew attention to unsafe automobiles and led to improved safety standards, and Rachel Carson's *Silent Spring* cautioned against the use of chemicals in the environment, precipitating calls for new environmental legislation. Other ideas— such as the inefficiency of many forms of economic regulation, the impact of research on development policy, or the efficiency benefits of marketable pollution permits—have had significant influence on the course of public policymaking in disparate fields (Derthick and Quirk 1985; Eviatar 2003; Robyn 1987).[2] That ideas matter is not the issue; rather, the issue is *how* some ideas—and not others—come to matter and what it means to *matter*.

The perceived gap between policy analysis and policymaking has generated various types of studies and critiques. At the broadest and most personal level are the observations of individuals who have participated significantly in the policymaking process. These range from journalistic accounts to accounts of individual policymakers and researchers. These individual accounts sometimes offer deep insight into the use of policy research, but their shortcoming is the inability of researchers to replicate their findings and generalize beyond individual perceptions, interpretations, and experiences. Nonetheless, taken together they represent important perspectives on the relationship of research to policymaking.

Perhaps the greatest concentration of informed observation occurs in the area of social policy, in part because so much policy research is applied in this arena but also because of the significant
policy changes in recent years—most fundamentally, the welfare
reform of 1996—and attempts to relate these policy changes to extant scholarship. Some of these scholars argue that social science
research and policy analysis had little impact over welfare reform
decision making. Sheldon Danziger, a prominent welfare policy research scholar, writes:

> Social scientists have conducted hundreds of empirical studies
> related to various aspects of welfare policies over the past thirty-
> five years since the War on Poverty was declared. Major findings
> of this research and their policy implications were virtually ig-
> nored, however, in the welfare reform debates leading up to Presi-
> dent Clinton's signing the Personal Responsibility and Work
> Opportunity Reconciliation Act of 1996 (the PRWORA). . . .
> Over this period [1969–1996], with the exception of the Family
> Support Act, social science research on welfare tended to be one
> cycle behind the welfare reform policy debate and to have had
> little impact on policy outcomes. Instead, policies, once they have
> been implemented, have influenced the nature of subsequent
> welfare reform research. . . . Now, welfare reform research is once
> again following policy as numerous studies are analyzing the ef-
> fects of PRWORA. (Danziger 2001, 137, 151, 152)[3]

In contrast, other welfare reform participants argue that policy
analysis has an impact, albeit only indirectly linked with policy outcomes. Ron Haskins, a long-time Republican congressional staffer
working in social welfare policy, concludes that "there is no question that social science research contributed substantially to creating the policy conditions in which welfare reform became possible"
(Haskins 1991, 628). He also states that much of the influence was
due to research results that were amenable to policymakers' predispositions and that "the domain of application for social science
research to public policy is more circumscribed than most scholars
think" (p. 630). He argues that "research played a large role" in the
fact that the 2002 Temporary Assistance to Needy Families (TANF)

reauthorization did not change much. According to Haskins, the research showed very good results from TANF and therefore suggested little change. However, he concludes, "Social Policy 101 says that it rarely happens that research trumps values" (Haskins 2002). Judy Gueron of Manpower Demonstration Research Corporation (MDRC), an organization long associated with high-quality policy evaluation research, argues that research played a role in what did *not* happen: "Large-scale harm did not occur" (Gueron 2002).

Part of the reason for these varying views is the divergent definitions of use and different political environments that the participants are using. Political context matters. Similar to Kingdon's policy windows, then, is the notion that research can be valuable only when ideological and political issues are at bay (Kingdon 1984). Peter Szanton reports that MDRC's randomized experiments had a decided impact on policymaking in the late 1980s because of certain conditions: "Ideologies were beginning to converge; regional differences were not at issue; no powerful constituencies opposed change. Congress, in short, was not data-proof" (Szanton 1991, 600). Predicting when these policy windows will open is far from clear and it is therefore difficult to predict the conditions under which policy analysis might be useful.

Having been involved in policy discussions leading to decisions and (often) producing research, knowledgeable policy participants bring a nuanced understanding of the use of policy analysis in decision making. They understand that, over time, although the influence of policy analysis is sometimes profound, it rarely affects decision making directly. Instead, policy analysis can eliminate poor options, provide support for positions already held by policymakers, and influence the ways in which the debate is structured or framed (Schon and Rein 1994).

More generally, Robert Wood, an academic and former adviser in the Kennedy and Johnson administrations, argues for the importance of social science research, particularly in comparison to the counterfactual:

> When social science is set aside, advocacy in place of evidence comes to command political debate. Deductive interpretations of

conditions and events, "obtained," in Daniel Lerner's works, "by some secret process" take precedence over politics extracted by detailed observation and experiment. Sweeping moral criticisms of existing institutions and systems—replete with moral fervor— take the place of rigorous evaluations of actual performance. As moral absolutes become prominent, compromise becomes an increasingly unacceptable option for political participants. So violence becomes increasingly a quasi-legitimate alternative, in protests before abortion clinics, in city street behavior, even in the conduct of everyday life: in the dissolution of family relations, the availability and use of firearms enhance the likelihood of unpremeditated accidental assault. (Wood 1993, 175)

Others note the subtle ways that professions can sometimes influence policymaking. One article, written by an economist then serving as a state legislator, argues that even simple economic concepts, such as the importance of opportunity costs or the irrelevance of sunk costs, are enormously helpful to policymakers, and that economists make strong contributions to legislators by their conception of the public good, framing issues, and other less technical contributions (Brandl 1985).

RESEARCHERS AS POLICY ADVOCATES

The policy analysis realm began to shift markedly in the late 1970s and the 1980s with the introduction of a more heterogeneous set of interest groups, think tanks, and others offering policy analysis as political rhetoric. Advocacy and research were in some venues nearly inseparable. Although universities as institutions are rarely viewed as important contributors to policymaking, at least in the conventional sense, many social science and policy researchers, qua scholars, began to apply their expertise in public settings, such as blue ribbon commissions, congressional testimony, meetings with executive and congressional staff, and publications aimed at a wide audience. This research dissemination included newspaper columns and articles in journals—such as the *American Enterprise* and the *Brookings Review*— aimed at reaching a wider audience than that of most academic journals. Because social science or policy research is rarely designed to address policymakers' immediate concerns, policymakers routinely ask reputable social scientists for their considered judgments about prospective policies, the impacts of possible changes, or whether evidence supports or opposes their favored positions. "Clearly, officials do not always want policy recommendations, not even from policy analysts. . . . Not on a specific study do they sometimes wish to draw, but on the whole intellectual experience of the professional investigator" (Lindblom 1990, 272), and social scientists have been eager to comply.

Although social science had lost much of its luster of the early to mid-1960s, social scientists continued to play prominent roles in both Democratic and Republican administrations. One observer notes that in the Republican-dominated 1980s, "at least for the economists, outside domestic policy experts never had it so good. . . . Economists were on top as well as on tap" (Wood 1993, 146). The "Laffer Curve" of this era represents the influence of an idea— thought to spark the large Reagan tax cuts of the early 1980s—with profound policy impact yet very little social science underpinning. Despite the fact that social science had appeared to lose considerable input into policymaking, at least as typically understood, the social science lexicon suffused media reporting.

> From program evaluation to cost-benefit analysis, environmental impact reporting to macroeconomic forecasting and public opinion polling, American newspapers were full of the language of social science, and their editors evidently expected that their readers would understand and appreciate this analytical perspective. (Anderson 2003, 51)

Immediate answers from reputable social scientists serve the immediate needs of policymakers to improve their knowledge base, expand their understanding of an issue, and provide legitimacy for their positions. However, there is a large potential gulf between the social scientist qua scholar and the social scientist qua policy adviser. The scholar has to submit work to a peer review process that includes other specialists; although not without flaws, this at least subjects research to the scrutiny of other scholars. When the researcher becomes a policy adviser, particularly outside the public eye, that researcher may succumb to the temptation to offer advice beyond his or her professional competence. "Getting good social science research is different from consulting good social scientists. The latter, unless watched carefully, will offer guesses, personal opinions, and political ideology under the guise of 'expert advice'" (Wilson 1978, 91). The problem is that the policymaker may be led to believe that the results emanate from social science research, not an opinion, albeit an educated opinion. Another scholar and policy participant notes, "[T]oo much of the time too many social scientists act too much like politicians" (Nathan 2000, 3).

Universities have encouraged researchers to become involved in policymaking circles; those who promote their work aggressively are rewarded with additional attention. Somewhat despairingly, one study notes, "It seems that researchers can enhance the probability that their findings will be used by policymakers by devoting considerable resources to communicating with such persons, even at the expense of communicating with their professional peers" (Greenberg and Mandell 1991, 652). Seen in a more positive light, informal connections between scholars and policymakers can convey more subtle messages than a strict interpretation of the accumulated results. "Conceptual and qualitative knowledge, together with some sense of the relevant magnitudes based on experience and analogy, may all be helpful in providing guidance on the likely effects of current and future programs" (Cook 2003).

Several observers are cautious about the role of researchers in policy debate. Ron Haskins concludes that, because of the lack of review, "researchers who would apply their knowledge to public policy have an obligation to avoid advocacy" (Haskins 1991, 631). He notes,

> The direct role of researchers in the policy process raises serious issues of quality control. Peer review, journal publication, and replication are the hallmarks of quality control in the social sciences. When researchers enter the policy arena, however, they can easily avoid the standard quality control mechanisms and take their views directly to policymakers through testimony and individual

or group meetings. Most politicians, especially when engaged in political fights, have little regard for quality control: They want support for their position and they take whatever they can get. (Haskins 1991, 629–30)

Richard Posner has studied (mostly academic) public intellectuals and argues that they are, in their direct effects, not terribly influential. He suggests that this may be especially true in the United States, and that there is no check on the authenticity of their predictions. "The more stable and complex a society is—also the more complacent it is—the less likely are its public intellectuals to be able to take it by storm" (Posner 2001, 158). He adds, "[P]ublic intellectuals are for the most part neither very prescient nor very influential" (p. 21). Posner argues that "public intellectuals are read for information but also for entertainment—educated people enjoy reading the writings of lively minds on current affairs even if they realize that the writers are opinionated, incompletely informed, and basically unreliable—and for buttressing the reader's predispositions, that is, for solidarity" (p. 147).

Echoing the views of Krugman, Posner acknowledges that a more subtle form of traditional influence may be involved. "I am not so thorough going a materialist as to doubt that ideas, even if they are not scientific or otherwise rigorously provable, can influence public opinion and public policy. . . . [A] steady diet of books and magazine articles by public intellectuals may contribute to the shaping of a person's values and outlook" (2001, pp. 157 and 160). He believes that some of the sloppy thinking of public intellectuals is because "academics tend to think of themselves as being on holiday when they are writing for the general public" (p. 105), and that an academic is like a "fish out of water when asked to opine on events that are unfolding before his eyes as he speaks" (p. 107).

Buttressing these views is the finding that research quality has little effect on policymaking influence. Researchers studying the application of social experiments on policymaking, using a knowledge utilization framework that allows for many types of use, conclude that the use of information does not depend crucially on the quality of research and may depend more on how the research is

communicated. "It appears that research findings from tests of incre-
mental policy changes, subject to little scrutiny, reported by a single
voice, and based on fairly simple estimation techniques, are more
likely to be used in policy-making than research findings for which
the opposite conditions hold" (Greenberg and Mandell 1991, 652).[4]

Despite their insights, what is lacking from these informed personal accounts is the ability to generalize to other issue areas and
other situations. Furthermore, because these generally are not formal
studies but instead reflections of knowledgeable policy participants,
the results are not replicable and therefore hinge crucially on the
personal views of each particular policy participant. To complement
these accounts, we turn to scholarly research that seeks to assess directly the relationship between research and policymaking.

WHAT DOES IT MEAN TO *USE* RESEARCH?

Scholars began to question and examine what it means to use
research. Two scholars who reviewed the knowledge utilization
literature conclude that, "studies of research utilization have been
unnecessarily burdened with narrow conceptions and measures of the
process of research utilization" (Rich and Goldsmith 1983, 110).
Carol Weiss writes (1979) that a significant impediment to scholars
connecting with policymakers was the ambiguity of the term knowledge utilization. What does it mean to use social science or policy
research in public policy decision making?

In light of the recognition that policy analysis was not up to the
task of providing incontrovertible policy advice to policymakers,
scholars began to look for other more subtle roles for policy analysis.[5]
Rather than looking for direct analytical social science contributions
to policy, Aaron (1978) suggests, "[T]he contribution of the social
sciences seems to be not so much specific information and conclusions as a perspective, an encouragement to evaluate programs in
terms of their demonstrable effects. This finding makes it important
to consider alternative ways of fitting analysis into a broader perspective" (p. 165). Scholars rushed to explain why social science and
policy research had so little impact on policy outcomes, and a new

journal—*Knowledge: Creation, Diffusion, Utilization*—emerged that published insightful perspectives on the conundrum.

By focusing on ways to improve the dissemination of research to policymakers, the early work on knowledge utilization sought to identify, embellish, and, ultimately, surmount the two-communities problem. Despite some thoughtful research suggesting that policymakers and scholars rarely cooperate even when potential mutual benefit appears likely (Szanton 1981), the attempts to link research with policymaking continued. Scholars realized, however, that mere dissemination of results was insufficient. "The task becomes one not of the wholesale force-feeding of ignorant policy-makers by knowledgeable disseminators but of the discovery of those types of transfer that are worthwhile under varying conditions" (Knott and Wildavsky 1980, 538).[6]

Weiss (1979) outlines seven different models for research use by policymakers, some encouraging and some discouraging to those aspiring to directly inform and improve policymaking. The *knowledge-driven model* is the traditional—some would say naïve—top-down understanding of knowledge utilization: scientists (social and otherwise) generate research that is transmitted to policymakers and used in decision making. The *problem-solving model* assumes a well-defined policy problem and the application of social science research to solve it; policymakers either use preexisting research findings in their decision making, or they commission research to help inform decisions. The *interactive model* presumes multiple sources of information, only one of which is social science research, but which nonetheless informs policymakers.

Two of Weiss's models cast use in a political context. Her *political model* sees research not as informing decisions, but as ammunition, in effect enabling policymakers to rationalize decisions and support previously held views on public policymaking. Her *tactical model* views research as a means of delaying decisions, deflecting criticism, and increasing the prestige of the policymaker. As Weiss notes, "It is not the content of the findings that is invoked but the sheer fact that research is being done" (1979, 429). Despite the unease some scholars have with these uses of policy research, this broader set of definitions shifts the focus away from the products of the scholarly community and toward the information and research needs of policymakers.

Weiss's final two models include more subtle means of informing policymaking. Weiss's *enlightenment model*, which she describes as the most frequent use of policy research, involves a body of research and perspectives "that permeate the policy-making process"[7] (Weiss 1979, 429). Policymakers may not be able to cite specific studies in support of their positions, but research provides a common understanding of problems and causes, and narrows the range of possible solutions for policymakers to consider. Finally, the *intellectual enterprise* model "looks upon social science research as one of the intellectual pursuits of a society" (p. 430).[8]

Weiss's other work points to a highly indirect path from research to policy utilization. In one study, she notes that only 7 percent of respondents (among federal, state, and local mental health officials) could provide specific uses of social science research, although through follow-up interviews she found that officials make frequent use of research. She concludes, "public officials use research more widely than previous laments on the subject have suggested. But they do not often use it by considering the findings of one study in the context of a specific pending decision and adopting the course of action recommended by (or derived directly from) the research. That kind of instrumental 'utilization' is what many observers have expected and looked for in vain" (Weiss 1980, 396–97). Furthermore, she notes the methodological difficulties of searching for knowledge utilization in a context where many public decision makers "do not believe that they make decisions" (p. 398). Nonetheless, her research had used a "common instrumental definition": "If a decision maker considers the findings of a study or a group of related studies for near-term resolution of a policy problem, then that research is being used" (Weiss 1978, 35).[9]

Many of these studies, and most in the knowledge utilization literature, explicitly or implicitly define a decision-making locus. One study, however, found that even persons in high-ranking positions "claim that they do not make decisions" (Weiss and Bucuvalas 1980, 173). Many officials contend that decision making is an inappropriate conception of their work, with one commenting "I haven't seen a decision made in some time" (p. 173). Instead, because of the dispersion of responsibility in many large organizations, the division of authority among federal, state, and local government levels, and the amorphous process of reaching a decision, Weiss and Bucuvalas (1980) argue that because many so-called decision makers do not conceive of themselves as such, attempts to link research findings with decisions through interviews are methodologically problematic.[10]

Larsen notes that nonutilization receives little attention, with the presumption that more utilization is always preferred to less, despite the fact that nonutilization may be a valid alternative in some instances. Larsen points to the need for greater theory building, standardization of terminology, and good empirical research. In particular, she notes the dearth of studies at the state, regional, and local levels. Larsen states that scholars have paid little attention to whether utilization changes over time, the extent to which utilization can be generalized, and which factors are related to utilization, such as different bureaucratic structures or institutional arrangements (Larsen 1980).

EMPIRICAL STUDIES OF THE USE OF POLICY ANALYSIS

The general scholarship on knowledge utilization is helpful in explicating numerous types of knowledge utilization that had heretofore escaped the attention of those seeking to show that research had a direct influence over policymaking. We turn now to studies that sought, empirically, to understand the same relationship between research and policymaking.

One review pointed to several methodological problems plaguing the study of knowledge utilization, many of which apply today (Mandell and Sauter 1984, 149–50). First, researchers have too often chosen sample populations they are familiar with (e.g., through a prior affiliation), which are therefore unlikely to be representative of the population at large.[11] Second, researchers have not carefully specified use, normally conceptualized as the dependent variable, and therefore the ability to aggregate study results is complicated by the multiple forms of use that are being measured. In specifying the dependent variable (use), they argue that too many researchers study populations with which they are familiar (convenience samples) and that they study a single sector, e.g., health, instead of multiple sectors whose results produce more generalizable findings. They also criticize "the tendency to focus only on certain echelons within an agency" (p. 151) rather than drawing wider samples. Third, they argue that researchers sometimes rely excessively on respondents' introspection and their abilities to remember clearly what motivated their policy actions.

Despite methodological problems, several researchers added empirical evidence corroborating Weiss's point that research has many more uses than simply assisting decision making. Martin Greenberger finds that in the case of energy policy, "it was striking . . . how often there was disparity between intention and result" (1983, 278). He finds that analyses were used for talent shows, personal education, communication, mass education, a forum for debate, delay, posturing, "eyewash," and moderating goals rather than just for making decisions (pp. 278–82).

In an extensive study of the use of models in urban policymaking (Pack 1974), the most important use of the models was indirect application, specifically the education of the agency staff and policymakers with respect to urban interdependencies, and stimulating discussion about regional issues among regional and local planners. The study concludes that the use of models is attributable largely to the skill of the analyst working with the model. If the analyst is skilled in the model's use, sensitive to the policymaker's needs, and adept at communicating the results, the models have a greater chance of being used in making decisions. (Note that these factors are quite apart from the technical adequacy of the model itself.) Steele reaches similar conclusions in his study of the use of econometric models by the Federal Power Commission (Steele 1971). Another study that focuses on the knowledge sources of consumers of information finds that on-the-job training, graduate education, and supervisors were the major information sources; information from books or journals was used minimally (DeMartini and Whitbeck 1986). In his study of the use of survey data, Rich concludes that the use of research rests not so much on factors the analyst can control or the appropriateness of the information to the specific policy area. Instead, knowledge is used if it is useful to bureaucratic interests; a politics of information precedes the decision to use certain information in making policy choices (R. Rich 2001).

Much of the empirical research investigating the use of policy analysis in decision making is in the field of social welfare policy, where prodigious intellectual resources have been employed to evaluate existing programs and predict the consequences of potential new ones. Perhaps in no other policy arena has such a determined effort by both scholars and research practitioners been given to connecting scholarly work with the policy world. Hundreds of scholars conduct social welfare policy research; top-level applied research organizations, such as the MDRC and Mathematica, provide high-level and nonpartisan applied policy analysis and evaluation studies; and congressional and executive branch staff are sophisticated consumers of policy research. All the ingredients are in place, it would seem, for the smooth transition from analysis to policymaking. Nonetheless, although most observers conclude that research has had an impact, that impact has been circumscribed and generally overwhelmed by the substantially value-based dialogue that infuses social welfare policy. Furthermore, the impacts, noted earlier, are at least as strong in the reverse direction: Policy influences research as much as research influences policy (Danziger 2001).

A review of the impact of social experiments on income maintenance and welfare or work programs concludes that, in terms of traditional measures, there was little discernable impact as a result of the experiments on policy outcomes; in other words, few if any new policies were adopted, and few if any existing policies were modified based on the study results. Instead, and in keeping with the results of the knowledge utilization literature more generally, the impact was more subtle, such as influencing microsimulation models, and the design of President Carter's welfare reform plan, providing "ammunition for those who argued [for or] against" particular policies, and so on (Greenberg and Mandell 1991, 639).

Peter Szanton's (1991) review of MDRC's assessments of experimental state programs prior to the passage of the Family Support Act of 1988 concludes that "those assessments were pivotal to the passage of the FSA and that they demonstrate the growing potential power of policy research" (p. 590). However, Szanton also argues that several conditions are necessary to effect change, ones that are important for policy analysts to remember:

> They must work their issues long enough to develop deep expertise. They must know the politics of those issues well enough to understand when change may be possible, what evidence might prove crucial, and when that evidence must be available. Their methods must appear authoritative to analysts and convincing to policymakers. And they must be determined to present their findings in as many forms, and to as many forums, as may be required. These are not easy conditions to meet. (Szanton 1991, 602)

Studies of the use of policy analysis have also ventured into many other policy areas. A study of Department of Interior offshore lease auction schedules finds that analysis matters but that "only major changes in the outcome of the analysis would affect the decision," and that "the implication is that cruder analyses may provide the same level of information to the decision maker [as the more sophisticated ones conducted at Interior]" (Farrow 1991, 176).

An early study interviewed 204 decision makers to understand their use of social science in public policy decisions, and concludes that "many of the self-reported instances of knowledge utilization involved strategically important applications of policy-related social science and would suggest reasons for modest satisfaction rather than the despair and cynicism so prevalent in the literature on social science utilization and public policy" (Caplan, Morrison, and Stambaugh 1975, 46).

A study of the impact of twenty national health evaluation studies finds that most definitions of use have been overly narrow and have, accordingly, underestimated use more broadly defined. Second, and consistent with a theme developed later in this book, people matter to research utilization:

> The translation, the interpretation, the meaning, the relevance are established through the interactions over time of individuals

is structurally impervious to policy analysis. Dreyfus argues that Congress is not primarily the originator of policy ideas but is largely reactive to ideas and policies that have been formed primarily in executive agencies: "Major policy decisions treated by the Congress are rarely the result of congressional formulation" (Dreyfus 1977, 103). As a result, "the role of Congress is to evaluate the political strengths of the various viewpoints, to assign political measures to the intangible and otherwise unquantifiable factors that make the decision controversial, and to arrive at either a political victory or a compromise that will result in a feasible and legitimate policy" (p. 103). He does not discount the importance of policy research, but simply "questions the feasibility and the need of making the legislative process a focal point of such research" (p. 106). He argues that "such analysis is simply superfluous to the summary role that Congress plays" (p. 106).[13] Schick agrees, noting, "Congress is not a natural habitat for policy analysis" because of "the institutional character of Congress as a representative, law-producing body" (Schick 1976, 216). Congress is, he argues, more concerned about distribution than efficiency or benefit-cost analysis, and therefore "the legislative and analytic processes are not natural or easy partners" (p. 217).

Charles Jones refers to policy analysis as a "tidy endeavor" (Jones 1976) not well suited to Congress. He notes the problems that congressional research agencies (GAO, CRS, CBO, and the Office of Technology Assessment [OTA]) face: controlling their agenda; maintaining objectivity; decision making filtered through committees or partisan staff; reliance on Congress for support, which compromises their aggressiveness; the short time frame in which analysis must be performed to be useful; and the political delicacy of promoting themselves without jeopardizing member support. He concludes that Congress can't do policy analysis (Jones 1976). Both Schick and Jones doubt that new analytical agencies can do much to promote policy analysis in Congress,[14] with Jones arguing that unless the agencies adapt to the political needs of Congress they will either be ignored or be reorganized. As Schick puts it, "For Congress, analysis is a sometime thing" (p. 233). Similarly, Davidson notes that congressional committees are "the toughest customers" to whom policy analysis may be sold (Davidson 1976).

One study of congressional use of expertise examines the quantity of news media and congressional visibility of sixty-six public policy think tanks. The type of organization supplying the advice mattered considerably to this definition of use. "My results suggest that the process by which expertise is selected and used by Congress and the media may be more conditional on the attributes of its suppliers than previously understood" (A. Rich 2001, 599). In general, Rich notes that policymakers and the media "prefer experts at larger institutions that are conveniently located. But they take note of sources' ideologies and strategies as well, depending more often on more neutral and staid sources for policy guidance than more ideological and aggressive sources for political support" (p. 600). Interviews with congressional staff by Carol Weiss (1989) reinforce the understanding that congressional staff place considerable importance on the source of the information. She states, "Staff value information more when they know and trust its source and understand its political motivations" (p. 411). Others have studied the use of information through congressional testimony, concluding, "[T]here was almost no support for our hypotheses about the impact of information on congressional action" (Burstein 2002, 13). However, given the strong theoretical support for the importance of information in policymaking, the author suggests, "More work is needed on the impact of information on the policy process" (Burstein 2002, 13).

Taking a different view, Robert Haveman acknowledges the institutional obstacles affecting Congress's use of policy analysis, yet argues, "[A] significant step can be taken to increase the analytical capacity of the Congress. With a well-trained, nonpartisan professional staff in both the committees and the Budget Office, it will be possible to reduce congressional reliance on the hearings process with its domination by special interests and the executive branch," thereby narrowing the gap in analytical capacity between executive and legislative branches (Haveman 1976, 249).

Implicit (if not explicit) in these accounts is the understanding that policy analysis will not have immediate and direct impacts on legislative decision making. Empirical evidence supports the assessment that Congress is unlikely to be a major institutional user of policy in this sense of use. Nonetheless, some empirical studies, using broader measures of use, paint a decidedly more nuanced picture of the way policy is and can be used in legislative institutions.

One study examines the use of OTA studies in congressional committees (Whiteman 1985). He distinguishes substantive use from elaborative use (to extend and refine existing policy positions), and strategic use (use to support policy positions already taken), and concludes that Congress uses policy analysis, although for widely varying purposes, strategic use being the most common. As he explains, "the political environment into which new analytic projects are sent has a clear effect on the type and area of subsequent use" (p. 308). One of the most comprehensive studies of policy information use in Congress is Whiteman's subsequent book, in which he measures both concrete use and conceptual use across twelve policy analysis projects from government agencies. Staffers report the greatest use of analysis for personal background, and only infrequently for formulating or advocating legislation. Whiteman (1995) concludes that there is little worry that policy analysis will dominate democratic values: "Within Congressional communication networks, policy analysts have little ability to dominate the multitude of other sources of information competing for the attention of congressional enterprises" (Whiteman 1995, 183).

An account of a prominent congressional research agency—the OTA—notes that several constraints operate to check the influence of research agencies. First, agencies must be careful to avoid harming any legislator with information that may run counter to her preferences or assist a rival; this obviously limits the independence of the agency. Second, although most researchers consider reports to be the primary policy research currency, OTA's experience suggests that personal relationships matter far more: "It is less an exaggeration than one might think to say that OTA's role in Congress would not have been diminished had the agency never published a written report" (Bimber 1996, 96). Nonetheless, Bimber argues that analysis has its place, even in Congress.[15]

In a study of congressional use of policy analysis, Weiss (1989) says that of several different types of use, "by all accounts, the most common form of legislative use is support for preexisting positions" (p. 425). She quotes one congressional staff as saying, "'Information is used to make a case rather than to help people make up their minds'" (p. 425). Furthermore, she notes, "members don't decide policy strategies on the basis of information" (p. 426). A CBO staffer explains:

> Almost always their mind is made up about the general direction they want to take. It's either because of a political mandate of some sort or their own concerns. They want to save dollars or this year they want to provide for expansion of Medicaid to this group. They never come to us for goals or direction of policy. That's what they're elected to do, and that's what their immediate staffs are there to translate in the first-level translation. . . . About options for achieving that goal, they're more often open-minded. (Quoted in Weiss 1989, 426)[16]

Nancy Shulock's more recent work (1999) provides empirical support for this more indirect enlightenment function, where the acknowledgement of a study or report is an indication that it at least factors into decision making, leaving aside whether it had any discernable influence over the policy outcome itself. Assessing the use of policy analysis in Congress by studying congressional committee use of policy analysis from 1985–1994, across several policy domains, Shulock finds that Congress is a frequent user of policy analysis, with use defined as specific mentions of policy research in committee reports. She concludes, "[D]espite its scientific origins, policy analysis may be a more effective instrument of the democratic process than of the problem-solving process" (p. 226). This interpretive view of policy analysis converts "speaking truth to power" into "speaking truths to powers."

Policy Analysis in the States and State Legislatures

Few studies have investigated the use of policy analysis in state legislatures. One review, undertaken more than twenty years ago, points to the dearth of studies focusing on knowledge utilization in states and localities; relatively little has changed since then (Larsen 1980). Studies of policymaking in state legislatures generally focus on the staff or the members themselves and the flow of information. A study of Minnesota state legislators finds that legislators' experiences and their constituents are the most important sources of information, but that "idea factories" play a minimal role (Gray and Lowery 2000). Another study of the Oklahoma and Kansas legislatures finds that legislators' personal values are the most important influence on decisions (Songer et al. 1985). Political scientists have studied how state legislators take their cues for policy decision making, and they have studied which sources of information—such as staff, universities, or lobbyists—are most utilized in supplying scientific and technical information (e.g., Guston, Jones, and Branscomb 1997). Legislators' experiences and values, grassroots organizations, and constituency are also found to be important (Gray and Lowery 2000; Ray 1982; Jackson-Elmoore, Knott, and Verkuilen 1998).[17]

Other studies focus on the influence of various information sources on policymaking. One study finds that even when states are considering important reform efforts, as in the case of welfare reform where three states implemented alternative reforms, the key experiments in other states "did not have a dramatic, decisive effect on policy-making" (Greenberg, Mandell, and Onstott 2000, 375). Officials were more interested in learning about how the programs operated in the field than in understanding the empirical findings of the studies themselves. Furthermore, studies find that universities, think tanks, and foundations play a minimal role in providing information, much less in decision making (Gray and Lowery 2000; Lester 1993; Sabatier and Whiteman 1985; Szanton 1981). One study of the Michigan House concludes, "Michigan legislators in particular feel that their supply of information on many questions which come before them is inadequate" (Porter 1974, 728). Another study finds that legislative sources of *written* information are quite limited. That study finds that state legislators gather the vast majority of their information from three sources: fellow legislators, interest groups, and executive agencies. Legislative staff, the media, academic sources, party officials, and others provided relatively little useful written information to the legislators (Mooney 1991b). Another study finds that among Nevada legislators, scientific and technical information came from two principal sources: committee hearings and the staff of the Nevada Legislative Counsel Bureau. Indeed, these two information sources were ranked well above all others, including public interest groups, state agencies, and so on.[18] Interested parties, public interest groups, and lobbyists supplied far less information (Bradley 1980). A final study shows that information sources for state legislative voting decisions—in this instance, the author studied legislators in Massachusetts, Indiana, and Oregon—tend to come from inside the legislature, whereas those involving persuasion and the development of legislation rely more on information from other sources (Mooney 1991a). Personal values and constituents are the most important sources of influence in another study of state legislators (Songer et al. 1985). "We find that legislators rely primarily on their own experiences and those of their constituents" (Gray and Lowery 2000, 573).

One study of state officials examines knowledge utilization in the context of a comparative state framework and finds that "utilization of policy information is best explained by state contextual variables and user characteristics. That is, agency officials in wealthier, more conservative, moralistic states used policy analysis in their work more than officials in poorer, more traditional, liberal states. In addition, more experienced and better educated officials used policy advice less than inexperienced and less educated officials" (Lester 1993, 267). He adds, "Those decision makers that do utilize policy analyses tend to reside in wealthier, moralistic states, as well as those with conservative tendencies" (p. 282).

Most studies of knowledge utilization start with research or analysis, and then try to determine its receptivity by policymakers. Only rarely is the organization itself the subject of study, and in only one case (Weiss 1992) were multiple policy research organizations studied.[19] One study focuses on science advisory boards for U.S. federal agencies in a comparative context (Smith 1992), another studies national policy advising internationally (Weaver and Stares 2001), and still another studies the impact of think tanks in the United States and Canada (Abelson 2002). Beryl Radin (2000) provides profiles of several policy analysis organizations, including one state-based organization, yet the work is intended to develop a typology of functions rather than to compare how and why they participate in the policy process (chap. 3). Scholars have provided a rich understanding of the many kinds of uses that may exist, but have contributed less empirically in promoting our understanding of policy research organizations.

CONCLUSIONS

The knowledge utilization literature has made important theoretical contributions, perhaps most importantly by shifting the theoretical emphasis away from the knowledge-driven and problem solving models and toward other uses of policy research, such as an interactive model (where policy analysis is but one source of information) or a tactical model (where policy research can be used for delaying decisions, increasing prestige, or other political ends; Weiss 1979). The empirical literature—both generally and in the U.S. Congress and among state officials—shows that policy research rarely has a direct impact on policymaking,[20] but nonetheless that it makes important contributions in more subtle ways, including those in interactive and tactical uses.

The proliferation of policy research could reasonably be viewed as prima facie evidence that policy analysis contributes to policymaking. Congress must, after all, value the work of the CBO, GAO, CRS, and the many think tanks and other organizations that ply them with information and analysis. Futhermore, some believe that the ideas generated by the scholarly community are highly influential, particularly in more general educational terms that underlie policy decisions:

> Much of what people learn about politics, through popular books and articles and discussions with friends as well as through media reports, originates in scholarly research or expert commentary. In many cases, experts and research studies have provided accurate and useful new information that has helped the public better to understand problems facing the country and better to estimate the costs and benefits of policy alternatives. Thus scholars, researchers, and experts, and those publicizing their work (for example, the experts appearing on TV who can so strongly affect public

opinion), have helped educate the public. (Page and Shapiro 1992, 358)[21]

Policy analysis has come to be seen, by some, as more a contribution to the discourse of policymaking than an exclusive expert–client relationship:

> Whether or not social science and scientists are invited into the inner circles of power seems a less fundamental marker of relevance than whether and how honest numbers are made accessible to the public and not just to government. Speaking truth to power, in a democracy, requires just that. And therefore as the social sciences move into the twenty-first century, their potential relevance to democracy may be even greater than their relevance to policy-making. (Featherman and Vinovskis 2001b, 14)

Carol Weiss (1979) adds that policy analysts need to be attentive to policymaking processes: "Perhaps it is time for social scientists to pay attention to the imperatives of policy-making systems and to consider soberly what they can do, not necessarily to increase the use of research, but to improve the contribution that research makes to the wisdom of social policy" (p. 431). Accordingly, the role of policy analysts also has changed. In this newer view of knowledge utilization, policy research is suffused throughout the decision-making process, and policy analysts are urged to throw off the green eyeshades, get away from their computers, and participate in democratic politics, if they want to be effective.[22] If anything is clear from the empirical literature studying the use of policy analysis, it is that there is little concern for policy analysis trumping political values, particularly in legislative settings.

Although the literature on knowledge utilization does not suggest that policy research plays a large and immediate role in decision making, particularly in the legislative arena, based on empirical research there is some reason to believe that policy research organizations—even those that serve state legislatures—may play a meaningful role. Compared with the U.S. Congress, it is true that state legislatures are poorly supported: Their pay, session duration, and staffing are far below that of national levels. Furthermore, the institutional problems that thwart the use of policy analysis in Congress, such as its inherently distributive and reactive orientation to politics, also plague state legislatures. Nonetheless, one study finds that the information source most highly rated across four criteria by legislative staff in the California legislature is the California Legislative Analysts Office, and that the most important factors bearing on information use were accessibility, convenience, and comprehensibility (Sabatier and Whiteman 1985).

Furthermore, much of the knowledge utilization literature treats the use of policy analysis over a limited time frame. Scholars rarely have studied empirically how changes in political context affect the use of policy analysis, although many have emphasized its importance in understanding how research will be utilized (Kingdon 1984; Szanton 1991). When examining a single point in time, researchers cannot control for the open policy windows seemingly necessary for the use of policy research. This book instead studies institutions that, although evaluated at a single point in time, reflect, to a large extent, the accumulation of past political practices and preferences that shape their form and function.

An enduring paradox is that legislative institutions are supposedly antithetical to policy research, yet Congress and virtually every state legislature sustain nonpartisan policy research organizations (NPROs). For all of the studies that have decried the lack of substantive information available to Congress, and the institutional obstacles to congressional use of policy analysis,[23] there is little examination of why Congress finances the extensive staff of the GAO, CBO, and CRS. Yet the legislative demand for nonpartisan policy research does not end with Congress: Virtually every state legislature—whether composed of part-time citizens or full-time professionals—finances an NPRO. The question of why these legislative institutions overwhelmingly support NPROs remains something of an enigma, given all of the reasons why legislative institutions are viewed as routinely data proof. Chapter 3 introduces the institutions that form the empirical backbone of this book: NPROs serving state legislatures. The chapter shows that NPROs are found in almost every state, and that a number support substantial operations, and yet the story is more complicated than that. There is significant variation in the size and type of NPROs, the nature and effects of which are explored in subsequent chapters.

NOTES

1. Table 2.1 represents dimensions that are actually continua in a 2×2 matrix for simplicity of exposition.
2. One example is the reported influence of development research on foreign aid policy. In one example, a study by Craig Burnside and David Dollar in a 2000 issue of *The American Economic Review* reportedly had a significant impact on President Bush's decision to provide billions of dollars in aid to countries that were committed to "ruling justly, investing in their people and encouraging economic freedom" (Eviatar 2003, A17). Students of knowledge utilization question whether the impact was purely that of scholarly thought influencing policy, or the right study for the right administration. Subsequent research using a similar methodology with new and better data discredited the Burnside and Dollar study findings, casting doubt on the efficacy of the Bush administration's aid policy guidelines. The authors of the new study conclude, "policymakers should be less sanguine about concluding that foreign aid will boost growth in countries with good policies" (p. A17). The relationship of scholarship to policymaking was called into question: "Why can one study trigger the flow of millions or even billions of dollars while another, equally valid work sits on the shelf?" (p. A17).
3. Echoing a similar view, Isabel Sawhill, another distinguished scholar of social welfare policy, argues that the Bush administration has made marriage promotion a major push, yet there is no evidence that it will work. She believes the effort is misguided, because research shows that a delay in childbearing is more effective, yet the administration still pushes for marriage for reasons unrelated to research. Although research has shown the beneficial effects of reducing early childbearing, the House bills do not permit funding of these effective programs. She also maintains that "the research is not there on abstinence education" (Sawhill 2002), yet it continues to receive administration support.
4. Scholars have drawn contradictory findings from earlier works studying knowledge utilization. One review states, "A number of recent studies . . . conclude that completion time is an important determinant of the use of ABI [analytically based information]. Yet, other studies . . . indicate that this variable has little or no effect. . . . Similar

contradictory evidence is found with respect to the effect of technical quality on the use of ABI. [One study] found research quality to be the most important determinant of an individual's use of ABI. Others, however . . . have found virtually no relationship between technical quality and use" (Mandell and Sauter 1984, 156).

5. Some of the knowledge-utilization literature centers on an assessment of the use of scientific and technical information, in which analysts may be expected to play a larger role. However, in this context, the definition of "scientific" is subject to some disagreement. Some of the scholarly literature on the effects of welfare reform involves sophisticated quantitative social science, yet most would not regard it as a science per se. One study asked legislators which issues they believed had important science and technology components. They found that legislators believed air pollution and power plant siting had important science and technology dimensions, whereas legislative redistricting and election abuses did not (Feller et al. 1979). This is despite the fact that sophisticated quantitative analysis often is involved in redistricting questions, in addition to obvious political dimensions. Therefore, assessments of science and technology advice can ignore important technical information sources, and it may not be possible to generalize from science and technology advising to policy analysis. Furthermore, the study cited above found that legislators have deep ambivalence about science and technology advice.

6. The review of studies trying to link policy research with policymaking reveals an implicit bias in the literature: Virtually all scholars assume that decision making based on policy research is preferable to other forms of problem solving. Despite the range of views on the appropriate use (or lack of use) of policy analysis in policymaking, it remains true that most studies that try to determine some kind of use do so with the presumption that policy analysis *should* be more integrated into policymaking.

7. The virtue of the enlightenment view was that it maintained an important, if indirect, role for policy research in public policymaking, and that it was empirically plausible. Scholars could continue to generate policy research, which was sometimes esoteric, with the thought that it might enlighten policymaking in some fashion. The sometimes highly indirect route of policy research to policymaking was judged to be sufficient. Unfortunately, at least from the point of view of scholars trying to understand and document knowledge utilization, it proved difficult to document use in a falsifiable way. To falsify the claim would require that no

policymaker either knew about a study or knew anyone who did, or that the ways policy is shaped could in any way be linked with a particular study. More cynically, enlightenment was virtually impossible to disprove. Merely presenting a paper at an academic conference may be said to influence the general enlightenment of the policy community. This is not meant as a criticism of the enlightenment model—indeed, it is a very important function of policy research. It does, however, underscore the way in which use became difficult to detect (in its narrowest interpretation) or impossible not to (in its broadest).

8. Various types of use are examined in chapter 6.

9. Weiss (1979) recognizes that her enlightenment model had its deficiencies, not least of which included the possibility that shoddy or inept work could become part of the policy milieu, leading to what she refers to as "endarkenment." As we saw in chapter 1, there are two types of endarkenment. First, endarkenment can be shoddy research or drawing inappropriate inferences from solid research. Second, it can be good researchers becoming policy advocates beyond their scope of expertise, or championing causes without the support of scientific evidence.

10. They state, "Given the slow and cumbersome process through which proposals often travel, many organizational members are not fully aware of the influence they have. They make a proposal and see nothing happen for months. Even if the proposal is eventually adopted with only minor modifications, they may lose sight of the connection between what they proposed and what eventually happens. And when a series of adaptations is made, they seem to conclude that they have little influence on the system" (Weiss and Bucuvalas 1980, 174).

11. Examples include Pugliaresi and Berliner 1989, and Nelson 1989.

12. A notable exception to the proliferation of policy-relevant information in Congress was the elimination of the OTA in 1995.

13. "The observations that have been made strongly suggest the futility of attempting to introduce sophisticated policy research into the congressional decision process. . . . Major policy decisions, alternatively, frustrate the timely preparation and introduction of independent policy research because of the very nature of the congressional decision process. The challenge to the Congress in such issues is not to discover new factual knowledge or previously overlooked alternatives" (Dreyfus 1977, 106).

14. Schick states, "I doubt that the establishment of a single center of analytic excellence would make more than a marginal difference in the overall performance of Congress" (Schick 1976, 229).

15. OTA's influence was subtler: "Legislators did not cast votes because OTA instructed them what was best; rather, they employed OTA's expertise to sift among problems and frame potential solutions" (p. 96). Although OTA was eliminated, he nevertheless concludes that "Congress is not as hostile an environment for expertise as is sometimes thought. The conventional wisdom about Congress' lack of receptivity to policy expertise is quite incomplete" (Bimber 1996, 98).

16. "Enlightenment" appeared far less frequently as a use of analysis. Weiss (1989) notes that "relatively few people talked about the influence of analysis on reconceptualizing problems" and that "enlightenment uses of analysis are infrequent in Congress" (p. 427).

17. One study finds that legislators and interest groups are important, but did not survey attitudes toward staff, because most legislators in the states surveyed did not have any staff (Ray 1982).

18. Bradley (1980) develops an index of importance for each source. Committee hearings were ranked 90, while the Legislative Counsel Bureau staff was ranked 89. The next-highest ranking was public interest groups, at 29.

19. The edited book is more a compendium of perspectives from different policy analysis organizations—virtually all of which are oriented to the federal government—rather than a truly comparative study.

20. The editor of the leading journal of its time on knowledge utilization states, "The deficiencies and deadly sins elaborated by Lindblom and Melsner are no doubt related to one of the more robust and troubling findings of research on the utilization of the social sciences by policymakers: Social science theory and research seem to play a secondary, minor, or insignificant role in policymaking" (Dunn 1986, 341). In some respects, little has changed. Henry Aaron (1978) explored the role of social science research in the war on poverty, and concludes, "The findings of social science seemed to come after, rather than before, changes in policy, which suggests that political events may influence scholars more than research influences policy" (p. 9). Writing twenty-three years later on the impact of welfare research on policymaking, Sheldon Danziger draws similar conclusions (Danziger 2001).

21. In another study, they use data on public opinion and news sources over time to track the influence of multiple factors over public opinion. One factor is the experts. They find that "those we have categorized as 'experts' have quite a substantial impact on public opinion," although they note that "the existence of a reciprocal process, influence by public opinion upon experts, cannot be ruled out (particularly to the extent

that the audience-seeking media decide who is an expert based on the popularity of his or her policy views" (Page, Shapiro, and Dempsey 1987, 35). They detail several issues in which experts were particularly influential (p. 36).

22. This more holistic view of the function of policy analysts, as well as the fact that highly trained students were being hired by private management consulting companies at historically exorbitant salaries, has led policy schools to reexamine their core principles. What, exactly, separates them from, say, business or law schools, which also train smart, interdisciplinary students? One answer was provided by Berkeley's Lee Friedman, who in his APPAM presidential address distinguished policy analysis from other forms of political persuasion and lobbying by its focus on serving the public interest (Friedman 1999).

23. See, e.g., Schick 1976 and Jones 1976.

CHAPTER 3

Policy Analysis in the States

Policy analysis is pervasive at the national level, with large, highly professional institutions advising Congress, including the General Accounting Office, the Congressional Research Service, and the Congressional Budget Office (CBO).[1] In addition, there has been substantial growth in the provision of policy analysis at the federal level, particularly through the proliferation in the number of so-called think tanks over the past thirty years. Policy research organizations assume disparate forms, from one-person nonprofit advocacy groups to large national nonprofit organizations such as the Brookings Institution, and from small, single-issue state and local agencies to large federal executive and legislative agencies such as the CBO that produce voluminous and sophisticated research.

Despite increases in staffing and professionalism following the widespread state legislative reforms in the 1970s, nonpartisan policy research organizations (NPROs) in U.S. state legislatures vary considerably. Some large, sophisticated, nonpartisan agencies—such as Maryland's Office of Policy Analysis or Kentucky's Legislative Research Commission (LRC) and Long-Term Policy Research Center (LTPRC)—provide their legislatures with policy analysis on a broad range of issues. Offices in other states are understaffed or, in several instances, nonexistent. The temporal development of policy analysis institutions also varies: Massachusetts abolished its Legislative Services Bureau (LSB) in 2001, Maryland reorganized to create a separate Office of Policy Analysis in 1997, and Kentucky established its LTPRC several years earlier, in 1992. Moreover, the preponderance of existing evidence about NPROs is anecdotal. Little has been written about the range and type of policy analysis institutions at the state level or about the analytical capacities of states to make informed decisions in the face of increasingly partisan debate and complex policy issues.[2] Furthermore, there is little comparative work devoted to policy analysis institutions.[3]

This chapter reports and analyzes data from two surveys and provides the first comprehensive review and assessment of nonpartisan policy analysis institutions serving state legislatures.[4] The chapter also examines the associations between NPROs and party strength, political culture, interest group influence, and other key political factors. (Various descriptions and sources are provided at the end of this chapter.) This chapter draws on a written survey of state nonpartisan policy analysis institutions as well as interviews with NPRO staff, and finds the following: there is significant variation in legislative nonpartisan policy analysis capacity; generally, states have modest policy analytic capacities; public policy agencies tend to react to legislative demands rather than behave proactively; and there are important political associations between the strength of nonpartisan policy analysis capacity and state interest group and party strength.

Perhaps most importantly, the chapter concludes that nonpartisan policy analysis is widespread in most state legislatures, and whereas the work performed by NPROs is often short term and descriptive, it confounds the prognosis that neutral policy analysis cannot survive legislative politics.

By examining how and why legislatures establish policy analysis institutions and define the scope of their activities, this chapter complements and advances earlier research focused on what legislators and staffers have said about the impact of policy analysis on their work. Furthermore, the study of NPROs is important due to the importance of legislative staff in policymaking. This chapter describes the range of policy analysis and research institutions serving state legislatures, analyzes commonalities among and differences between them, and provides initial observations about their relationship to the political institutions that sustain them.

SURVEY AND DATA COLLECTION

The fact that legislatures, in rich states and poor, create and finance institutions to provide nonpartisan policy analysis underscores its importance. States are a good comparative vehicle to examine differences in political institutions and public policy. They share a common language and have broadly similar populations, political cultures, and institutions. At the same time, there is considerable variation in their implementation of specific policies and procedures, including the development and use of NPROs for decision making. As one author notes, "These 50 bodies provide significant, but limited, variation on structural, cultural, and political variables that can influence lawmaking, while still being far more comparable than, say, most national legislative bodies" (Clucas 2003, 387).

To understand how NPROs operate, a written survey was conducted of all nonpartisan legislative research organizations, as identified by the Council of State Governments (CSG 2000, 460–65) and the National Conference of State Legislatures (NCSL 1999). The goal was not to identify all sources of policy information to legislatures—indeed, that would include vast numbers of organizations both inside the legislature and beyond—but to begin to identify those states that sustain institutions that provide nonpartisan advice for their legislatures. The survey asked leaders of these organizations about their staffing, budgets, workflow, time allocation, and so on. The survey defined policy analysis as "systematic research that assesses the impacts of and alternatives to various public policies."[5]

Organizations received the survey both in hard copy and electronically. Organizations not responding to the mail or Web survey were contacted by telephone. The survey was mailed to 105 agencies that were identified, by title, as nonpartisan,[6] and ninety-five responded, yielding a response rate of 90 percent. Seven organizations did not respond, despite follow-up phone calls. Of the research organizations surveyed, based on the CSG and NCSL sources, thirteen reported that they did not conduct any form of policy analysis or activities related to policy analysis, such as evaluation and budget analysis. These agencies were removed from the analysis, leaving a total of eighty-two NPROs that engage in some form of policy analysis. The following sections describe and analyze the survey results.

In the spring and summer of 2003, follow-up telephone surveys were conducted with the directors of the NPROs. Organizations that had participated in the written survey and whose work was limited to fiscal or budget analysis or auditing services were excluded from the seventy-seven telephone interviews. The telephone surveys used the same definition of policy analysis that was used for the written survey. The telephone survey focused on the type of work the office produces, including the proportion of time spent on long- and short-term projects and how much, if any, original research the office conducts. Some questions focused on staffing, including staff size, education levels, and experience. Other inquiries included the types of work the office conducts, including bill drafting, committee staffing, and other responsibilities. NPRO directors were asked to identify other sources of nonpartisan and partisan policy analysis or research services or capacity within the legislature.

A PROFILE OF THE AGENCIES

State legislatures underwent considerable changes in the 1960s and 1970s, including the addition of new staff, longer terms, better pay, more space, and longer sessions. Although these changes were driven in part by the need for increased access to information to make better-informed decisions, the changes also served to provide a counterweight to the informational and analytical hegemony enjoyed by many governors. From 1960 to 1980, the number of permanent state legislative research councils grew from just thirteen to forty-three (Rosenthal 1998, 53).

The impetus for the growth in state NPROs mirrored that in Congress. At the federal level, Weiss (1989) notes,

> One of the main reasons behind the zeal for increased analytic capacity was the Congress' distrust of the information it received from the executive agencies. Congress believed that agencies' information was self-serving, designed to bolster their programmatic proposals and budget requests. Congress wanted its own capability to amass and review data and to make sense of competing claims. (p. 417)

State NPROs were established for similar reasons. As one NPRO director stated, "Back in the 1970s, we were totally reliant on the Governor's office for information." In addition, the information from the executive branch was viewed as suspect. A legislator stated, "The reason we needed [a legislative research office] was simply trying to get the best information possible that we could make a decision on, from somebody who did not have an agenda. And when you get stuff from the administration . . . you've got to assume that there's an agenda there" (Guston, Jones, and Branscomb 1997, 457). One NPRO director stated that "the state legislature needed more muscle"; before, the legislature was "at the mercy of the executive branch for budget info., legal advice, lobbyists, etc."

The Importance of Nonpartisan Research

Two significant political trends emerged from the survey and through interviews with NPRO directors and staff. First, nearly all agreed that their legislatures were becoming more partisan. One director stated, "The bipartisanship spirit has evaporated, and we've seen it mostly on [the] Republican side. We used to host a retreat every year, but it was cancelled because Republicans didn't want to attend." This director noted that, as a result, Republican leaders were relying more on their own individual staff. In addition to noting an increase in partisan political debate, NPRO directors and staff perceive that the role of partisan staff is changing; as one nonpartisan director stated, "Partisan staff think they do the real work. They view nonpartisan staff as the 'eggheads' with the cushy jobs." In many states, however, particularly those with citizen legislatures, research staff are nonpartisan.

Second, almost all believe that the nonpartisan nature of their agency is crucial to their success. Nonpartisanship is viewed as important, not only because it is more economical to have one nonpartisan agency than two partisan ones, but, as one NPRO director explained, being nonpartisan "identifies us with the institution rather than with its occupants." Therefore, the nonpartisan role is seen as protecting the legislature as a whole more than it protects individual legislators.

Another director pointed to the importance of nonpartisanship in hiring qualified staff who, in turn, create a solid research base for the legislature and strengthen its position in relation to the executive branch. "Nonpartisanship is absolutely critical. Thirty years ago the legislature was completely under the thumb of the governor, and [it] has now developed independence through a great nonpartisan staff. . . . If the staff were partisan, then there would be pressure to hire people based on political relationships, acquaintances, etc." The NPRO director stated that his "agency would cease to exist" were it not for its nonpartisan role.

Finally, at a pragmatic level, NPRO directors indicate that legislators place a higher value on their product and feel it is more effective because it is nonpartisan. One director noted that "[m]embers can trust what you produce because you don't have an agenda." Another argued that, for legislators, "[b]usiness is far easier to do when you're dealing with one set of facts rather than six to twelve sets of facts. . . . We are the credible, central source of information. When our reports are discussed, that tends to establish the facts and allows members to deal from a consistent basis of information. This makes the process work better."

Organizations with obvious partisan affiliations were not included in this survey. At one time, partisan staff were involved with providing policy advice, but evidence suggests that both the trend and dominant patterns of current partisan staff assistance are overtly political, with partisan staff focusing mainly on reelecting members. Indeed, there has been a shift from policy research to political staffing in some states. Speaking of partisan staff, one observer notes, "The policy experts have been replaced by political hired guns whose main job is to get their bosses elected" (Rosenthal 1998, 193–94). Furthermore, legislators view partisan staff differently. As one New Mexico legislator stated, "Partisan information is not credible" (Guston, Jones, and Branscomb 1997, 461). The study notes, "Even partisan staff from Ohio and New York concurred that nonpartisan policy support was preferable" (p. 461).

Political actors and staff alike make a clear distinction between nonpartisan and partisan policy analysis. Indeed, in follow-up interviews with policy research directors, virtually all stated that the non-partisan dimension of their work was extremely important for one or both of the following reasons: The first reason was economy—having partisan staff serving both parties would require a substantial increase in legislative staff support, as much as doubling research staff to provide equal assistance to both parties. Particularly in citizen legislatures, nonpartisan staffing was viewed as more economical given budget constraints. Relatedly, one legislator expressed concern for a dilution of talent if staff were all partisan:

> The staff that serves legislative leadership is obviously partisan, although the speaker's staff often manages to serve all the membership. There is obviously an occasional strain on the non-partisan staff, but because the system is as it is, there is a tremendous amount of talent that is not split four ways between houses and parties. I just hope we can keep it intact.

More commonly, staff directors believe that the credibility of nonpartisan research is much stronger than from other sources, and all were scrupulous in trying to maintain the perception and reality of their nonpartisanship. As another NPRO director noted, non-partisanship "contributes to the credibility of the agency. . . . If we don't jealously guard objectivity, then people will raise the issue of partisan staffing."

Term Limits

Term limits are too new in most states to have produced widespread and observable institutional changes in NPROs. As a result, although this volume does not address term limits directly, the subject arose in interviews with NPRO directors. One NPRO director noted that because term limits create a cadre of less-experienced legislators, "we are becoming the institutional memory" for the legislature and are thereby building a strong potential base of political power.

Most expressed concern about the general directions that term limits have been taking in the legislature. Directors believe that term limits increase the partisan nature of debate in the legislature, leading to fewer—or at least different—demands on their work. One director stated, "We used to get requests that would take us a year to process. Now the requests are all short-term. Legislators have short attention spans, especially for out-year issues. There is less concern for the long-term." Another attributed the immoderate behavior of legislators in term-limited states to the life cycle of legislators: "Legislators are ideological initially, but become more moderate with time. But now, there is no time for moderation due to term limits. They are much more concerned with the party agenda, and the [NPRO] can't help them with this." Furthermore, term limits have, according to some, led to increased demand for partisan caucus staff, which in some states has gone into the development of press offices. Some directors perceive this as a threat to NPROs, and their concerns are not unfounded.

Agency Age

The survey results indicate that, although agency founding dates span almost a century, the most prolific years for agency formation were the 1960s and 1970s; the median year of NPRO establishment is 1969. This coincided with a time of substantial growth in state legislative capacities where legislatures were trying to maintain information parity, or at least competitiveness, with the executive branch. Just two agencies were founded before 1920—the Virginia Division of Legislative Services (1914) and the nation's oldest, the Wisconsin Legislative Reference Bureau (1901)—and only eight were founded before 1940. There are some notable changes in functions over time. Newer agencies are oriented more to policy analysis: Of the eight agencies that report establishment since 1981, all eight report policy analysis as one of their principal functions, with seven of them also reporting program evaluation. Furthermore, six of the eight report spending more than 30 percent of their time conducting policy analysis, with a mean of 43 percent, significantly higher than the overall mean of 32 percent. By contrast, only two of the eight report legal analysis as a principal function, and only one reports drafting bills. In addition, there is a significant correlation between the propensity to conduct legal

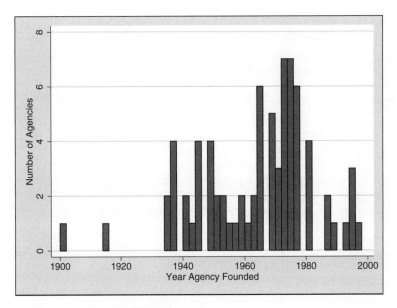

Figure 3.1 Most NPROs Established after 1960

analysis and the agency's age. Figure 3.1 details the frequency distribution of the agency founding dates.

Agency Reporting Duties

Most agencies serve multiple clients within the legislature. Table 3.1 indicates the percentage of agencies reporting to various state legislative bodies. Although all agencies serve the state legislature in some fashion, most agencies report serving the leadership, a joint committee, or the entire legislature, in nearly equal percentages. Indeed, thirteen agencies report to all three bodies, and only fifteen of seventy-nine agencies do not report to any of them. Relatively few report serving a specific chamber committee. Because most agencies have many clients, the evidence suggests that their products are likely to be distributed widely in the legislature. One NPRO director expressed the variety of means and openness with which they convey

Table 3.1
Most NPROs Report to Several Clients (N =79)

State Legislative Body	Agencies (%)
Joint Committee	48.1
Legislative Leadership	45.6
Entire Legislature	44.3
Specific Committee	21.5
Other (e.g., speaker, specific chamber, etc.)	19.0
Other State Agencies	3.8

Note: Percentages do not sum to 100 because agencies can report to more than one body.

information, in attention-grabbing terms: "We're like a full-service arms dealer. We sell to both sides, big weapons and little weapons."

Agency Size

Whether measured by budget or personnel, agencies vary widely. Reported agency budgets vary considerably, from $300,000 to $37 million annually. (Note that budgets for most agencies include activities well beyond policy analysis; this is reported below.) Generally, though, these agencies are small. Most agencies (fifty-five, or 79 percent of those reporting) have annual budgets of less than $5 million, and only five agencies reported budgets exceeding $10 million. The median reported annual budget is $2.2 million, with a mean of $4.2 million.

Measured by the number of personnel, the size of policy analysis agencies also varies considerably, with reported professional staff sizes ranging from 3 to 362, and clerical staff size ranging from 0 to 120. Mean staffing size by agency is thirty-four professional staff and twelve clerical staff. Most agencies, however, have fewer than twenty professional and ten clerical staff, with median values of nineteen professional and five clerical staff.

Larger agencies are less likely to report policy analysis as a principal activity. In terms of budget, number of full-time equivalent staff,

and the number of professional staff, agencies that report conducting policy analysis as a principal activity are substantially smaller
than those that do not. Agencies that do not conduct policy analysis report mean budgets of $9.2 million and seventy-four professional
staff, while those that conduct policy analysis report mean budgets
of $3 million and twenty-five professional staff.

Agency Functions

Most agencies surveyed perform multiple functions, with policy
analysis, general staff assistance, legal research, and evaluation reported by more than half the agencies. This suggests that agencies
only rarely focus exclusively on policy analysis. Of the six functions
specified in the survey, 55 percent of agencies (out of eighty responding agencies) reported performing at least four functions, with a mean
of 3.5 functions per agency. Only six agencies reported performing
only one function, although for four of these policy analysis was the
sole reported function. Table 3.2 displays the results of reported
agency functions.[7]

Because the vast majority of NPROs perform work for both committees and individual legislators, they respond to a high volume of

Table 3.2
Most NPROs Perform Several Functions (N = 80)

Agency Functions	Agencies Conducting This Function (%)
Policy Analysis	81.3
General Staff Assistance	65.0
Legal Research	60.0
Evaluation	58.8
Bill Drafting	50.0
Budget Analysis	37.5

Note: Percentages do not sum to 100 because many agencies reported performing
more than one function.

requests. The fact that they can effectively handle such high demand each session is a source of pride for some. One NPRO director states that his agency completes most requests within two days, and that "We rarely turn away work [and] always try to do as much as we can within the timeframe." Furthermore, they perceive that their work is greatly appreciated by legislators. One director in a citizen legislature states, "Our legislators are volunteers, and while they are not always sophisticated, they are very smart and hard-working and read everything we give them." The substance of their operations varies substantially. One called his agency "the law firm for the legislature," while another described her NPRO's chief function as "providing information that gets the ball rolling to file legislation." Many NPROs do not offer recommendations unless asked. One director stated, "That's their business. We're not elected and we're bipartisan."

Agencies vary widely in the ways they conduct their operations. A few strictly protect client confidentiality; in Georgia, for example, the work of their NPROs is not subject to public inspection. An NPRO director stated emphatically that the NPRO's success in part derives from the fact that "we won't betray a confidence" and that "our members can rely on our information." In most states, however, information is public or confidential for a designated period of time. In Colorado, for example, the information remains confidential for one week and then becomes available publicly; if the work relates directly to a bill, however, a legislator can request that the information remain confidential permanently.

There is a close relationship between the principal functions of bill drafting and legal analysis. Three-quarters of all agencies that report conducting legal analysis also report bill drafting as a principal function, and 90 percent of bill-drafting agencies also report conducting legal analysis. Furthermore, of the thirty-two agencies that do not conduct legal analysis, twenty-eight also report that they do not draft bills. Six agencies report that they do not conduct policy analysis, budget analysis, or evaluation, and every one conducts both legal analysis and bill drafting.[8] Of the thirty agencies that report conducting budget analysis as a principal function, twenty-two also report program evaluation as a principal function.

There are significant correlations among several reported principal functions, including budget analysis and evaluation, staff assistance, legal research, and bill drafting. NPROs that conduct policy analysis are less likely to provide bill-drafting services for the legislature. Consistent with the results reported above, the larger the staff, the less time agencies spend on policy analysis. Agencies with more than the median number of professional staff spend on average 23 percent of their time on policy analysis, compared with nearly 40 percent for agencies with smaller professional staffs.

Type of Research and Policy Analysis

Based on the survey results as well as telephone interviews with NPRO directors in all fifty states, agencies generally fell into one of three distinct types with respect to research and policy analysis functions, independent of the size of the agency. Type A agencies primarily conduct information gathering and descriptive research. They field many requests for information from legislators and provide quick, brief responses; they seldom, if ever, conduct longer-term policy analysis. Georgia's House Research Office, for example, concentrates most of its attention on providing short-term analysis and prides itself on the quick turnaround it provides for legislators. As one staffer said, "We provide whatever the members want, and we make sure it's fast and accurate."

Type B agencies primarily carry out descriptive research, but also conduct some analytical research between legislative sessions, and they frequently provide staff for interim study committees. For example, the Maine Office of Policy and Legal Analysis staffs committees and conducts short-term analysis during the session, while providing longer-term analysis and research between sessions.

Type C agencies spend considerable time conducting policy analysis and longer-term research throughout the year. California's several NPROs, including the Legislative Analysts Office (LAO), the Senate Office of Research, and the California Research Bureau, conduct longer-term research and analysis throughout the session in addition to short-term work.

Table 3.3
Type of Work in NPROs by State

Type of Policy Analysis and Research Available	No. of States
A (Information gathering and descriptive research)	16
A/B	8
B (Primarily descriptive research, periodic analytical research)	14
B/C	1
C (Substantial policy analysis, including long-term analytical research)	10

Source: Author survey and typology.

The typology was applied to the states based on the aggregate agency policy analysis and research capacity, as summarized in table 3.3 above. Some states span two of the categories because of a mixture of activities or because the type of nonpartisan policy analysis and research available differs in each chamber of the legislature. In sum, most state NPROs conduct mainly short-term descriptive research with little ongoing analytical policy research.

How Policy Analysis Is Initiated

Because it provides an indication of an agency's ability to pursue independent mandates and interests, agencies were asked the means by which policy analysis is initiated. Respondents were asked to indicate the percentage of instances in which policy analysis is initiated in different manners; the results are listed below in table 3.4. The results indicate that the most common means of initiating policy analysis is through requests from individual legislators, but several other sources of interest also emerged.

The frequency and type of requests that agencies receive may vary considerably from year to year. Across the sixty-seven responding agencies, policy analysis was self-initiated just 16 percent of the time. In only five agencies was policy analysis self-initiated more than 40 percent of the time, and in 30 percent of responding agen-

Table 3.4
Policy Analysis Is Frequently Initiated by Individual Legislators (N = 67)

Method of Initiation	Mean Percentage of Time That Policy Analysis Is Initiated in This Way
Requests from Legislators	39.1
Committee Directive	19.4
Self-Initiated	16.0
Legislative Leadership	12.1
Statutory Directive	11.4
Requests from the Executive Branch	1.2

cies policy analysis was never self-initiated. Most agencies either rely solely on external mandates or are free to pursue their own interests only a small fraction of the time. Indeed, there is a strong correlation between the proportion of time that work is self-initiated and the time an agency spends on policy analysis, budget analysis, and program evaluation.[9] This suggests that institutions more oriented to policy analysis have greater latitude to initiate studies on their own. Furthermore, agencies that spend more time conducting policy analysis, budget analysis, and program evaluation are less likely to have their work originate from the legislative leadership. Nonetheless, most NPROs take their cues from external sources and only occasionally initiate their own work, generally taking directives rather than initiating policy analysis. This limits their independence and constrains their ability to provide new ideas and analysis to the legislature.

Spending on Policy Analysis

Responding agencies reported that their total annual budgets ranged from $300,000 to $37 million, although an agency's overall function could be as specific as a dedicated policy analysis or as broad as a general legislative council. Only thirty-eight organizations reported the

Table 3.5
Reported Spending on Policy Analysis

Reported Percentage of Budget Spent on Policy Analysis	No. of Agencies
0	6
0–20	12
>20–40	7
>40–60	1
>60–80	4
>80–100	8
TOTAL	38
Reported Annual Spending on Policy Analysis	
$0	6
$0–$500,000	14
$500,000–$1 million	5
$1 million–$1.5 million	5
$1.5 million–$2 million	4
$2 million+	3
TOTAL	37

percentage of their budget dedicated to policy analysis, with several noting that their budget did not specify a line item allocation for policy analysis. Using those thirty-eight organizations, table 3.5 indicates the percentage of the agency budget spent on policy analysis and the corresponding implied dollar amounts. These figures indicate that most agencies are spending relatively small percentages of their budgets on policy analysis and relatively small amounts overall.

HOW MUCH POLICY ANALYSIS DO THE AGENCIES CONDUCT?

Representing the level of policy analysis in state legislative organizations is conceptually difficult. First, the agencies surveyed as a part of this study are only those that work directly within state legislatures. They do not include executive agencies, partisan staff, policy analysts working under contract to the state, analysts working at the local level who might inform state policy, or nongovernmental organizations analyzing state policy (e.g., lobbyists or think tanks). Second, definitions of policy analysis vary; although the survey instrument provided a definition for respondents and distinguished policy analysis and budgetary functions, some agencies may have included such tasks as budgetary analysis under the general rubric of policy analysis, and others may have separated the two functions. Also, to the extent that respondents interpreted the term "policy analysis" differently, the potential exists for sometimes-incomparable results.

Using agency reports of the number of policy analysts, table 3.6 indicates one measure of the quantity of policy analysis conducted: the reported number of analysts per agency. The first two columns of figures in table 3.6, "By Agency," show the number of policy analysts reported by agency; the second set of columns reports these data aggregated by state. The "Reported" columns are the number of analysts reported by the agency or aggregated by state. To provide

Table 3.6
Number of Policy Analysts

Per Agency or State	By Agency		By State	
	Reported	Implied Measure	Reported	Implied Measure
None	15	5	12	7
0–5	20	27	3	7
5–10	11	13	2	4
10–15	19	21	8	9
15–20	2	3	6	7
20+	12	12	13	15
TOTAL	79	81	44	49

Note: "0–5" includes anything greater than 0 and less than or equal to 5; other categories are constructed similarly.

another representation of the number of policy analysts working in state agencies, a second measure was developed, calculated as the number of reported professional staff multiplied by the percentage of time the agency reports spending on policy analysis. This measure is reported in the "implied measure" columns. This alternative measure relies on the respondent's sense of how much time is spent within the agency on policy analysis activities rather than relying on respondents identifying individuals as "policy analysts."

Regardless of the measure used, it is clear that even among agencies that are reported to be the chief policy analysis and research institutions in their state legislature, most do not dedicate substantial human resources to conduct policy analysis.[10] Similarly, the data aggregated to the state level indicate that relatively few state legislatures have a sizeable pool of nonpartisan policy analysts. When the implied measure is used, fewer than one-third of states (fifteen) have more than twenty policy analysts working for nonpartisan organizations in their state legislature. This implied measure suggests that slightly more nonpartisan policy analysis-related activity is happening in states than is observed when one focuses only on the job title of policy analyst. The results also suggest that many states do not have the ability to conduct traditional policy analysis of prospective policy changes. Over one-fourth of states reported having no official policy analysts working for their legislature; this figure is reduced to 14 percent when the implied measure is used.

POLICY ANALYSIS BY STATE

Figure 3.2 provides a graphic representation of the number of policy analysts per state measured as the larger of the reported number of policy analysts and the implied measure that multiplies the number of professional staff by the percentage of time spent on policy analysis. By either the reported or the implied measure, seven states—Arkansas, Delaware, Massachusetts, New Jersey, New York, Rhode Island, and Wyoming—report that no nonpartisan policy analysis is conducted in their state legislative agencies.[11] This does not imply, of course, that policy analysis is not conducted in these states, but only that nonpartisan policy analysis is not reported by the state leg-

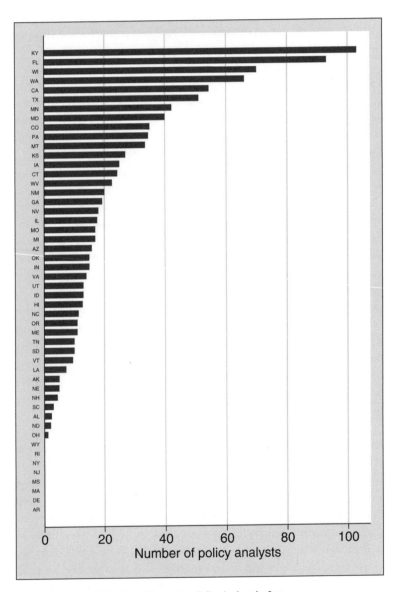

Figure 3.2   Reported Number of Nonpartisan Policy Analysts by State

islative agencies. Indeed, several of these states—including Massachusetts, New Jersey, and New York—have large partisan staffs. Other states with large partisan staffs, such as California and Illinois, have substantial nonpartisan research staff support as well.

Furthermore, a calculation comparing the number of policy analysts per state legislator does not markedly change state rankings; the top five states based on this measure are Kentucky, Florida, Wisconsin, California, and Washington; the lowest five (not including those with zero reported policy analysts) are, in ascending order, Ohio, New Hampshire, North Dakota, Alabama, and South Carolina.

One factor commonly used to explain variation in state politics and policy is the degree of legislative professionalism. For example, the world's most professional legislature (traditionally measured by staffing, duration, and salaries)—the U.S. Congress—has copious policy analysis capabilities at its disposal. A well-known measure of professionalism of state legislatures, developed by Peverill Squire, compares state legislatures with the U.S. Congress and encompasses several facets of legislative activity.[12] Therefore, it is a particularly useful measure against which policy analysis capacity can be viewed. Nonetheless, the direction of influence is unclear. Because of their longer legislative sessions and full-time legislators, more highly professionalized legislatures may be expected to have greater capacity to promote more policy analysis; alternatively, demand for policy analysis may be greater from citizen legislatures whose members have less time to gain knowledge of complicated policy debates.

Figure 3.3 depicts the relationship between the number of policy analysts and the three major categories of legislative professionalism. Although in general there is a positive correlation between professional legislatures and policy analysis capacity (although not always statistically significant),[13] there are important exceptions in both directions: professional legislatures where there is little or no nonpartisan institutional policy analysis capacity (e.g., Massachusetts) and citizen legislatures where significant policy analysis capacity exists (e.g., Montana and West Virginia). It is notable that for each level of legislative professionalism at least one state within each category contains one or more agencies with no policy analysis capacity and several states with more than one policy analyst for every five

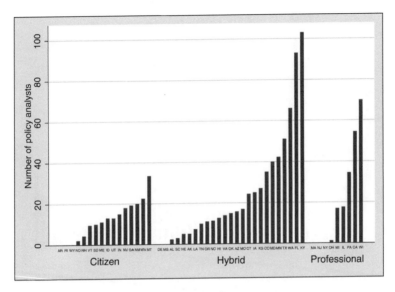

Figure 3.3   Legislative Professionalism and Policy Analysis Capacities

legislators. While generally correlated, NPRO capacity does not derive simply from legislative professionalism.

Given the inherently political nature of policy analysis, one might expect party and interest group strength to be related to policy analysis capacity; specifically, I expect strong parties to limit growth in nonpartisan staff. Party strength is classified as weak, moderate, or strong based on governors' percentages of the primary vote in gubernatorial primaries over a twenty-year period (Morehouse and Jewell 2003, 79). Interest group strength is classified as subordinate, complementary, or dominant (or some combination) based on a study by Thomas and Hrebenar (1999) that compared perceptions of the strength of interest groups across all fifty states (Morehouse and Jewell 2003, 79). Figure 3.4 depicts the relationship between the number of policy analysts per state and three types of party strength. Among strong-party states, none reports more than thirty-five nonpartisan policy analysts.[14] However, this is also true of weak-party states; Kentucky is the only state with a weak party system that has more than twenty-seven nonpartisan policy analysts. By contrast,

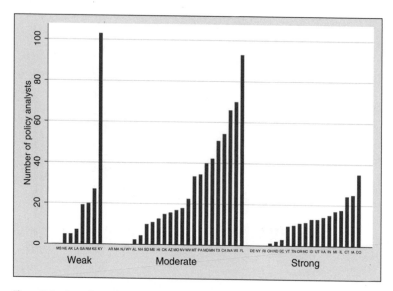

Figure 3.4   Party Strength and State Nonpartisan Policy Analysis Capacities

nine states with moderate party strength report more than thirty-five policy analysts. A statistically significant relationship exists between the reported number of nonpartisan policy analysts and the presence of moderate party strength. This nonlinear relationship suggests that both weak and strong parties may serve to discourage NPRO development; the next chapter tests this hypothesis more rigorously.

There also is a statistically significant relationship between the number of reported nonpartisan policy analysts and the level of interest group strength, as depicted in figure 3.5. Of the four states with complementary or subordinate interest groups, only Minnesota has more than a dozen nonpartisan analysts, with a mean of 16.6. The mean number of policy analysts for the successively stronger interest group categories is 19.9 (for complementary interest groups), 33.3 (dominant and complementary), and 40.8 (dominant). As a countervailing source of information and analysis, strong nonpartisan policy analysis staffs may be more likely to exist in states with a strong interest group presence. The relationship between the size and type of NPROs and interest group and party strength is examined in chapter 4.

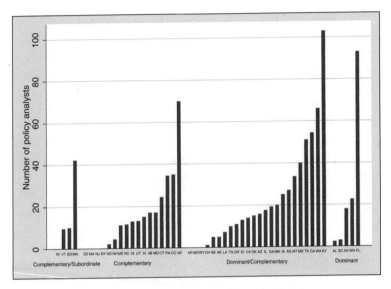

Figure 3.5   Interest Group Strength and Nonpartisan Policy Analysis Capacity

TWO ANOMALIES: KENTUCKY AND MASSACHUSETTS

The preceding sections examined the general attributes of NPROs in the fifty states and found significant variation along a number of dimensions. Two states, however, support extreme—and, given their wealth and level of legislative professionalism, one might say surprising—differences in the way nonpartisan policy analysis is supported. In 1992, Kentucky created the Kentucky LTPRC despite the presence of the large and well-regarded LRC, established by statute in the 1940s and now one of the largest state policy research organizations in the country. In contrast, in 2001 the Massachusetts General Court (its legislature) eliminated funding for and thereby abolished a modest LSB that at one time provided basic information and assistance to legislators, leaving the Commonwealth without an NPRO. Both unusual steps, at least in relation to the rest of the country, can be traced largely to the actions of legislative leaders and the conduct of the agencies themselves.

Kentucky's LTPRC was established when legislative leaders recognized that several important opportunities were missed by the state in the late 1980s; they believed that by establishing an organization focused on long-term issues, the state could avoid some problems and capture opportunities. Both executive and legislative branch officials met and agreed to establish the LTPRC to do just that. Kentucky's LTPRC has a twenty-one–member board of directors: Ten are state government officials (six legislators, both Republicans and Democrats, and four from the executive branch), and eleven are at-large members, six of whom are appointed by the governor and five by the legislature. Although the LTPRC is attached formally to the assembly, it is designed to serve both the legislative and executive branches. Participants believe that this unusual structure provides them with additional legitimacy in the state. Some board members serve lengthy terms—indeed, some are original members—and, as a result, long-term relationships have developed that further the LTPRC's agenda.

Every two years, the LTPRC engages in a formal process of soliciting from both executive and legislative branch members research topics of enduring importance to the state. With the board's active participation and mindful of staff capabilities and interests, they then select topics to focus their work. They are careful to "be perceived as objective and above the fray," and they do not usually present recommendations explicitly, unless they are "motherhood and apple pie" recommendations, such as investing in education.[15] The LTPRC widely disseminates its work through print and electronic media.

The LTPRC has been judged to be highly successful and has gained press attention for its work. A Republican legislator stated, "Because the Center is nonpartisan, it is trying to raise awareness instead of dictate policy, and I think it is doing it" (Stuart 2001, 10). A prominent journalist in Kentucky remarked, "I really believe in this agency. I really use them. . . . The Center does not shrink from serious problems and is able to give the best accounts of anyone I know" (p. 11). Keon Chi, editor of *Spectrum: The Journal of State Governments*, states that it is the only institution of its kind in the United States and praises the agency in saying, "No other state produces reports on such pertinent issues" (p. 10).

In contrast to the success of NPROs in Kentucky, the Massachusetts General Court has no NPROs. Even in budget projections, one person from the Massachusetts Taxpayer Foundation, a well-regarded business-financed research organization, called themselves "the CBO [Congressional Budget Office] for the legislature," an assessment corroborated in interviews with several Massachusetts legislators. At one time, the legislature supported the LSB, which in its early years enjoyed some success. The LSB was established in 1972 by Speaker David Bartley; at that time, the House had 240 members (later reduced to 160), no staff, and no offices, and they used a set of lockers in the statehouse and a bank of telephones to conduct chamber business. The LSB originally had a staff of approximately thirty and, like many current NPROs, provided staff assistance to committees and served as the conduit to national organizations such as the NCSL and the CSG.

In 1978, the House shrank to 160 members and added new staff in an effort—as in many state legislatures in the 1970s—to become more professional. Members slowly began to acquire offices, committee chairs in particular were able to add new staff, and, ultimately, during the 1984 "revolution," committee chairs were permitted to hire their own staff and the LSB staff was downsized. (Some LSB staff went to work directly for the committees, while others were reassigned.) This was a pivotal moment for the LSB, because it now became a more generic institution not tied specifically to legislative committees, who now had their own staffs. The information provided by the LSB thus became more general in nature, and the agency tended to work for individual members, many of whom had their own small staffs. Although it was formally located in the House, the LSB served both the House and Senate chambers.

Because it was decoupled from committees, the LSB's influence began to be tied directly to the interests and inclinations of the House Speaker, a powerful position in Massachusetts politics. Speaker Flaherty focused relatively little attention on the LSB in the early 1990s. It became less a research organization and instead performed more general services for legislators, such as providing orientation sessions for new legislators, conducting training sessions and seminars, shepherding visitors and foreign delegations around the statehouse, and undertaking a variety of other services. The LSB's work turned increasingly to compiling short memos and bibliographies and arranging meetings and conversations, rather than preparing reports and memos that are the hallmarks of many NPROs.

Some legislators became frustrated by the LSB's work. One reported that, although the bureau used to be effective, she was frustrated that a person rarely answered the phone and that she had to wait far too long for research results. Another member claims to have never received a quality product from them. There also were challenges that the LSB was "a reputed patronage haven" (Sandler 1990b). Former Republican state representative Deborah Mazzola expressed frustration that "Democrats continue to keep ex-legislators on our state payroll collecting thousands of dollars each week for doing nothing. They [the LSB] are not really a productive force in our state government, and yet we continue to keep them" (Sandler 1990a). With the loss of support from rank-and-file legislators, coupled with a Speaker who wanted to centralize power (reportedly, neither the House nor the LSB had Internet access until 1999), the LSB had no strong constituency defending it. Furthermore, Massachusetts has a long-standing Democratic majority in both houses, and controlling information in partisan committee staff was effectively unchallenged. (The last time Republicans held a majority in the state Senate was in 1958; in the House it was in 1954.) For both internal and external reasons, the LSB was effectively abolished in 2001.

There remains no NPRO serving the Massachusetts legislature; nevertheless, legislators still have access to policy research. The strong (partisan) committee staffs and, for some members, personal staffs provide the potential for access to policy-relevant information and analysis. Furthermore, Massachusetts hosts a professional legislature with, by national standards, well-paid full-time legislative positions. Finally, there are numerous interest groups, from the Pioneer Institute on the right, to the centrist Massachusetts Taxpayer Foundation and MassInc, to the Massachusetts Budget and Policy Center on the moderate left. The abundance of universities in the state adds to the air of ready access to information and policy-relevant research.

These examples suggest that the external environment in which NPROs operate is crucial to their success. Policymakers in Kentucky were able to act on their realization, at least among political leaders, that more forward-thinking analysis was needed. Through a relatively modest investment, they were able to create the still-small LTPRC. In Massachusetts, however, the shifting political environment that empowered the committees by providing them with their own staff signaled the demise of the LSB.

The other implication, however, is the importance to the organization of carving out its own area of expertise of importance to the legislature. In the case of Kentucky's LTPRC, their success is owed to their inclusion of many stakeholders on their board, their wide solicitation of advice for research topics, their visibility in disseminating reports in both electronic and print form, and the general perception that they are very good at what they do.[16] In Massachusetts, the LSB did not adjust effectively to the external political changes of the mid-1980s. If they had recast themselves as serving legislators by providing quick information turnaround and short-term analysis, and been effective in doing so, they might have been able to win the support of legislators who, despite having professional legislature status, still have few staff with time and resources to conduct any kind of policy analysis. Instead, they chose other tasks and, when called upon, were reported by several legislators to be unresponsive. Although it might have always been a challenge for the LSB to succeed with house speakers eager to acquire and dispense information for their own benefit, it is also true that the LSB was unable to effectively widen its constituency or to gain sufficient support from rank-and-file legislators. Ultimately, this failure to identify and serve a supportive constituency led to its quiet demise; several people I interviewed did not even know the LSB had been eliminated.

CONCLUSIONS

The survey results showed significant differences in the institutional provision of nonpartisan policy analysis capacity among state legislatures. A few have robust, well-staffed offices with the ability to initiate policy analysis, while legislators in other states have no such office to rely on for nonpartisan policy analysis or research. Within the survey results, some patterns are detectable. Most large and wealthy states—including California, Florida, Texas, and Illinois—have strong nonpartisan as well as partisan policy analysis capabilities. However, there are important exceptions to this pattern, as evidenced by states like New York and Massachusetts, which are wealthy states with professional legislatures that have little or no legislative institutional capacity for conducting nonpartisan policy analysis. Although states like Montana and Kentucky have relatively low per capita incomes and citizen or hybrid legislatures, they nevertheless have significant nonpartisan policy analysis capacities serving their legislatures. Therefore, it is difficult to generalize about the ability of state legislatures to acquire nonpartisan policy analysis, and definitive judgments about legislative capacity to understand complex policy issues require more-detailed investigation. Furthermore, the simple pairwise relationships noted above need to be studied more systematically to explain the level of nonpartisan policy analysis capacity. Quantitative and qualitative research, as discussed in subsequent chapters, begins to uncover both the causes for this variation in policy analysis capacity at the state level and the assessments of nonpartisan policy analysis institutions by legislators.

NOTES

1. A notable exception to the proliferation of policy-relevant information in Congress was the elimination of the Office of Technology Assessment (OTA) in 1995.
2. Anecdotal information is available, such as Hill 2003.
3. An exception is Weaver and Stares 2001. See also Weiss 1982, which examines several policy research organizations, but only one of which (California's LAO) was at the state level.
4. For the purposes of this paper, nonpartisan refers to institutions without partisan leanings, i.e., that describe themselves and their work as either nonpartisan or bipartisan.
5. The survey instrument is available from the author on request. Although the definition is effective in distinguishing traditional policy analysis from, for example, information retrieval, this definition potentially may cause respondents to underreport other related

functions, such as information brokering and interpreting studies for policymakers.

6. Initially, surveys were mailed to 124 agencies. In several instances, agencies reported that their functions were redundant with other agencies, that they had subsequently merged, or in two cases that the agency had been eliminated. Furthermore, three responses came from subunits of organizations that had already replied, and these responses were also removed to eliminate redundancies.

7. Agencies that did not conduct any form of policy analysis were removed from the survey results; therefore, we would expect that policy analysis would be prominent among the functions of those agencies that remain.

8. In one part of the survey, some agencies indicate that they do not conduct policy analysis, yet in other sections indicate either that they employ policy analysts or that they spend some portion of their time on this function, or both. Therefore, based on the survey results, this outcome is not inconsistent with including these agencies in the analysis because, in other parts of the survey, they indicate that they do conduct policy analysis.

9. This relationship—significant at the 5 percent confidence level for this broad definition of policy analysis—is strongly positive but not statistically significant for the narrower definition of policy analysis, the reported number of policy analysts.

10. There are, of course, notable exceptions to this generalization, such as in Florida and Kentucky, among others.

11. Mississippi reported too little information to generate a state total.

12. Peverill Squire's typology of professionalism in state governments is based on a comparison with the U.S. Congress using the following formula:

Professionalism index =

$$\frac{\frac{legislator\_salary(state)}{legislator\_salary(federal)} + \frac{number\_of\_days\_in\_session(state)}{number\_of\_days\_in\_session(federal)} + \frac{number\_of\_legislative\_staff(state)}{number\_of\_legislative\_staff(federal)}}{3}$$

This index has since been updated, dividing states into three categories: professional legislature, hybrid legislature, and citizen legislature (Hamm and Moncrief 1999).

13. There is a positive correlation between the number of policy analysts and hybrid legislatures, although it is significant at only the 10 percent confidence level.

14. Connecticut and Iowa both report approximately twenty-five nonpartisan policy analysts, using the broader definition.

15. Interview with Michael T. Childress, executive director of Kentucky's LTPRC, March 25, 2003.
16. One staffer says of the executive director, Michael T. Childress, "He is absolutely the best, a leader by example who inspires people to do good work" (Stuart 2001, 17).

Variable Sources and Definitions

Variable Title	Source	Description
Party Competition	Bibby and Holbrook 1999	Ranney State Party Competition Index: Measures how close states were to perfect party competition between 1995 and 98 (0.5=no competition; 1=perfect competition).
Party Strength	Morehouse and Jewell 2003	Party system strength (1=weak; 3=strong).
Unified Government	Morehouse and Jewell 2003	=1 if usually unified Democrat or Republican government; =0 otherwise.
Interest Group Strength	Morehouse and Jewell 2003	Impact of interest groups in the late 1990s (5=Dominant, 3=Complementary, 1=Subordinate).
Governor's Institutional Strength	Beyle (www.unc.edu/~beyle)	Beyle index, excepting party control (accounted for separately).
Think Tanks	Rich 2002	No. of think tanks in each state that focus on state politics.
Policy Liberalism	Erikson, Wright, and McIver 1993	Public opinion measure of state policy liberalism.
Moralistic, Individualist, or Traditional Culture	Gray 1999	Indicator measures developed by Elazar to identify three major state subcultures (binary measure for each type of political culture).
Gross State Product	Bureau of Economic Analysis	1999.
Per Capita State Income	U.S. Bureau of the Census	1999.
Total Legislative Staff	NCSL (www.ncsl.org)	Total staff during session, 1996.
Legislative Membership	NCSL (www.ncsl.org)	Total no. of state legislative members, 2001. Both houses combined.
Population	U.S. Bureau of the Census	Total state population, 1999.
Legislative Professionalism	Hamm and Moncrief 1999	Based on data from 1996–98 (0=Citizen, 1=Hybrid, 2=Professional).
Legislative Session Duration	Hamm and Moncrief 1999	1996-67 days in session.
Average Legislative Salary ($)	Hamm and Moncrief 1999	1997-98 for state legislators

CHAPTER 4

Explaining Variation in Policy Research Organizations

Why does nonpartisan policy expertise manifest itself in so many different ways? Why, to take one example, would a bicameral professional legislature in a wealthy, progressive, and largely Democratic state like California invest so heavily in nonpartisan policy research, while another bicameral professional legislature in a wealthy, progressive, and largely Democratic state like Massachusetts invests nothing in an NPRO? This chapter addresses two principal questions. First, why do so many states support NPROs, in some cases with substantial resources? This is particularly vexing in light of scholarship suggesting that once-neutral experts become increasingly politicized the closer they get to the locus of power; in short, that power distorts knowledge. I evaluate several alternative theoretical explanations—drawing on distributive, agency, and information theories—based empirically on the survey results from chapter 3.

Second, why is there such variation in NPROs across states, and what factors account for those differences? To begin to understand observed differences in policy research organizations—institutions established for the express purpose of serving the legislature—the second part of this chapter examines why legislatures organize their policy analysis capacities in their current forms. Although there is no extant theory to explain these differences, and much more work is required to draw more broadly generalizable conclusions, the second part of this chapter tests political hypotheses explaining the size and type of nonpartisan policy analysis organizations that states have sustained.

THEORETICAL EXPLANATIONS FOR THE EXISTENCE (AND PERSISTENCE) OF NPROs

Although NPROs vary substantially across states, at one level consistency reigns: The vast majority of states support one or more NPROs. Why they do so is explored in the first part of this chapter, by examining theoretical perspectives on the demand for legislative institutions. North's work on institutions underscores the importance of information and how institutional imperatives influence organizational change.[1] "Both what organizations come into existence and how they evolve are fundamentally influenced by the institutional framework" (North 1990, 5). North argues that "Competition forces organizations to continually invest in knowledge in order to survive" (North 1993, 68), and in the highly competitive world of legislative politics the benefits of this investment in information are, apparently, well understood by state legislators.

The widespread existence of NPROs in state legislatures—particularly NPROs that are perceived as nonpartisan by their clients and a source of pride to themselves—forces us to question the received wisdom that neutral policy advice cannot survive politics and proximity to power (Heclo 1975; Rourke 1992). Because this is the first detailed study of state NPROs, we cannot be certain that NPROs have not become more politicized with time, but the decades-old institutions retain their nonpartisanship in principle and perception. Therefore, neutral expertise is intact, in some institutions for more than fifty years. Specifically, we examine one assertion that "the best one can hope for is to attempt to slow the inevitable tainting of experts by politics [and] . . . the way lies in the design of political structures and the incentives to which experts respond" (Bimber 1996, 23–24).

Scholars have long studied the strong influence that elected leaders have over the agencies that serve them. Some studies even point to legislative influence over agency structure and functions (e.g., Weingast and Moran 1983), although there are important challenges as well (Moe 1987). Although scholars most often study the impact of political representatives, in particular U.S. legislators, on agency functions, they also have conducted detailed research on executive and independent agencies (Arnold 1979; McCubbins and

Schwartz 1984). Therefore, if Congress can have substantial influence over executive and independent agencies, not just on policy issues but on their structure and management, it suggests that the legislature and general political environment will have a powerful influence on legislative organizations. Existing theories can be extended to generate testable hypotheses regarding the existence of NPROs. As shown below, distributive, agency, and information theories produce distinct predictions of NPRO existence and use.

Distributive, Agency, and Information Theories

Distributive Theory.   Distributive theory posits that self-interested legislators organize committees and other legislative machinery to confer local benefits to legislators in order to gain approval from voters and win reelection. In this context, distributive theory incorporates several strands of inquiry, including industrial organization, the "new institutionalism," and game theoretic approaches. Based on the work of many scholars (e.g., Arnold 1979), distributive theory isolates the different types of goods conferred by legislatures as general benefits (i.e., public goods), group benefits (i.e., those that accrue to one group), and local benefits that accrue to one geographic area.[2] In effect, legislators are assumed to maximize net benefits to their districts, their probability of reelection, or similarly self-interested goals, and thereby collectively organize the institution to efficiently pursue these goals. The focus of inquiry, almost exclusively, has been the U.S. Congress.

In a narrow definition of distributive theory, the policy implications can be described quite simply. If legislators maximize their probability of reelection (or, more directly, if they maximize district benefits), one way to achieve local support is to direct federal projects and awards to their constituents. But how can legislators garner local benefits when, presumably, a majority of legislators would oppose a project that benefits just one congressional district? This is accomplished, argue distributive theorists, through the formation of committees composed of "preference outliers," legislators whose district-based interests coincide with committee jurisdiction. For example, this model hypothesizes that legislators from coastal districts choose maritime committees, those from farm states choose agricultural committees, and so forth. Through the strength of the committee system, which depends on institutional deference to committee decisions, legislators channel projects to their districts based on the needs of their constituents rather than those of the nation as a whole. If a sufficient number of legislators benefits from this distribution of resources, a majority will support the institutional form that sustains it. Writ large, we have in theory the institutional creation of a wide range of inefficient government projects for the benefit of individual legislators. In effect, legislators will sacrifice economic efficiency for political efficiency . . . or so the story goes. Although many empirical studies provide evidence supporting distributive theory, the scope and even magnitude of the effects have been called into question.[3]

Distributive theory therefore extends beyond "pork barrel politics" to include the design of the institution itself. Because a majority of legislators theoretically would oppose an inefficient flood control project in Mississippi without a complex configuration of compensatory side payments, other institutional structures—such as strong committee systems—are needed to sustain the system. Individual legislators are assumed to exercise some degree of choice over committee assignments, and, as a result, committees are composed of the preference outliers that sustain particularistic benefits to a membership of "high demanders."

Agency Theory. Much of principal-agent theory posits general principles that apply to the delegation of power from the "principal" to the "agent." In this context, citizens (the principals) delegate powers to elected representatives (agents); similarly, Congress (the principal) delegates power to regulatory agencies (e.g., Weingast and Moran 1983). However, when institutions such as Congress establish agencies to serve their ends, an agency problem results: "The problem is like walking a dog with a rubber leash on a dark night. The leash is not a perfect instrument of control to begin with, and control is made more difficult by being able to see only shadows and fragments of what is going on" (McCubbins and Page 1987, 410).[4]

The dimension of principal-agent theory most relevant here involves the problem that the principal (the legislator) has in using an agent (the NPRO) to provide information and analysis. Because information is powerful, and power can be used to the advantage or detriment of any one legislator, the legislator's decision to use information gleaned from elsewhere must be made carefully. To delegate power—in the form of information gathering, analysis, synthesis, and interpretation—the legislator must be reasonably sure not only that the expert or institution is likely to produce something of value that could not be obtained otherwise, but also that the expert will not use the information to the detriment of the legislator.

One study argues that in order to overcome the principal-agent problem, delegation to an expert takes place most effectively when the legislator is able to trust the motives and content of the information provider (Lupia and McCubbins 1994). "When legislators delegate some of their policy-making authority to expert agents, they can and do create institutions within which they can learn about the consequences of their agents' actions" (p. 374). This is consistent with chapter 3's finding that NPROs often serve committees and even individual legislators scrupulously, drawing legitimacy and power by serving all legislators. Put another way, legislatures can be seen as creating NPROs that will be responsive to their needs and, as a result, are easily monitored.

Information Theory.   A newer theoretical approach repudiates the local, decentralized distributive approach and challenges scholars to understand why legislators and their staffs spend so much time reading policy reports, talking with lobbyists and interest groups, holding hearings, and financing elaborate and expensive legislative organizations such as the General Accounting Office (GAO), Congressional Budget Office (CBO), and Congressional Research Service (CRS). After all, if the legislator is concerned only with the effect of a particular policy on a district, it is hardly necessary for him or her to expend resources to understand the broad policy impacts of proposed legislation beyond district boundaries. The information approach argues that the efficient organization of information and

majoritarian rule are central to understanding the structure and functions of legislative organizations (Krehbiel 1991).

Krehbiel applies two principles to legislative organization. The
"majoritarian postulate" states that legislative majorities over time
choose chamber policies and procedures; policies or institutions that
frustrate the will of the majority are ephemeral. Krehbiel's second
principle, the "uncertainty postulate," is of particular theoretical
interest here. This principle asserts that, although legislators understand the content of legislation, they are uncertain about the connection between legislation and its policy effects. For example, when
legislators pass complex legislation such as the Clean Air Act, the
actual impact on air quality, not to mention the effects on industry,
international competitiveness, automobile design and safety, costs to
consumers, etc., are far from certain. Therefore, uncertainty is in-
herent in legislating, and because legislators are presumed to be most
concerned with effects, reducing uncertainty is a key dimension of
legislative organization. Although there is some disagreement over
whether information theory is truly distinct from gains from exchange theories (Shepsle and Weingast 1994), information theory
represents a significant expansion of the role of uncertainty and information in legislative structure and policymaking.

Implications for NPROs

Information is powerful; therefore, NPROs can threaten other legislative institutions and legislators themselves because of their role
in developing and controlling information. As one review observed,
"[W]hen certain information-gathering activities become centralized,
the autonomy of congressional policy subsystems may erode. . . .
A new body of experts available to anyone in Congress would
threaten the power of committees by allowing challenges to their
authority on technical matters" (Bimber 1991, 590). Therefore, the
existence of NPROs comes at the expense of alternative political
power arrangements, and the nature of NPRO activities helps define power relationships within the legislature.

Distributive theory relies on the assumption that legislators are
rationally self-interested and achieve their electoral goals by channel-

ing resources to their districts.[5] Accordingly, legislatures structure the institution to maximize the potential for benefits from mutually advantageous trades, e.g., logrolling. Distributive theory is normally associated with hypothesizing a different set of institutional structures than considered here—largely involving committees and procedures—but the implications of this theoretical approach can be explored within the context of state NPROs. If legislative institutions are organized to maximize distributive benefits, then a priori we would expect little need for NPROs. After all, if analysts are trained—as they are in schools of public affairs—to represent the public interest,[6] and if NPROs widely share the information and analysis they generate, then it follows that the distributive nature of legislative actions—economic costs in exchange for political benefits—is more likely to be revealed. Transparency does not serve distributive politics well. Distributive theory predicts that information will be maintained within committee structures rather than in agencies representing and disseminating information to the entire legislature.

Gathering, analyzing, and disseminating information is a specialized task that is best delegated. Agency theory predicts that agents will delegate power to information agencies, but only if they are able to monitor their work both to maintain quality and to avoid the production or dissemination of information that could be detrimental to individual legislators or committees. Therefore, principal-agent theory suggests that NPROs are likely to exist, but will be monitored closely and maintain institutional checks to avoid agency problems.

Information theory, in contrast, suggests that if information is valuable, particularly that which reduces uncertainty between legislation and policy outcomes, then legislators can be expected to try to exploit its power. Information theory suggests that information—particularly that which reduces uncertainty between proposed legislation and actual impact—is valuable to legislators more generally. Therefore, information theory supports ex ante the existence of NPROs to help state legislatures reduce the uncertainty between policy proposals and their impacts.

Current theory can help formulate testable hypotheses related to the existence and functions of NPROs, which can be summarized as follows:

- *Distributive theory*: Legislatures do not support NPROs that share information with the entire legislature. Information and analysis are contained in committees, which is the source of power needed for distributive policies to prevail.
- *Principal-agent theory*: Legislators support NPROs to the extent that they provide information that is verifiable and controllable. Principals seek to minimize the independence of NPROs.
- *Information theory*: Legislatures support NPROs; information and analysis are shared widely in the legislature.

Assessing Theories of the Existence of Policy Research Organizations

How well do these hypotheses match the empirical data gathered on NPROs? Information theory provides the strongest theoretical support for the widespread existence of NPROs, which exist in most states, while agency theory supports the type of development and functions of many NPROs. Initial evidence rejects distributive theory's prediction that NPROs will restrict information,[7] while providing strong support for the information and agency theories of NPRO formation and behavior.

Principal-agent theory stresses the importance for agents of maintaining the credibility and trust of their principals, and NPROs make substantial efforts in this direction. First, in order to develop trust, some NPROs allow legislators to review their work prior to publication, and some even retain something akin to attorney-client privilege. There are many variations in how agencies manage this process. At the other extreme, California's Legislative Analysts Office does not divulge publicly even that a legislator made a request to its office, much less divulge the product itself. A similar model is Nevada's Research Division, which produces work products confidentially for legislators requesting information; findings, which are usually presented in memo form, can be released publicly only by the legislator. Therefore, much of its work product never becomes public information. In these states, the principal-agent problem is managed by the principal (legislator) by ensuring that some of the information provided by the NPRO is confidential.

In most states, however, nearly every legislative request and work product is part of the public record, although there may be variations with respect to how and when this information is released. For example, Connecticut's Office of Legislative Research allows legislators to retain the work for five days prior to its public release. Others have changed their procedures over time. Montana's Legislative Fiscal Division used to preserve anonymity for legislative requests; it now provides the information to outsiders who make such a request. Therefore, although most NPROs produce work that is ultimately available to the public, the legislator normally sees the work first and, therefore, can control its dissemination to some extent.

Second, NPROs frequently go to great lengths to preserve the appearance and reality of being nonpartisan, sometimes even in states traditionally controlled by one party. Virtually every research director interviewed stressed the importance of nonpartisanship. One reason was purely financial: It is less expensive to have one NPRO than two partisan ones. Nonpartisanship was also viewed as important in providing credibility to legislators, many of whom prefer clear, unbiased facts from a dependable source to more sophisticated analysis from an undependable source. Many research directors said that their credibility derived substantially from their nonpartisan orientation, that they would be far less effective without it, and that this distinguished their organization from other political actors in the legislature.

Finally, the vast majority of NPROs is highly responsive to individual legislator requests, and for many, these requests occupy much of their workload during the legislative session. Some agencies pride themselves on never turning down a work request from a legislator, although this sometimes strains staff resources and compromises the NPRO's ability to conduct longer-term research. Many NPROs—particularly those in part-time legislatures—reported that their staffs work long hours during session and compensate by taking vacation and working fewer hours between sessions. This attention to individual legislators and committee requests from both sides of the aisle is key to fostering the perception that the institution is credible and trustworthy. Therefore, agency theory explains much about the way NPROs conduct their business in order to preserve credibility and maintain the trust of their clients.

NPROs comply with legislatures in different ways, and some, such as the LSB in Massachusetts, are effectively eliminated because they do not serve the legislative power structure effectively. Some NPROs, for example, scrupulously avoid making policy recommendations in their reports, while others are permitted to do so, at least occasionally. Some NPROs are permitted to initiate their own analyses, while others take their cues directly from individual legislators or committees. Finally, some NPROs focus on providing information and short-term analyses to members, while others are permitted to conduct longer-term analyses. These all are examples of different ways in which state legislatures and agencies have adjusted to policy research capabilities and needs. The information needs of legislators—following the lead from information theory—have produced NPROs in nearly every state, but it is nevertheless clear—following from agency theory—that NPRO behavior is monitored closely by legislators (principals) and that NPROs have been molded to serve the interests of their clients. Surprisingly, that molding has not included overt politicization in most cases.

EXPLAINING VARIATION IN NPROs

Scholarly writing on legislative organization focuses almost exclusively on the U.S. Congress, and its application has little direct bearing on explaining variation in the institutional structure of information providers in state legislatures. Although there are studies that examine individual agencies, such as the OTA (Bimber 1996), there is no theoretical literature that develops testable hypotheses applicable to NPROs or other information providers in the legislature. One recent review notes, "What is needed is comparative research into the factors that affect staff levels and organization and the consequences these changes have had on the state policymaking environment" (Grossback and Peterson 2004, 27). The theoretical approaches examined in brief above—distributive, agency theory, and information—have little direct application in terms of explaining variation in state NPRO size and structure. For example, the distributive and informational approaches to legislative structure have developed hypotheses that apply to committee formation, the choice of legislative rules that restrict joint action, and procedures adopted after floor debate. However, existing theory falls short of explaining the structure of legislative institutions, such as NPROs, and does not begin to explain the substantial variation of these organizations across different political-institutional frameworks. Nonetheless, the literature on congressional use of policy analysis—reviewed earlier in chapter 2—yields some tentative explanations for variation in information provision across legislative structures.

Schick argues that legislative demand for policy analysis is a function of several factors, including independence from the executive branch, staff resources, the analytic resources available to the executive branch and private interests, and the openness of the legislative process (Schick 1976). Other studies suggest that Congress "is actually very effective as a consumer of expertise." Bimber's analysis of the former Congressional OTA, like many NPROs a "captive organization of experts," concludes that such organizations "can provide depoliticized expertise—if institutional arrangements reward it" (Bimber 1996, 98). Bimber also maintains that more decentralized legislative organizations will tend to reward organizations of experts that are inclusive. Whiteman's study of the use of policy analysis in Congress draws attention to the personal relationships that can develop between congressional staff and experts (Whiteman 1995). Others argue that "information is so central to the formation of desired public policies and the power of policy actors, that we see it as the driving force in the development of legislative structures and staff organization" (Grossback and Peterson 2004, 30–31).

The study of institutions is central in politics. "If observers of politics have learned anything over the past two decades, it is that institutions do matter" (Bimber 1996, 21). Because the overwhelming majority of policy-relevant work is intended to help inform policymaking, policymakers' needs shape the type of analysis they receive. In an earlier article, Bimber adds that "institutional arrangements shape the relevance of expertise to political outcomes.

Whether knowledge is power or whether it is irrelevant to political outcomes depends in part on features of the institution" (Bimber 1991, 587). This section examines whether and how the state political and economic environment affects the size and type of NPROs.

The overwhelming majority of knowledge utilization studies have examined the impact of expertise on policymakers and policymaking. Rarely has the impact of policymakers on policy expertise been examined, despite the fact that future policy analysts are taught to tailor their analyses for the needs of their clients (Bardach 2000; Weimer and Vining 1998). The simple schematic in figure 4.1 typifies the relationship between policy analysis, which in knowledge utilization studies is always treated as the independent variable, and public policies or policymakers, which are always treated as the dependent variable. This presumes an independent and unidirectional relationship between policy information and policymaking. The relationship is framed so that the research question is, inevitably: How do we gauge the impact of policy analysis on public policymaking?[8] Although it is an important question worthy of considerable research, the reverse direction of causality remains unexplored. One study of expertise in legislatures—in this case Congress—states, "[I]t is indeed possible for political institutions to elicit the production of neutral-tending expertise. . . . The key is how institutional structure aggregates individual politicians' demands for information" (Bimber 1996, 97). Some of the effects of politics on policy analysis are examined below.

If policy analysts begin to fit the more participatory role that

Figure 4.1   Directions of Causality in Studies on Knowledge Utilization

many champion (e.g., deLeon 1997), then policy analysis is more accurately depicted as endogenous to the model, not purely an independent factor, and is viewed as being shaped by political institutions rather than influencing political institutions and policymaking. For instance, some researchers bemoan the fact that sound bites and stories dominate policymakers' expositions of policy problems and solutions (Kirp 1992), and that policymakers' use of policy analysis supports positions already in keeping with their ideological orientation. Yet, one of the most significant recent trends in applied policy analysis has been the growth of partisan think tanks, such as the Heritage Foundation or the Center on Budget and Policy Priorities. Virtually all think tanks go to great lengths to be relevant by publishing short summaries of scholarly research, testifying on Capitol Hill, promoting events where researchers and policymakers interact, and generally making their work more accessible. Furthermore, since their inception policy schools have emphasized the role of the client in training policy analysts. It is clear that, in general, the needs of policymakers have had a profound influence on the way that policy analysis is conducted. Nevertheless, researchers' focus on knowledge utilization has almost completely neglected the potentially large impact of policymaking on the conduct of policy analysis and, by extension, on the institutions that promote it.

The research methodology is predicated on the belief that to learn about the intentions and needs of government institutions it is useful to study what these institutions actually do, as well as what government officials say. If legislators create the types of institutions that best serve them, we expect those institutions to reflect policymakers' information and research needs. State variation in political and economic institutions helps determine the reasons for variation in what policymakers demand from policy analysis. This section seeks to determine whether the wide variation in the types of policy analysis organizations is a product of economic circumstances, state political culture, the professionalization of the legislature, or other factors.

NPRO Measures

Two indicators are used to test hypotheses regarding the influence of politics on legislative structures. The first dependent variable is the size of the NPRO capacity for policy analysis, where policy analysis is "defined broadly as systematic research that assesses the impacts of and alternatives to various public policies." This measure includes the number of policy analysts working in each state's NPRO.[9] The second variable measures the type of work performed by the NPROs in each state. In many states, staffing levels and the demands of the legislature preclude anything more than responding to individual requests and performing largely descriptive research. In other states, legislatures have developed agencies that regularly conduct studies over the course of many months, or even many years. Based on the typology developed in chapter 3, states are assessed and ranked on a three-point scale based on the type of work performed by their NPRO.[10]

Factors Affecting NPROs

Although the theoretical foundation for explaining state variation in NPROs is underdeveloped, independent variables explaining NPRO size and type are derived from the theoretical literature reviewed above as well as results from the extant empirical literature on state politics. The justifications for variable selection and their expected effects on NPRO size or type are provided below.

Political Competition. Political institutions respond to competition, and legislatures respond to competition from multiple sources. Accordingly, because knowledge can be used to advance political and economic interests, political competition from external sources can increase the demand for information internally. "Competition is the key force that causes organizations to invest in the knowledge and information necessary to maintain or enhance their power" (Grossback and Peterson 2004, 31).[11] Evidence also suggests the importance of political competition and party strength on state policymaking (Barrilleaux 1997).

Because individual legislators are unlikely to be able to exploit information for their own purposes—we saw in chapter 3 that the vast majority of NPROs make their general studies available to all legislators, although dissemination is sometimes delayed—they must use other institutional means to exploit the power of information from their NPROs. The most apparent means of organization is by party (Cox and McCubbins 1993). Political parties are a means of organizing interests and attenuating internal competition. Therefore, we would expect that where parties are strong institutions, and where their supremacy is consistent over time, the institutional importance of maintaining a NPRO is more limited. If a single party is dominant over time (e.g., Democrats in the Massachusetts legislature), there is little incentive to provide information to the opposition party as long as there is little chance of the minority party taking control of the legislature. By contrast, and coupled with information theory described above, in states where parties are competitive over time, NPROs can be expected to be better developed and play a more significant role in legislating. Legislatures in states with strong parties can be expected to suppress information, not invest in it, whereas those with competitive parties can be expected to support stronger NPROs.[12]

The effects of political competition are measured in three ways. The first uses the Ranney measure to identify the level of two-party competition within the state from 1980 to 2000. This approach measures the proportion of state senate seats won, the proportion of votes won for governor, the proportion of state house seats won, and the average proportion of time that the state senate, house, and governorship were controlled by a particular party. The value increases in relation to higher levels of two-party competition in the state. The second variable measures state party strength, which is classified as weak, moderate, or strong. States with strong parties are expected to have weaker NPRO capacity because they compete for political power and the influence that information begets.[13] Finally, as a measure of sustained political power over a longer time frame, an indicator variable is used to measure whether one party, either Republican or Democrat, has controlled both houses of the legislature and the governorship from 1979–2002.[14] If so, we would expect smaller and more descriptive NPROs that deliver little analysis.

Political Culture. Political culture relates to different historical and political developments that shape a state's political culture, which are hypothesized to influence the development of political institutions. Elazar's widely used typology divides states into one of three types of political culture: moralistic, traditionalist, or individualist (Elazar 1984). Some research supports the conclusion that officials in moralistic states are more likely to use policy analysis (Lester 1993); other research suggests that moralistic cultures are more likely to support government activities and are more likely to innovate (Johnson 1976; Karning and Sigelman 1975). Other studies find that political culture has a strong impact on the general policy liberalism in a state (Klingman and Lammers 1984). Moralistic states tend to emerge from a progressive orientation and may be favorably disposed to the role of policy analysis in public policymaking. As one study puts it, "The moralistic culture views government in a much more positive light. It becomes a vital force in the search for the good life, in the quest for a common weal" (Morgan and Watson 1991, 33). Therefore, we would expect legislatures in states with moralistic political cultures to support larger and more analytical NPROs.

Policy Liberalism. A state's overall political ideology is expected to influence the type of government that develops, as well as legislative demand for information (Erikson, Wright, and McIver 1993). States that are more politically liberal can be expected to support more activist governments, which in turn demand more information to develop new or modified policies. Policy liberalism is measured using the composite policy liberalism scale developed by Erikson, Wright, and McIver (EWM), which is derived from public opinion on eight issues. At first, the hypothesis—that more liberal states will support larger or more analytical NPROs—appears questionable: New York and Massachusetts, states without much nonpartisan policy research capacity, receive the highest scores on the EWM policy liberalism index. The relationship between policy liberalism and NPROs is tested more systematically below and includes other intervening factors that may explain NPRO variation.

Interest Group Strength.   Interest groups are an essential part of politics; as one study notes, "If we want to understand the major changes that have taken place in state politics—particularly changes in power relationships—interest groups and lobbying are among the best elements of state politics to study" (Thomas and Hrebenar 1999, 113). Others find that state legislators find interest groups to be an important source of information (Mooney 1991b; Ray 1982; Sabatier and Whiteman 1985). The verification of information from delegated agents (such as NPROs) is essential to solving the principal-agent problem in legislatures[15] (Lupia and McCubbins 1994). Based on this theoretical orientation, the greater the availability of independent information to verify the output of the NPRO, the greater the likelihood that the legislature will support such an institution. Therefore, this information-verification perspective hypothesizes that states with powerful interest groups will have more robust independent nonpartisan research capacity.

An alternative view of the role of interest groups in shaping legislative analytical capacity leads to a similar conclusion, yet for different reasons. Allen Schick believes that Congress will use analytical resources, but in a different way. He argues, "The extent to which Congress uses analysis depends at least as much on external capabilities as on what it does to bolster its own analytical resources. If very little analytic work is being done outside Congress, the prospect is dismal for much of it inside" (Schick 1976, 227–28). This, too, suggests that stronger external interest group involvement will lead to more internal demand for analysis. State interest group strength is measured on an increasing scale from subordinate to dominant, as described in chapter 3. Stronger interest groups are hypothesized to be associated with stronger NPROs, although the specific reason for this will need to be examined using other means.

Think Tanks and State Economic Resources.   Legislators absorb information from many sources; in addition to interest groups, think tanks are increasingly an influential source of information in Washington and in many states. The nature of think tanks in states is currently unexamined across states. Data do not yet exist on the political strength of think tanks in states; one simple measure of this strength is the number of think tanks in each state that make state politics part of their mission.[16] Some states have many think tanks— California leads the way with twenty-one—whereas eight states have no state-based think tanks; the mean number of think tanks per state is 2.34. As with interest groups, I hypothesize that greater competition from information providers would lead to larger and more analytical state NPROs.

The literature on state politics has long found that the level of state economic development is strongly correlated with policy outputs (Sharkansky and Hofferbert 1969). The economic resources of the state are important independent variables in predicting the level of support to different groups, such as to the economically disadvantaged.[17] As with any normal good, economic theory predicts that greater aggregate economic wealth can be expected to increase government functions, in this case including the size and capacity of NPROs generally. Similarly, I hypothesize higher state per capita income to be associated with larger NPROs.

Legislative Professionalism and Staff Support. Legislative demand for information can be expected to be related to the professionalism of the legislature. While noting important impediments to Congress using policy analysis, scholars have suggested that because Congress is becoming more professionalized it is likely to be increasingly receptive to policy analysis (Weiss 1989). Similarly, the professionalism of the legislature also affects knowledge use in state legislatures (Guston, Jones, and Branscomb 1997). I hypothesize that more professionalized legislatures will be less dependent on external information sources and more likely to have larger and more analytically sophisticated NPROs.

State legislatures are categorized in relation to three levels of professionalism depending on staffing, salaries, and session duration. Citizen legislatures rank lowest, followed in ascending order by hybrid legislatures and professional legislatures. However, it is unclear whether more professional legislatures would or would not demand more policy analysis. In professional legislatures, full-time legislators can devote substantially more time to policymaking, and therefore may demand more analytical support staff (independent of other staff support, which is controlled for in this analysis). At the same time, it may also be true that, because they are part time, citizen legislators have a greater need for policy analysis, research support, and larger NPROs. Theory provides little guidance on expected impacts, but generally I expect more professional legislatures to have larger and more analytical NPROs.

Finally, the size and type of NPRO are likely to be influenced by the overall staff support available to the legislature. Legislative staff are widely recognized as important contributors to knowledge diffusion and developing policy alternatives (Jones, Guston, and Branscomb 1996; Whiteman 1995). States that provide significant staff support can be expected also to provide strong NPROs. Included in the analysis are measures of the level of staff support per legislator and the square of that term to identify possible nonlinearities.

Gubernatorial Strength. The strength of the legislature in relation to the governor can be expected to play a significant role in the legislature's ability to acquire and use policy analysis. Because they compete for political power, gubernatorial strength can be expected to affect the information needs of legislators. In a supply-side view, institutionally strong governors are likely to be associated with more-limited policy analysis capacity in the legislature (what good is more information and analysis if the institution is unable to act upon it?) while states with weaker governors may be expected to have stronger legislative analytic capacity. However, seen from the perspective of the demand for information, states with institutionally strong governors challenge the legislature to develop its own expertise; in fact, this reality was instrumental in driving the state legislative reforms of the 1970s. Therefore, the expected impacts of gubernatorial strength on NPRO size or type are ambiguous, and theory provides no clear guidance for predicted impacts. Gubernatorial strength is measured using a modified version of Thad Beyle's six measures of the structural powers of the governor.[18]

THE POWER OF POLITICS OVER INSTITUTIONS

Each of the independent variables above is regressed in bivariate models on the two measures of NPRO capacity: the number of analysts and the type of work the NPRO performs. The results are shown in table 4.1, for both ordered probit and ordinary least-squares regressions.[19] The direction and significance of the coefficients are consistent across different model types and, often, across the two measures of NPRO capacity.

There are several clear associations in the bivariate models. First, and consistent with expectations articulated above, stronger political parties are consistently associated with smaller and more descriptive NPROs in every bivariate specification. Second, there is some support for moralistic political cultures being associated with larger and more sophisticated NPROs, although the magnitude is consistently positive the statistical significance is not consistently strong. Third, policy liberalism is related to more analytical NPROs,

Table 4.1
Bivariate Relationships

Independent Variable	No. of Analysts		Type of Work	
	OLS	Ordered Probit	OLS	Ordered Probit
Party Competition	0.02	0.001	0.001	0.002
Party Strength	−9.31**	−0.39*	−0.27*	−0.44**
Unified Government?	2.06	0.17	−0.04	−0.04
Moralistic Culture?	8.06	0.54*	0.41*	0.59*
Policy Liberalism	2.90	0.04	0.23**	0.35**
Interest Group Strength	5.54	0.28	0.06	0.10
Think Tanks	1.75*	0.07	0.07**	0.13*
Staff per Legislator	1.58**	0.05	0.05**	0.08**
Legislative Professionalism	11.06*	0.56*	0.18	0.27
Governor's Institutional Strength	0.08	0.006	0.03	0.04
Gross State Product (ln)	7.62**	0.34**	0.22**	0.34**
Per Capita Income (ln)	1.91	−0.48	0.78	1.07

Note: Dependent variable is number of policy analysts in each state or type of work performed by NPRO.
*Coefficient is significant at the 90% confidence level; **significant at 95+% level.

although not to larger ones. Fourth, the existence of more think tanks in a state is associated with larger and more analytical NPROs. Fifth, legislatures that employ more staff per legislator are more likely to support larger and more analytically oriented NPROs. Sixth, more professional legislatures are associated with larger, but not more analytical, NPROs. Finally, larger NPROs are strongly associated with states with larger economies, although only in the aggregate; there is no significant impact when wealth is measured in terms of per capita income.

Contrary to expectations, the bivariate comparisons revealed no relationship between NPRO size or type and party competition, a unified government, interest group strength, and the institutional strength of the governor. These relationships are explored more fully below in the more complete multivariate models.

The results of the multivariate estimations are shown in tables 4.2 and 4.3. Table 4.2 presents estimates of models where the dependent variable is the number of policy analysts; table 4.3 uses the typology measuring the type of work the NPRO performs as the dependent variable. Both tables show the results of both ordinary least squares (OLS) and ordered probit model specifications.[20] Overall, the results indicate that several factors independently influence the number of policy analysts and the type of work performed by NPROs across states. In particular, party strength, a unified government, a moralistic political culture, and the number of staff per legislator are strongly correlated with the number of policy analysts as well as more analytical, longer-term policy research organizations. In short, politics has a powerful influence over the nonpartisan policy research conducted in state legislatures.

The most consistent finding is the influence of the state's political environment over the size or type of NPRO. Party competition is positively correlated with the number of analysts in every model specification, but in only one case is it associated significantly with the type of work performed. This corroborates the hypothesis that more party competition is likely to be associated with stronger NPROs, although the results suggest this association holds more consistently for the size of the NPRO, not its analytical capacity. This suggests that party competition increases the demand for information

Table 4.2

Determinants of the Number of Nonpartisan Policy Analysts Serving the State Legislature (N = 45)

Independent Variable	OLS— Unweighted	OLS— Weighted[a]	Ordered Probit— Unweighted	Ordered Probit— Weighted[a]	Elasticity[b]
Party Competition	0.01*	0.01**	0.01**	0.01**	2.69
Party Strength	−1.39**	−1.64**	−0.93**	−1.28**	−0.79
Unified Government?	3.46**	4.80**	2.17**	3.02**	0.64
Moralistic Culture?	2.08**	2.00**	1.21**	1.28**	0.13
Policy Liberalism	0.62	0.84	0.43	0.59*	0.05
Interest Group Strength	0.64	1.13**	0.47*	0.92**	0.88
Think Tanks	0.23	0.25*	0.18*	0.22**	0.27
Staff per Legislator	1.00**	1.04**	0.63**	0.67**	2.01
Staff per Legislator (squared)	−0.05**	−0.06**	−0.03**	−0.04**	−1.58
F (or Likelihood Ratio) Statistic	4.75**	9.32**	38.11**	54.37**	
Adjusted R^2	0.4338	0.6298			

Note: Dependent variable is the square root of the number of policy analysts in each state.

*Coefficient is significant at the 90% confidence level; **significant at 95+% level.

[a]Weighting is by total state population.

[b]Elasticities from OLS weighted model, evaluated at the means of the independent variables.

gathering and other more routine research tasks rather than for more sophisticated policy analysis. Party competition is also substantively important, shown by elasticities.

In contrast, state policy liberalism is closely related to the type of work the NPRO performs, and yet is unrelated (the effects are positive but not usually significant) to the number of policy analysts. Taken with the effects of party competition noted above, it appears that greater party competition is associated with more nonpartisan policy analysts, but that state policy liberalism is most closely associated with more analytical NPROs.

As expected, stronger parties are associated with smaller NPROs and those with less long-term capacity. This corroborates theoretical

Table 4.3
Determinants of the Type of NPROs (N = 46)

Independent Variable	OLS— Unweighted	OLS— Weighted*	Ordered Probit— Unweighted	Ordered Probit— Weighted[a]	Elasticity[b]
Party Competition	0.00	0.00	0.00	0.01*	2.19
Party Strength	−0.54**	−0.60**	−1.35**	−1.53**	−1.27
Unified Government?	0.95**	1.29**	2.21**	3.20**	0.76
Moralistic Culture?	0.50**	0.39*	1.24**	0.97*	0.11
Policy Liberalism	0.42**	0.44**	1.01**	1.01**	0.11
Interest Group Strength	0.11	0.19	0.28	0.52	0.65
Think Tanks	0.03	0.08**	0.06	0.22**	0.38
Staff per Legislator	0.27**	0.37**	0.61**	0.84**	3.10
Staff per Legislator (squared)	−0.01**	−0.02**	−0.03**	−0.04**	−2.30
F (or Likelihood Ratio) Statistic	7.58**	12.17**	44.22**	55.62**	
Adjusted R^2	0.5682	0.6907			

Note: Dependent variable is the typology of the analytical capacity of NPROs.
*Coefficient is significant at the 90% confidence level; **significant at 95+% level.
[a]Weighting is by total state population.
[b]Elasticities calculated from the weighted OLS model at the means of the independent variables.

expectations that states with stronger parties are less likely to support strong NPROs that would share information widely and threaten party control of the legislative agenda. Contrary to expectations, however, the presence of unified government—defined as either Republican or Democratic—is associated in every model specification with larger and more analytically oriented NPROs. Theory predicted that unified government would be associated with smaller organizations, not larger ones, and certainly with organizations that have less, not more, analytic capacity. This effect was not visible in the bivariate estimates, yet the effects are robust across a number of multivariate model specifications.

The theoretical predictions of the effects of interest groups on NPROs stemmed from two views: One orientation held that strong state interest groups, as information providers, would be associated with larger NPROs required to verify their information output. Another held that interest groups raised the demand of information from within the legislature. Both views predict a positive association between interest group strength and NPRO size or type, and the results provide empirical support for this hypothesis. However, as with party competition, the association is stronger between interest group strength and the size of NPROs than with their analytical capacity. This may lend greater credence to the Lupia and McCubbins prediction that NPROs are necessary to verify information (requiring a larger number of analysts rather than greater sophistication) more than Schick's argument about the overall quality of analysis. Nonetheless, the relationship between interest groups and nonpartisan research production in state legislatures will require further study.

The results further support the importance of political culture in the size and type of institutions supporting the legislature. As expected, across all model specifications, states with moralistic political cultures are strongly and consistently associated with larger NPROs and NPROs with more long-term research capacity. Although culture is not a manipulable policy variable, the findings do suggest that there may be limits to which states with traditional political cultures can create large NPROs or ones that will be rewarded for producing sophisticated policy analysis.

The number of think tanks in each state—expected to be positively related to NPRO size and type—is positively related to nonpartisan policy research for legislatures, although their statistical significance varies across model specifications. Finally, overall staffing is strongly associated with NPRO size and type. States whose legislatures have larger staffs tend to have substantially larger and more sophisticated NPROs, although the marginal influence declines with additional staffing.

CONCLUSIONS

The clear and unambiguous conclusion from this chapter is that political influence over institutional form is profound and generally consistent with theoretical expectations. A more pluralistic distribution of power, through greater party competition and less party strength, is associated with stronger and larger NPROs. This suggests that the knowledge utilization literature, which has for decades focused on the effects of policy analysis and research on politics, should begin to emphasize the reverse influence: the effect of politics over the nature and conduct of policy analysis. In particular, the effects of state party organizations, state interest groups, state political culture, policy liberalism, the number of think tanks, and legislative staffing are significantly associated with the size and type of institutions created to provide nonpartisan policy advice to the legislature. Coupled with the observation that a substantial portion of the variation in the size or type of NPROs is explained by these factors, the prospects for significant change in state NPROs appears limited. With overall staffing and a series of external political factors influencing the size and type of NPROs, there seems to be little latitude to establish stronger NPROs or to significantly weaken or change them. Therefore, the investigation of the use of policy analysis should emphasize at least as much the influence of politics over analysis—both on individual studies and researchers and on entire policy analysis institutions—as the influence of policy research on political decision making. NPROs are substantially affected by their political environment, which contributes to their neutrality and lack of independence noted in chapter 3. The fact that NPROs are reactive rather than proactive results from the profound influence of politics over policy research institutions.

One implication of these findings is that NPROs will need to be particularly attentive to external political forces, such as the increasing partisanship of think tanks and interest groups, and to forces within state legislatures that foster greater partisanship. Although the increasingly partisan tenor of political debate is not unique to state legislatures, it does not imply an important role for NPROs. As state legislative leaders are able to add partisan staff—Massachusetts may be a telling example—the demand for information from a nonpartisan source may be attenuated. State NPROs may find themselves either adapting to a changed political environment that requires adopting an overt political perspective within their analysis, or else establishing a unique contribution to state political discourse. The former would be anathema to the internal cultures of many state NPROs, but some may risk losing resources and being devalued if they ignore the larger political environment in which they operate. The latter requires effective and entrepreneurial NPRO leadership in states where the political conditions are changing rapidly.

NOTES

1. North takes a broad view of institutions: "Institutions include any form of constraint that human beings devise to shape human interaction" (North 1990, 4).
2. For more background on the distributive approach to legislative organization, see Krehbiel 1991 and Arnold 1979.
3. Empirical studies on distributive theory, many of them focusing on water resource projects, include Ferejohn 1974 and Maass 1951. Others have questioned whether the emphasis on water projects—a small portion of the federal budget—extends to other areas as forcefully. For example, I suggest that even in the area of water resource policy, the inefficiencies from pork-barrel politics are not particularly significant and are, in fact, economically superior to some other forms of allocation (Hird 1991). More generally, Wittman argues that political institutions are more efficient than normally recognized (Wittman 1995).
4. There are two types of agency problems: shirking and slippage. Shirking occurs when, most often as a result of goal conflict, the agent fails to comply with the wishes of the principal. Slippage occurs when the agent, though perhaps trying to serve the principal's wishes, is institutionally unable to do so (McCubbins and Page 1987). Ambiguous signals from the principal (especially true in a legislative body), unclear collective preferences, or institutional agency structures that obscure or thwart effective compliance are all factors that may lead to slippage.
5. This does not preclude other motivations of legislators, asserting only that electoral self-interest is one of them.
6. See, for example, Friedman 1999. See also, for the importance of the public interest in training policy analysts, Weimer and Vining 1998.
7. In a broader sense, distributive theory suggests that treating information as a private rather than a public good may increase NPRO power and influence. This trade-off—between increasing NPRO legitimacy by being open to legislative requests and providing information to all, and restricting information to powerful members or committees—is something with which NPROs regularly grapple.

8. This research focus is ironic, because students of policy analysis traditionally are taught that a client orientation is an important dimension of their success as analysts, and it is assumed that one's client will have a substantial impact on the type of analysis that is appropriate to deliver and how the analyst decides which projects to undertake. Yet, in researching how knowledge and analysis are used in policymaking, the impact of policymakers is presumed to be an unimportant vector of influence on policy analysis or the analysts themselves.

9. See chapter 3 for an explanation of the derivation of this figure.

10. For the purposes of the statistical analysis, a Type A state is assigned the value of 1, a Type B state is assigned 2, and a Type C state is assigned 3.

11. The state politics literature conjectures that variations in state policy outputs can be explained by, among other things, the threat of political competition *within* the state. For example, officials in two-party states are alleged to have a greater likelihood of serving the interests of the economically disadvantaged than those in one-party states. Because they represent the largest block of potential voters, politicians in two-party states will craft policies to appeal to economically disadvantaged voters (Dawson and Robinson 1963).

12. At the theoretical level, one could argue that the direction of causality is reversed, i.e., that strong NPROs promote greater party competition by providing information to all members. Although this cannot be eliminated formally as a possibility with the empirical means available, theoretically it is sufficiently implausible to believe that NPROs affect party strength—as opposed to the reverse—that further investigation here is unwarranted. Nevertheless, we might expect some reinforcing influence of strong NPROs in sustaining parity among party access to policy-relevant information.

13. Both variables are from Morehouse and Jewell 2003, pp. 79 and 107.

14. The political control of state legislatures has changed dramatically over the past thirty years. In 1975, Democrats controlled thirty-seven state legislatures compared with only five controlled by Republicans; the other seven states were split or there was a tie. By 2000, Democrats controlled sixteen legislatures, Republicans controlled eighteen, and fifteen were split or tied. The major jump in Republican control occurred in 1995, when the number of legislatures they controlled jumped from eight in 1994 to nineteen in 1995 (U.S. Bureau of the Census 2003, 251).

15. They write, "A prerequisite for verification is that there be a second information source who is knowledgeable and has an incentive to

reveal what he knows. To qualify as a verifier, this second information provider must be subject to action costs or penalties for lying or must be known to have preferences over outcomes that are in direct conflict with the preferences of the first information provider. In either case, the presence of a verifier creates competition in information provision, since the first information provider is aware that the effectiveness of any statement he makes could be affected by the verifier's statement. Thus, in legislatures where the likelihood that there will be informed adversaries is high, so is the probability of verification" (Lupia and McCubbins 1998, 370). In short, the greater the competition among information providers, the greater the ability of the legislature to verify the results emanating from their NPROs. Contrary to popular opinion, interest groups that are effective over the long term may present legislators with biased information but rarely with factual misstatements, which would jeopardize their credibility. The Washington, D.C., experience is illustrative. "Because there are literally thousands of interest groups lobbying in Congress for every conceivable cause, the competition among interest groups is likely to be fierce. It follows . . . that the wise interest group is one that guards its access jealously by providing legislators with accurate, succinct information on its favored issues, because once a member of Congress's trust has been broken by an over-zealous lobbying effort, there may be little opportunity to win it back" (Lupia and McCubbins 1998). Therefore, the presence of strong interest groups in the state is a good indicator of the ability of legislators to use independent verification of the results of NPROs, leading in turn to the creation of strong NPROs.

16. Andrew Rich kindly supplied these data. For the purposes of these data, he defines think tanks as "independent, non-interest-based, nonprofit organizations that produce and principally rely on expertise and ideas to obtain support and to influence the policymaking process" (interview for survey). These data measure the number of think tanks in 1996 (Rich 2002).
17. Sharkansky 1968.
18. Beyle's measure aggregates whether governors are separately elected, their appointment power, their budget authority, and so on. Party control, one of the six measures, is measured separately in this analysis and was therefore excluded from this particular analysis. A new index on a five-point scale measures the institutional strength of the governor. For Beyle's source data, see http://www.unc.edu/~beyle/gubnewpwr.html.

19. For completeness, the analyses reported below include both ordinary least squares and ordered probit formulations, and weighted and unweighted estimates. The weighted equations are weighted by the state's total population to account for the substantially different sizes of states, in effect making the individual rather than the state itself the unit of observation. For the number of policy analysts, OLS is most likely the more appropriate measure as the magnitude of the differences is accounted for, e.g., twenty analysts are counted as twice as large as ten analysts. In contrast, where the dependent variable is the type of NPRO, the ordered probit specification may be more appropriate because the magnitude of differences is not proportionate to its numerical designation. (For example, California's NPROs, coded as "3" are not three times the level of Alabama's, coded as "1.") Also shown are the equations, both unweighted and weighted by the size of the state's population.

20. Several independent variables from above are highly correlated, and several were dropped from the multiple regression analyses for this reason and for model parsimony. The focus of the analysis is on political relationships between NPROs and their states and legislatures. The variables dropped include legislative professionalism and the governor's institutional strength, due to multicollinearity, as well as the gross state product and per capita income. Including these variables does not change the direction of the effects shown in tables 4.2 and 4.3, but because of the high degree of collinearity lessens their individual statistical significance. In separate analyses, richer states—defined as those with large economies, although not in per capita terms—are associated with larger NPROs but only weakly with NPROs that conduct more long-term research. This association therefore says more about state population than wealth per se.

CHAPTER 5

Legislators and Policy Analysis

The study of the use of policy analysis is incomplete without under-standing something about what policymakers need to make decisions. What is their perception of the importance of policy analysis in making political decisions? Chapter 4 showed the degree to which NPROs are affected by their political environments; this chapter turns to policymakers' preferences and attitudes toward information and policymaking in the legislature as well as their assessments of NPRO effectiveness. Previous studies have surveyed legislators, their staffs, and others on their use of technical and scientific information in policymaking. In many of these studies, personal interviews with legislators have provided insight into their motivations for using research, the conditions under which they do so, and the sources they consult in reaching public policy decisions.[1] This assessment of policymakers' demand for policy analysis reaches across a wide range of states and samples hundreds of legislators, soliciting detailed in-formation on legislators' views on the use of information, the influ-ence of various policy actors, their own varied uses of policy analysis, and information on their ideology, party, formal education, and other personal characteristics. It represents a broad yet detailed assessment of legislators' views of the relative importance of policy analysis in policymaking, as well as their perceptions about the performance of NPROs in delivering the sort of information and analysis they need. The results suggest that legislators value the contributions of NPROs mostly for gathering and summarizing information and least for critically reviewing policy proposals or bringing new ideas and fresh perspectives to the legislature. NPROs are valuable to, albeit not influential in, the legislature, and yet their value in general is measured by their more modest analytical contributions to their clients.

The states where legislators were surveyed were chosen to represent variation along several important dimensions of legislative and political behavior, principally variation among three factors: professionalism of the legislature (professional, hybrid, and citizen); variation in the political culture (traditional, moralistic, and individualistic); and the size and type of nonpartisan policy analysis organizations (see chapter 3).[2] In addition, an attempt was made to achieve geographic distribution. This variation is depicted in table 5.1. (Note there are no professional legislatures in states with traditionalist political cultures.)

Seven hundred and seventy-three legislators returned completed surveys. Legislator response rates were tested against known state and national figures for representativeness. Figure 5.1 compares survey responses with those surveyed as well as nationwide averages by legislative professionalism, chamber (Senate or House), party, and gender. Although national, surveyed, and respondent averages were close for most measures, the greatest discrepancy is between national figures for legislators from citizen and hybrid legislatures; the sampled states oversurveyed citizen legislators and undersampled hybrid legislators. Subsequent analyses account for these discrepancies: Data are adjusted (weighted) where statistically significant differences emerged.[3]

THE CONTEXT: OVERVIEW OF RESPONDENTS

The 773 respondents represent a diverse group of legislators. Figure 5.2 represents the individual characteristics of the respondents. Seventy percent are men, nearly two-thirds are between ages fifty-one and seventy, and 94 percent are white. The respondents are a formally well-educated group, with 79 percent college graduates (including 55 percent who have had some postgraduate education), and just 5 percent not pursuing education beyond high school. Forty-six percent described their primary occupation as "legislator" (note that

Table 5.1
Sampled States by Legislative Professionalism and Political Culture

Culture	Citizen (16)	Hybrid (23)	Professional (9)
Individualist (16)	**Nevada (I)** **Indiana (I)** **Rhode Island (I/M)** West Virginia (I/T) Wyoming (I/M)	**Maryland (I)** **Delaware (I)** **Connecticut (I/M)** Nebraska (I/M) Missouri (I/T)	**Illinois (I)** **Massachusetts (I/M)** Pennsylvania (I) New Jersey (I) Ohio (I) New York (I)
Moralist (17)	**Maine (M)** **Vermont (M)** **Montana (M/I)** **New Hampshire (M/I)** Utah (M) North Dakota (M) Idaho (M/I) South Dakota (M/I)	**Minnesota (M)** **Colorado (M)** Washington (M/I) Kansas (M/I) Iowa (M/I) Oregon (M/I)	**California (M/I)** Wisconsin (M) Michigan (M)
Traditionalist (15)	**Arkansas (T)** **Georgia (T)** New Mexico (T/I)	**Alabama (T)** **Kentucky (T/I)** Florida (T/I) Texas (T/I) Louisiana (T) Virginia (T) Oklahoma (T/I) South Carolina (T) Mississippi (T) Tennessee (T) Arizona (T/M) North Carolina (T/M)	None

Notes: Sampled states are depicted in **bold**. Alaska and Hawaii are not included. Political cultures are noted parenthetically, e.g., Rhode Island (I/M) is individualist/moralist, and Georgia (T) is traditionalist.

many states have part-time legislatures), followed by 21 percent in "professional services" (e.g., medicine, law); 8 percent in education; 4 percent in farming, mining, or construction; and the others sprinkled across six other categories. (Other reported professions

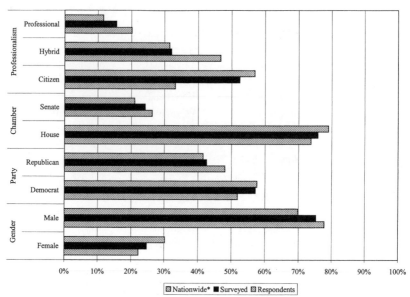

Note: Nebraska is excluded from the nationwide figures because it has a unicameral legislature and its legislators are not identified by party affiliation.

Figure 5.1 State Legislators: Survey Respondents, Total Surveyed and Nationwide, by Professionalism of the Legislature, Chamber, Party Affiliation, and Gender

included such diverse occupations as dry cleaning, landscape designer, waitress, fire chief, retired, and "between jobs at the moment.") Finally, reflecting technological proliferation and suggesting improved potential access to citizens, 74 percent of legislators say they use e-mail every day, 12 percent weekly, and 6 percent less than weekly; just 7 percent say they never use e-mail.[4]

Figure 5.3 presents the political characteristics of the survey respondents. Nearly half of respondents describe their political ideology on economic issues as fairly or very conservative, with less than 20 percent fairly or very liberal. Legislators generally represent themselves as more liberal on social (e.g., civil rights) than economic issues (e.g., taxes); 343 rank their social liberalism higher than their economic liberalism, while just 78 are more liberal on economic issues. In terms of party affiliation, 57.6 percent are Democrats, 41.5

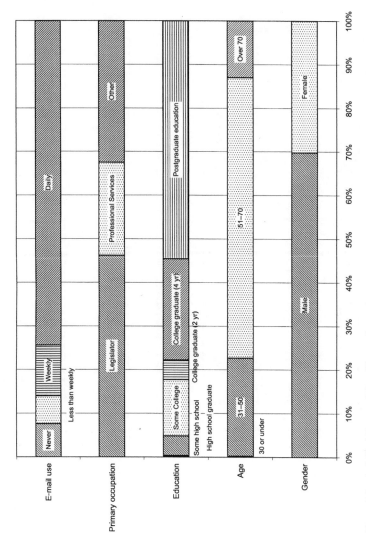

Figure 5.2 Individual Characteristics of Survey Respondents

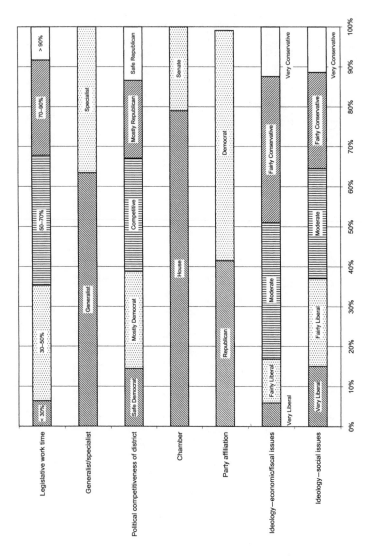

Figure 5.3 Political Characteristics of Survey Respondents

percent Republicans, and 0.9 percent are independents or of another party.

Two-thirds of respondents describe their roles as committee members, with 22 percent describing their roles as leaders and 27 percent as committee chairs. Sixty-two percent describe themselves as "generalists," with 38 percent "specialists." The types of specialization were remarkably diverse, covering almost anything legislatures might handle, such as forest ecology, gambling, labor law, the environment, finance, growth management, and retirement planning. Fully 89 percent served as state representatives, on average for eight years, while 30 percent were senators for an average of seven years. (Approximately one in eight respondents served in both chambers.) In terms of the political competitiveness of their districts, their description yielded a normal distribution: 29 percent rate their district as "competitive" (the median category), 24 percent say "mostly Democrat," and 20 percent "mostly Republican," with 14 percent rating it as "safe Democrat" and 13 percent "safe Republican."

Because of the diversity in the types of legislatures, including part-time citizen legislatures and full-time professional legislatures, just 8 percent of respondents said they spend more than 90 percent of their time on legislative responsibilities; 24 percent spend between 70 percent and 90 percent of their time on legislative responsibilities; 33 percent spend between 50 percent and 70 percent of their time; 29 percent spend between 30 percent and 50 percent of their time; and 6 percent report spending less than 30 percent of their time on legislative matters (see the top row of figure 5.3). As expected, legislators from states with professional legislatures report spending more time on legislative matters than those from other states. Five percent of citizen legislators, 11 percent of hybrid legislators, and 13 percent of professional legislators report spending more than 90 percent of their time on legislative matters. However, legislators who report spending less than 30 percent of their time on legislative matters comprise 8 percent of citizen legislators, just 2.5 percent of hybrid legislators, and (disconcertingly) fully 8 percent of professional legislators who responded. The vast majority—85 percent—of legislative respondents reported that they would be returning to the legislature, while 6 percent had not sought reelection, 3 percent were term-limited, and 6 percent had lost the last election. Therefore, most respondents were reelected and serving in the legislature.

LEGISLATORS' ASSESSMENTS OF THE IMPORTANCE OF VARIOUS INFORMATION SOURCES

Overall Results.   Legislators were asked to rate the importance of sixteen different information sources—from legislative leaders and the Governor to their constituents and the Internet—in helping them reach policy decisions. Although many sources were judged to be important, legislators' constituents are clearly the most important reported information source for helping legislators understand and reach public policy decisions. On a scale of 1 to 7, with 1 being "never important" and 7 being "always important," 88 percent of respondents rated the importance of constituents as 5 or higher, with fully 40 percent rating constituents as "always important."[5] (The next highest source was nonpartisan legislative staff, selected as always important by 21 percent of respondents.) The mean score of 5.92 is substantially higher than that of other information sources.

Figure 5.4 presents the mean ratings of the importance of various information sources, in descending order. Other highly rated information sources included nonpartisan legislative staff (the next highest overall ranking), other members, local grassroots and community organizations, legislative leaders, and special committees or task forces. The lowest scoring information sources included the Internet,[6] political party organizations, and print and broadcast media, all of which were rated as relatively unimportant overall.

In terms of the relative importance of NPROs to other sources, 69 legislators rate their NPRO at least as important as all other information sources; however, 205 legislators rate their NPRO as at least as *unimportant* as all other information sources. Thirty-nine legislators rate their NPRO as less important than all other information sources, whereas just six rate their NPRO as more important than all other information sources. Among states, California's legislators rate the importance of their NPRO—in terms of providing important information—with a higher mean score than any other state surveyed.

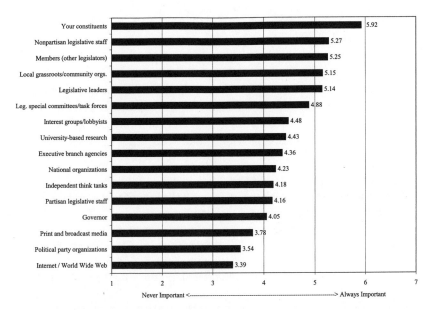

Your constituents	5.92
Nonpartisan legislative staff	5.27
Members (other legislators)	5.25
Local grassroots/community orgs.	5.15
Legislative leaders	5.14
Leg. special committees/task forces	4.88
Interest groups/lobbyists	4.48
University-based research	4.43
Executive branch agencies	4.36
National organizations	4.23
Independent think tanks	4.18
Partisan legislative staff	4.16
Governor	4.05
Print and broadcast media	3.78
Political party organizations	3.54
Internet / World Wide Web	3.39

Never Important <--> Always Important

Figure 5.4   Mean Importance of Information Sources

Perhaps most significantly, NPROs were judged to be far more important than partisan legislative staff in providing information; the latter earned a mean score of just 4.16 compared with 5.27 for NPRO staff. Fully 404 legislators rated the nonpartisan staff more highly than partisan staff, with just 106 legislators ranking the partisan staff as more important. Corroborating this result, 61 percent of legislators agreed that "nonpartisan staff are far more valuable to me than partisan staff"; only 20 percent disagreed. One legislator commented on the importance of the state's NPRO as well as nonpartisanship:

> The [NPRO] provides year-round support of legislators' needs. They staff committee meetings, do research, draft bills, and generally make things happen for us. They, however, have several rules. They leave partisanship at home. They keep personal opinions to themselves. While they are not perfect in these areas, they usually do a pretty good job. Obviously, the down side of this

arrangement is that we legislators are completely free to create whatever disasters we wish, independent of the pool of institutional knowledge under our noses.

Table 5.2 indicates the importance of NPROs as information providers in relation to other sources. By a substantial majority, in every case except for constituents, NPRO staff are deemed more important as information providers than every other interest shown.

Table 5.2
The Importance of NPROs as Information Sources for Understanding and Reaching Public Policy Decisions, as Revealed by Legislator Survey

	More Important Information Source Than Nonpartisan Staff	Less Important Information Source Than Nonpartisan Staff
Your constituents are . . .	378	155
Local grass-roots and community organizations are . . .	250	316
Legislative leaders are . . .	231	301
Members (other legislators) are . . .	222	279
Legislative special committees or task forces . . .	184	336
Statewide interest groups/lobbyists/ associations are . . .	148	445
University-based research is . . .	142	444
Executive branch agencies are . . .	119	456
Independent think tanks are . . .	118	485
Governor is . . .	118	488
National organizations (e.g., CSG, NCSL) are . . .	117	476
Partisan legislative staff are . . .	106	404
Print and broadcast media are . . .	82	546
Political party organizations are . . .	80	556
The Internet/World Wide Web is . . .	77	592

n=765; where rows do not sum to 765, legislators rate the influence as equal or data are missing.
Note: Shaded rows indicate where a majority of legislators believe that nonpartisan staff are more influential.

The importance of nonpartisan staff in providing information does not imply, by extension, that partisan staff are unimportant to this process. On the contrary, when asked whether they agreed with the statement, "Information from partisan sources is not credible," only one-fourth of respondents agreed (ranking it 5 or higher), one-fourth were neutral, and fully 49 percent disagreed.

Institutional Differences.   Institutional differences do not produce dramatically different perspectives on the role of information sources; nevertheless, there are a few areas where these differences persist. Professional legislators are more likely to place a heavy reliance on information from other members (perhaps because the other legislators are also professionals), independent think tanks, print and broadcast media, and partisan legislative staff. (The last observation must be tempered by the fact that several states do not have any partisan staff.) Significantly, with respect to their views on the importance of nonpartisan legislative staff, there is neither a significant difference between senators and representatives, nor between different levels of professionalism in the legislatures.

Political Culture.   The differences among the responses of individual legislators based on the state's political culture are striking and add credence to the notion that political culture does indeed connote a consistent difference among governing styles in the states. The most important differences are between legislators from states with moralistic and traditional political cultures. Legislators from moralistic states place much greater emphasis on information from nonpartisan staff, and traditionalists place much less.[7] In turn, legislators from moralistic states place far *less* emphasis on information from a wide variety of sources: legislative leaders, national organizations (such as the National Conference of State Legislatures—NCSL), the governor, statewide interest groups, local grassroots organizations, and their constituents. In all of those instances, traditionalist legislators place far greater emphasis on these information sources than do legislators from other political cultures. Other than placing higher value on information from statewide interest groups and associations, legislators from individualistic states do not systematically respond

differently from other legislators. Nonetheless, overall political culture is associated with substantial differences in the importance of
various information sources to policymakers.

Legislative Position.   Perhaps not surprisingly, the legislator's
position in the legislature is associated with varying perceptions of
the importance of information sources. Unsurprisingly, legislative
leaders and committee chairs are among those who rate legislative
leaders as the most important sources of information. However, legislative leaders generally place greater importance on a wide range
of information sources, including partisan staff (to whom they are
more likely to have access than are rank-and-file members), legislative special committees (who are likely to be established through the
influence or at least cooperation of the legislative leadership), national organizations, the governor, and their constituents.

Politics and Ideology.   Legislators' perceptions of the importance
of different information sources are strongly associated with their
political ideologies. (The legislator's party is strongly associated with
the legislator's self-professed political ideology on both economic and
social issues; therefore, in most cases, the results are similar for both
party affiliation and political ideology.) Republicans and political
conservatives tend to place greater emphasis on the importance of
the governor and their constituents; in contrast, Democrats and
political liberals tend to place more emphasis on a wider range of
sources, including special legislative committees, national organizations, state-wide interest groups, university-based research, local
grass-roots organizations, print and broadcast media, and the
Internet. For all of the differences they place on information sources,
there is no correlation between party or ideology and the importance
legislators place on NPROs. (Correlation coefficients between Republicans and conservatives and the importance of NPROs are negative but not statistically significant.)

Demographics.   There are observable demographic differences
among legislators' use of information. Female legislators tend to place

greater importance on some information sources outside the legislature—such as national organizations, university-based research (and to a lesser extent, think tanks), and print and broadcast media—and less emphasis on information from grassroots organizations. Those with more formal education place less importance on legislative leaders, partisan staff, the governor, political party organizations, and their constituents. Older legislators place greater importance on special committees and the governor, and less importance on statewide interest groups and the Internet. Finally, and not surprisingly, legislators who use e-mail more often place greater emphasis on the Internet for information.

POLICYMAKING IN THE LEGISLATURE

It comes as no surprise that most legislators believe the legislature in their state is the most significant participant in public policy decisions. However, the process by which those decisions are made cannot be viewed, at least for rank-and-file members, as broadly democratic. Most members describe decision making as highly partisan, and most agree that a small number of legislators make most of the decisions. In terms of public policy, most legislators say they spend a lot of time developing policy expertise and that they generally need policy analysis to reach policy decisions. Legislators generally agree that politics can be distinguished from the substance of public policy decisions, reflecting an old politics-administration dichotomy and perhaps fueling their interest in policy analysis. These responses are explored below in detail. Figure 5.5 illustrates legislators' responses to various statements about policy analysis and policymaking in the legislature.[8]

Legislative Institutional Decision Making.   Legislators were asked about the importance of the legislature in state policymaking and whether most policy decisions are made in committees, whether their chamber is highly partisan, and whether a small group of legislators makes most of the decisions. Legislators from citizen legislatures are significantly more likely than professional legislators to believe that

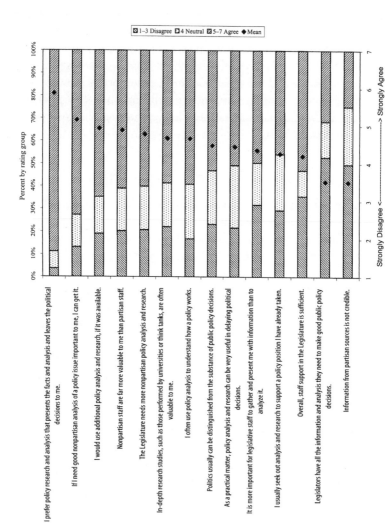

Figure 5.5 Legislators' Use of Policy Analysis

most decisions are made in committees; professional legislators are more likely than citizen legislators to agree that a small group of legislators makes the policy decisions in their chamber. Representatives are likely to agree with this characterization of decision making, but senators are not. Finally, representatives are significantly more likely than senators to believe that decision making is highly partisan.

Political culture is strongly associated with legislators' views of their institutions. Legislators from moralistic political cultures are more likely to agree that most decisions are made in committees and that decision making is highly partisan, yet they disagree that a small group makes most legislative decisions. Individualist legislators, in particular, believe that decisions are not made mostly in committees, and they do not believe that decision making is highly partisan; nevertheless, they do believe that a small group of legislators makes most of the decisions. Although traditionalist legislators disagree that decision making is highly partisan, their views are uncorrelated with respect to the other three propositions. Finally, Democratic legislators agree that a small group makes most of the decisions; Republicans and political conservatives (on both economic and social matters) tend not to believe this.

Legislators' Personal Style and Roles.   Two survey questions explored the extent to which legislators view their role largely as a "trustee" or a "delegate." To that end, the first question asked whether legislators agree with the statement, "My role is to look out for the needs of my district, more than the state as a whole." The second question asked, "If there is a conflict, I would tend to vote for what the people of my district want, rather than my own view of what is right."

Citizen legislators are more likely to be district-oriented; professional legislators tend to look out for the state as a whole. (There is no association between senators or representatives along this dimension.) Legislators from moralistic states tend more to view their role as district oriented, and individualist legislators are more state-oriented. There is no significant association between institutions and the degree to which legislators vote their district views or their conscience, but traditionalist legislators are statistically more likely to be district-oriented. There are two notable personal correlates. Those with more formal education tend to be more state oriented and, if pressed, to vote their own views rather than those of their constituents; those who use e-mail more often share similar orientations.

Political culture is strongly associated with legislators' views of their individual roles. Political conservatives (both social and economic) tend to be more district-oriented rather than looking out for the needs of the state. Democrats perceive that they are elected—and therefore tend to make decisions—based on their personal views and what they bring as individuals, but Republicans perceive that they are elected—and therefore tend to make decisions—based on what they believe to be the views of their constituents. In short, Democrats perceive their roles to be more as trustees whereas Republicans report their role more as delegates.

Legislative Information and Staffing.   As in other responses, the type of legislature and the legislator's political ideology strongly condition responses to information and staffing of the legislature. Political conservatives tend to find most of their information from within the legislature, as do those with less formal education. Conservatives and Republicans tend generally to believe that staff support is sufficient, and do not describe themselves as spending a lot of time developing policy expertise. Democrats report the opposite: that staff support is insufficient and that they spend a lot of time developing policy expertise. Citizen legislators tend to believe that staff support is insufficient, and yet they do not report spending a great deal of time developing expertise. Hybrid and professional legislators tend to give opposite responses, stating that they believe staff support is sufficient and that they spend a great deal of time developing policy expertise. Finally, demographic characteristics are strongly correlated with these responses. More formally educated members, as well as female legislators and those who are frequent e-mail users, get most of their information from outside the legislature, tend to believe that staff support is insufficient, and spend a lot of time developing policy expertise.

Legislators' Views on Politics and Policy.   Although it is somewhat surprising to learn that legislators believe public policy can be separated from politics, there are also some strong correlates with those responses. Professional legislators, those with more formal education, and those from moralistic political cultures tend to believe that politics and policy are inseparable; older legislators and those from individualistic legislatures are more likely to see a distinction. Most legislators respond that they need policy analysis to make policy decisions, yet those responses vary significantly based on demographic and ideological characteristics. Republicans, conservatives, and older legislators are more likely to state that they make policy decisions without the need for policy analysis; on the other hand, professional legislators, Democrats and liberals, women, those with more formal education, and frequent e-mail users state that they require more analysis in order to make policy decisions.

INFORMATION AND POLICY ANALYSIS IN THE LEGISLATURES

U.S. legislators and other federal officials have access to copious information sources, sources that are increasingly sophisticated and aggressive in disseminating research. But state legislators—and there is considerable variation in the nature of the work required of legislators in different states—respond to different sets of pressures and have less staff support than their federal counterparts. Do state legislators feel overwhelmed by the information available to them? Can they get the policy analysis they need to make effective policy decisions?

Although less than one-third of legislators believe they have all the information and analysis they need to make good public policy decisions, at the same time, a majority of state legislators (61 percent) report feeling overwhelmed by the volume of policy-related information available. Individual responses are uncorrelated with either political party or degree of legislative professionalism, although female legislators are significantly more likely to report feeling overwhelmed than their male counterparts.

Just 5 percent of legislators strongly agree that they often use policy analysis to understand how a policy works, although another

54 percent agree to some extent. Furthermore, a substantial portion (45 percent) of respondents uses policy analysis instrumentally, to support a position they have already taken, supporting Weiss's contention that knowledge utilization has many political possibilities. Most legislators—fully 88 percent—prefer policy analysis that presents the facts and analysis, yet leaves the political decisions to them. This is consistent with the view of some that policy analysis and politics are separable in policymaking.[9] Can policymakers get the information and analysis they demand? Most state legislators do not believe they have all the information they need to make good policy decisions; they also believe that the legislature needs more nonpartisan policy analysis. Nearly two-thirds say they would use more policy analysis and research if it were available, yet a large majority—nearly three-fourths—agree that they can get good nonpartisan analysis if they need it.

Institutional Differences.   The demand for and use of policy analysis vary substantially by chamber and, particularly, by the professionalism of the legislature. Senators are less likely to believe they have sufficient information to make good policy decisions, and they are more likely to believe in the credibility of information from partisan sources. The main institutional differences emerge from variation in the professionalism of the legislatures in which they serve; citizen legislatures differ significantly in this regard from their hybrid and professional counterparts. Consistently, citizen legislators are less likely to report using policy analysis to understand how a policy works; at the same time, they also are less likely to believe that legislators have sufficient information or that they are able to get good nonpartisan analysis when they need it.[10] Therefore, the lack of use of policy research reported by citizen legislators may simply be due to poor access to policy analysis. Furthermore, when compared to legislators from hybrid and professional legislatures, citizen legislators are more likely to report that their legislatures need nonpartisan policy analysis and that they would use more, if available. Finally, citizen legislators are more likely to agree that information from partisan sources is not credible; hybrid and professional legislators disagree significantly with that position; accordingly, citizen legislators place far more value on nonpartisan rather than partisan staff.

Political Culture.   Legislators from states with individualist cultures have different views on the importance of nonpartisan policy analysis, particularly when compared to legislators from states with moralist political cultures. Legislators from individualistic political cultures are less likely to believe that the legislature needs more nonpartisan policy analysis and less likely to believe that nonpartisan staff are more valuable than partisan staff. They also reject the claim that information from partisan sources is not credible. Furthermore, they are more likely to believe that legislators have access to all the information they need to make good policy decisions. Legislators from moralist political cultures, in contrast, believe that nonpartisan staff are more valuable than partisan staff and that information from partisan sources is not credible.

Legislative Position.   Committee chairs and rank-and-file members report similar preferences for policy analysis. Yet, not surprisingly, legislative leaders are more confident that they can obtain good nonpartisan policy analysis and more likely to believe that legislators have sufficient information to make decisions. More tellingly, they are significantly less likely to agree that nonpartisan staff are more valuable than partisan staff, in large part because many legislative leaders rely on partisan staff for support and because they occupy positions of political as well as institutional leadership in the legislature.

Legislators who report spending a larger percentage of time in their role as legislator are more likely to report spending more time developing policy expertise and using policy analysis to understand how a policy works. They are also more likely to agree that they can find good nonpartisan policy analysis if they need it. Legislators who spend most of their work hours as legislators also are more likely to agree that their NPRO performs well overall.

Political Orientation.   Not surprisingly, a legislator's political orientation is strongly correlated with demand for and use of policy analysis.[11] In general, Democrats and liberals are more likely to believe that legislators need more policy analysis and are more likely to use it if available. Republicans and political conservatives (on both economic and social issues) are less likely to use policy analysis and, consequently, are more likely to believe that legislators have sufficient information to make policy decisions. They also are less likely to believe that more policy analysis is needed. Therefore, we might infer that attempts to bring more policy analysis to state legislatures will be met with greater receptivity in those with a strong base of Democrats and more liberal legislators.

Individual Characteristics.   One of the most striking differences among legislators is gender-based. Consistently, female legislators report feeling more overwhelmed by the volume of policy-related information available to them. Female legislators are less likely to believe that they have sufficient information to make policy decisions, and they report far greater demand for additional policy research and analysis than their male counterparts. Legislators who report higher levels of formal education are less likely to feel overwhelmed, are less likely to believe they have enough information to make good policy decisions, are less likely to believe that they can obtain good nonpartisan policy analysis when they need it, and would use more policy analysis if it were available. Although the legislator's age is not highly correlated with many indicators of information demand or need, older legislators are more likely to value the work of nonpartisan over partisan staff.

POLICYMAKING INFLUENCE

Legislators appear to draw a clear distinction between *information sources* in reaching policy decisions and *influence* over those decisions. An important finding is that, in the minds of most legislators, the strong impact of NPROs in providing information and analysis to legislators does not translate as strongly into policymaking influence, at least compared with other policymakers and institutions. According to legislators surveyed, NPROs rank tenth among thirteen policymakers or institutions in their influence over policymaking,

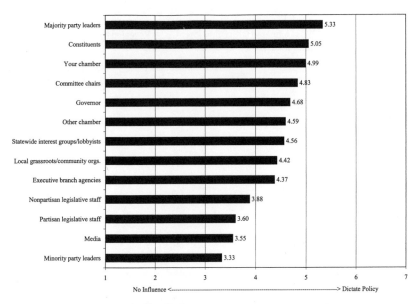

Figure 5.6   Mean Influence of Political Actors

ahead only of minority party leaders, media, and partisan staff, and trailing far behind majority party leaders and constituents (see figure 5.6). The mean score of 3.88 on the 7-point Likert scale from "no influence" to "dictate policy" suggests their perceived degree of policymaking influence is quite low. In comparison with their partisan staff counterparts, however, nonpartisan staff are considered more valuable by many more legislators than those who believe the reverse, although the mean score is only slightly higher.

Table 5.3 shows legislators' perceptions about the relative influence of various political actors in comparison to NPROs. By nearly a five to one majority, legislators believe that majority party leaders and constituents are more influential than NPROs; committee chairs are perceived to be more influential by nearly a 4 to 1 margin, and governor and executive branch agencies are perceived to be more influential than NPROs by a 2 to 1 margin. Although NPROs are deemed more influential in policymaking than minority party leaders, partisan staff, and the media, the numbers are not overwhelming. Clearly, in terms of aggregate policy influence, NPROs are not

Table 5.3
The Influence of NPROs Compared with Other Interests, as Revealed by Legislator Survey

	More Influential than Nonpartisan Staff	Less Influential than Nonpartisan Staff
Majority party leaders are . . .	523	109
Constituents are . . .	496	90
Your chamber is . . .	487	106
Committee chairs are . . .	450	125
Governor is . . .	440	190
Other chamber is . . .	417	182
Statewide interest groups/lobbyists/ associations are . . .	405	165
Executive branch agencies are . . .	357	187
Local grassroots and community organizations are . . .	356	167
Media are . . .	218	349
Minority party leaders are . . .	196	379
Partisan legislative staff are . . .	182	273

n = 765; where rows do not sum to 765, legislators believe the influence is equal or data are missing.
Note: Shaded rows indicate where a majority of legislators believes that nonpartisan staff are more influential.

viewed as important political actors. The contrasting perceptions of NPROs are stark: Legislators see them as one of the most important sources of information in helping them to understand and reach public policy decisions, and legislators view them as distinctly not influential over policymaking itself.

THE PERFORMANCE OF NPROs

Overall, NPROs receive high marks from their principal clients. In evaluating their overall performance in serving the legislature, 70 percent of legislators rate them excellent or good, with 22 percent rating them average and just 8 percent rating them poor. However, their performance on individual tasks varies considerably. Figure 5.7 shows legislators' ratings of their NPROs, from "poor" to "excellent";

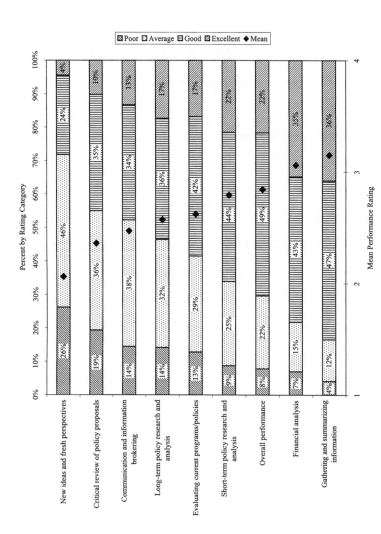

Figure 5.7   Performance of NPROs

the black diamonds indicate the mean rating by function. State NPROs are seen as being most effective in gathering and summarizing information, and least effective in communication and information brokering, providing a critical review of policy proposals, and bringing new ideas to the legislature.[12] Legislators rated the agencies as more effective in conducting short-term rather than long-term policy research and analysis; two-thirds of the legislators rated their effectiveness as excellent or good for short-term policy analysis, and nearly half rated their effectiveness in conducting long-term policy analysis as average or poor.[13] Therefore, the generally positive ratings that NPROs receive are tempered by the fact that their work is perceived mostly as information provision and short-term analysis rather than for their capacity for critical or long-term analysis.

Similarly, legislators report that their NPROs are well respected in the legislature, that the staff is capable of conducting in-depth policy research, and that the office (offices) is truly nonpartisan. Perhaps most tellingly, as reported above, legislators report that NPROs are one of the most important sources of information to them, trailing only constituents among the most important of sixteen possible information sources. Finally, fewer than one-fourth of legislators agreed to some extent with the statement, "I usually can make policy decisions without the need for policy analysis or research."

However, legislators also report significant information overload, with nearly three-quarters agreeing that they often feel overwhelmed by the volume of policy-related information available to them. Therefore, although it appears that many NPROs are established to perform information gathering and synthesis functions—and apparently perform them quite well—state legislators are nevertheless still pressed to absorb all of the information available to them.

Overall Performance of NPROs.   State NPROs are generally perceived to be effective, overall and in gathering and summarizing information and conducting financial analysis, and reasonably effective in conducting short-term policy analysis and evaluating programs. They are seen as decidedly less effective in bringing new ideas and fresh perspectives to the legislature, although the extent to which legislators actually are interested in "new perspectives" is unclear. In general, legislators give their NPROs high marks for serving all legislators (as opposed to serving, for example, only legislative leaders or committee chairs), for being truly nonpartisan, and for being well respected in the legislature. The belief that NPROs can conduct in-depth research is more circumspect, with only slightly more than average believing that NPROs have the ability to conduct long-term research.

There are no significant differences among legislators based on leadership position in the legislature, the political safety of their districts, or the legislator's sex. There are, however, some substantial differences, which are detailed below, in how different groups of legislators perceive the performance of their NPROs.

Institutional Differences.   Whereas house and senate perceptions of their NPROs are only minimally different, the views of legislators from hybrid legislatures and those from citizen and professional legislatures differ markedly. This is an unexpected finding, since hybrid legislatures are by definition those that fall between citizen and professional legislatures in terms of session duration, salaries, and staffing. Overall, hybrid legislators give the NPROs strong marks in virtually all measures of success (except bringing fresh perspectives to the legislature), while citizen and professional legislators generally give lower evaluations of the effectiveness of their NPROs. Similarly, hybrid legislators are more likely to agree that their NPRO is able to conduct in-depth research, that the NPRO is well respected, that it is nonpartisan, and that its resources are appropriate. Citizen and professional legislatures tend to perceive the opposite: They have less respect for the NPRO, believe it is more partisan and less likely to be able to conduct long-term research, and that its resources are inadequate.

Political Culture.   There is little relationship between political culture and legislators' evaluation of NPRO performance in eight individual areas. Culture is, however, strongly associated with legislators' evaluations of the NPRO overall. Legislators from moralist political cultures tend to believe that their NPRO is well respected, that it is nonpartisan, and that it serves all legislators. In contrast, legislators from individualistic states believe just the opposite: NPROs are not well respected, they are partisan, and they are not there to serve all legislators. There is no statistically significant relationship between these measures and those for legislators from traditionalist political cultures.

Politics and Ideology. Ideology and party affiliation are not strongly associated with specific NPRO performance measures. However, there are strong differences between ideology and party affiliation in terms of assessing whether NPROs are nonpartisan and whether they have sufficient resources. Democrats and liberals are more likely to agree that NPROs are truly nonpartisan; conservatives and Republicans are likely to disagree. Similarly, conservatives are far more likely to agree that the NPROs have sufficient resources.

Demographic Differences. Although female legislators have markedly different views on the importance of policy analysis, their evaluations of their NPROs are not substantially different from that of male legislators. The most significant correlates with perceptions of NPRO performance emerged from formal education. Legislators with more formal education were consistently likely to give their NPROs lower marks for many indicators of success. They also were less likely to agree that their NPRO could conduct in-depth research, less likely to agree that the NPRO was well respected in the legislature, and less likely to believe that it was there to serve all legislators.

Legislative Roles. Legislators who view their roles as promoting their district more than the state as a whole are more likely to view their NPROs as influential than are legislators who view their roles as promoting the state before the district. Similarly, legislators who view their roles as delegates, or promoting the views of their constituents over their own view of what is right, are more likely to view NPRO influence as substantial than are legislators who see their role more as trustees. These associations hold true even when controlling statistically for the legislator's party.

Are NPROs Perceived as Truly Nonpartisan? Legislators were asked whether NPROs were truly nonpartisan, and the results strongly affirm that belief. Legislators were asked to indicate, on a scale of 1 to 7 with 1 representing "strongly disagree" and 7 "strongly agree," their assessment of the statement, "The 'Legislative Services Office' is truly nonpartisan." Overall, fully 70 percent of respondents rated their office 5 or higher, with just 17 percent rating the office 3 or lower (the other 13 percent rated it a 4). There is no significant difference in the responses from female and male legislators, or between various levels of formal education. Similarly, rank-and-file legislators, chamber leaders, and committee chairs report similar views on nonpartisanship.

Republicans and Democrats have somewhat different views on the nonpartisanship of the NPRO, however. Among Democrats, 76 percent agree that the NPRO is nonpartisan, compared with 63 percent of Republicans; 12 percent of Democrats disagreed compared with 22 percent of Republicans. Legislators' views vary significantly by state. There is a significant correlation between Democrats and the tendency to agree that the NPRO is nonpartisan in Kentucky, Illinois, and Connecticut, and a significant correlation between Republicans and the view that the NPRO is nonpartisan only in New Hampshire.[14] Among states that are described as "unified Democratic," Democrats are significantly more likely to believe that the NPRO is nonpartisan than are Republicans; this is no surprise. However, among states that are "unified Republican," there is no statistical difference between Republican and Democratic perceptions of NPRO nonpartisanship.

There are significant differences by state in legislative perceptions of NPRO nonpartisanship. Among the nineteen states surveyed, legislators in Minnesota, Colorado, Arkansas, Indiana, Maryland, and New Hampshire report relatively high levels of nonpartisanship in their NPROs, and those in Rhode Island and Georgia report relatively low levels. Furthermore, there is a strong correlation between the perception of nonpartisanship and type of the NPRO itself. (This relationship, although positive, is not significant for the size of the NPRO.) Using data from nineteen states, bivariate regressions indicate that nearly 25 percent of the variation in the perceived nonpartisanship of the NPRO can be explained by the type of work the NPRO performs, based on the three-point typology developed in chapter 3. Legislators in states where more of the NPRO's functions focus on longer-term (and less purely descriptive) research are more likely to strongly rate NPRO nonpartisanship.

Are NPROs Well-Respected by Legislators?   In general, state NPROs enjoy the respect of their clients. Fully 76 percent of respondents agreed—and only 11 percent disagreed—that the office was well respected in the legislature. There is no statistical difference between Democrat and Republican legislators in this regard, nor between senators and representatives, older and younger legislators, those who read e-mail frequently or not, or liberals or conservatives. However, legislators from states with moralistic cultures were more likely to believe that their NPROs were well respected, even accounting for the size and type of policy analysis agency in the state. Among different types of legislatures, hybrid legislators are significantly more likely to believe their NPRO is well respected, while professional legislators are least likely to respect their NPROs.

IMPLICATIONS AND CONCLUSIONS

A more nuanced story about NPROs has emerged. Although legislators value NPROs highly, and rate them highly for their ability to gather information and perform short-term analysis, they do not view them as influential in the policymaking process, nor do they credit them with bringing new ideas or fresh perspectives to policymakers. Rather, legislators report that they are best at and most valued for less analytical contributions. Furthermore, Democratic legislators are more likely to rate their NPROs highly and to view them as nonpartisan than Republicans. Corroborating the findings of chapter 4, we find substantial differences in legislators' perceptions, based on political factors, of NPROs as influencing policy or providing information. Taken together, the fact that legislators rate their NPROs highly and believe them to be most useful in providing short-term information and analysis suggests that legislators are getting what they want from their NPROs. With 71 percent of legislators rating overall NPRO performance good or excellent, and 72 percent rating NPROs as fair or poor in providing new ideas and fresh perspectives, legislators overall clearly value other dimensions of their work more highly.

These results, however, represent average legislator responses for a wide range of states, states where NPROs vary substantially in size and type of work. The next chapter takes up the question of whether these views of NPRO performance and influence are associated with differences among NPROs. In other words, does institutional form affect performance? For example, do larger or more analytically sophisticated NPROs earn higher ratings from their clients than NPROs that conduct mostly short-term descriptive analysis and information gathering? Chapter 6 analyzes the relationship between legislators' views of the usefulness of policy analysis and the types of NPROs that provide it.

NOTES

1. See chapter 2 for a review of these studies.
2. In fall 2002 and spring 2003, surveys were mailed to legislators from nineteen states. These surveys solicited their views on several dimensions of legislating and policy research: the influence of various groups over legislative decision making (e.g., interest groups, legislative leaders, constituents); the importance of several information sources (e.g., lobbyists, governor, nonpartisan staff); the importance of policy research and analysis generally; their role as a legislator (e.g., as a trustee or delegate); their political views and party affiliation; and demographic information (age, ethnicity, occupation, education, and so on). Postcards were mailed to legislators, reminding them to return the survey; a complete second copy of the survey was mailed; finally, a second follow-up postcard was mailed. In each case, this study followed standard mail survey methods, providing legislators with stamped, self-addressed envelopes, multiple means of contact (phone, e-mail, address), follow-up post card reminders, and personalized correspondence (Dillman 2000). In all, 3,150 legislators were surveyed and 773 legislators returned detailed responses, for an overall response rate of 25 percent. This is lower than hoped for, but it is not inconsistent with other legislator (elite) surveys, especially for forms that ask for such detailed responses (Maestas, Neeley, and Richardson 2003). The survey instrument, including the percentage of responses by question, is included in appendix 5.1.

3. Where differences between the survey results and population characteristics were identified, a variable was created representing its proportionate representation (Berman 2001). For example, if legislators in one
state were oversampled (e.g., New Hampshire), the weighting variable,
which initially is set at a value of "1" for all legislators, was multiplied
by the expected number of NH representatives (based on population
totals) divided by the actual. In this example, this would reduce the
weight variable based on the level of overrepresentation in the sample.
Similar adjustments were made for the other categories depicted in figure 5.1.

4. There is no statistical association between e-mail use and a linear measure of the professionalism of the legislature; for example, fully 82 percent of legislators in hybrid legislatures report using e-mail daily, yet
just 69 percent in professional and 71 percent in citizen legislatures.

5. This is true despite the location of "your constituents"—listed third
from the bottom—among the sixteen information sources on the
survey.

6. This may understate the importance of the use of the Internet since
respondents were overwhelmingly legislators rather than staffers who
may be more likely to gather information from the Internet. Further
investigation of the use of the Internet in legislative decision making
is needed.

7. One needs to exercise care in interpreting these results. The differences
may reflect as much about the quality of the information available from
NPROs as about differences in legislative interpretation of their worth.

8. The responses ranged from 1 (strongly disagree) to 7 (strongly agree).
The first shaded bar of figure 5.5 includes the percentage of responses
that were 1, 2, or 3 (disagree to some extent); the second bar represents the mean number who were neutral (4); and the third bar represents the percentage of legislators who agreed to some extent (answered
5, 6, or 7). The black diamond represents the mean score.

9. There is a significant correlation between legislators who believe politics and policy decisions are separable and those who prefer policy
analysis designed simply to present the facts while leaving the political
decisions to the legislators.

10. Interestingly, only legislators from hybrid legislatures believe they can
get good nonpartisan analysis when they need it; citizen and professional legislators are significantly less likely to believe they are able to
acquire good analysis.

11. In contrast, the political orientation of the legislator's district—i.e., whether it is described as safely Democratic, competitive, or safely Republican—is not correlated with legislators' survey responses.
12. In each of these instances, more than 50 percent of legislators rated their performance as average or poor.
13. Legislators from states with citizen or hybrid legislatures give higher marks overall compared to those from professional legislatures. This dimension is addressed formally below.
14. There is no statistically significant correlation in the other states.

CHAPTER 6

The Effectiveness of Nonpartisan Policy Research Organizations

The focus of this chapter is on how institutions affect performance. In this case, how do NPROs influence information access and policymaking influence, and how effective are NPROs in meeting client needs? Institutions are critical to the development of ideas; as North notes, "Ideas and ideologies matter, and institutions play a major role in determining just how much they matter" (North 1993, 68). Do legislators value larger or more analytically oriented NPROs over smaller ones, or those that produce material that is more descriptive? Do larger or more analytically oriented NPROs promote different types of use of policy analysis? And does the NPRO's ability to promote different types of use of policy analysis matter to its clients? More theoretically, does institutional form affect performance?

This chapter examines the relationship between the analytical capacity of state NPROs and various meanings of use in a comparative framework. The purpose of this examination is to improve the understanding of the use of policy analysis or research in several ways. First, I compare the survey responses of legislators in nineteen states—reported in chapter 5—with the types of NPROs identified in chapter 3. This comparative institutional approach permits the assessment of different NPROs in terms of the numbers of policy analysts they employ and the different institutional and political settings in which they work. Second, the effectiveness of policy analysis institutions is measured directly both by the degree to which they are associated with various types of use of policy analysis and by legislators' assessments of the institutions themselves. This is measured directly through a survey of legislators' assessments of the NPROs and indirectly by the degree to which legislators believe their various information needs are being met. Taken together, this chapter evaluates how clients use policy analysis differently across various NPROs, and the effectiveness of different types of NPROs in providing useful policy analysis to their clients.

This study seeks to expand the study of use empirically by including more subtle forms of assistance to clients in addition to the traditional written policy reports that academic policy researchers normally use as a reference point (Mooney 1991a, 1991b; Shulock 1999). Many earlier studies based their assessments on either the individual policy research report/analysis or a single policy research organization. The focus of the knowledge utilization literature on written reports is not surprising. "Academically trained experts are often focused on the presentation of written claims" (Bimber 1996, 96). One study notes that at the Congressional Office of Technology Assessment (OTA), "expertise was often conveyed in the context of personal relationships rather than published words" (Bimber 1996, 96). Studies that overlook these informal relationships are missing an important component of knowledge utilization.

These other, less obvious forms of assistance may include oral briefings of legislators by NPRO staff, the development of trust between legislators and staff over time, and other institutional linkages that promote the use of policy analysis. Carol Weiss notes that the U.S. Congress, like most legislatures, "is an institution with a largely oral tradition. . . . [Members] collect information through personal interaction, and they take pride in their ability to 'read people' rather than read reports. . . . Because they are able and experienced politicians, they have faith in their judgment about the wisdom of alternative policies. . . . Congress produces and uses enormous quantities of paper, too," but Weiss argues, "the oral tradition is paramount" (Weiss 1989, 414). Likewise, state legislators (and frequently their staffs) rarely have time to read long reports and, consequently, often are briefed orally. Therefore, focusing only on written research reports would understate the impact of policy research in the policymaking process. Furthermore, as one study notes, it is problematic to link research findings with policy decisions using individual interviews because many decision makers do not conceive of themselves as such (Weiss and Bucuvalas 1980). By examining the performance of institutions rather than individual studies or research reports, this study attempts to assess the impact of many routes—whether in writing or orally—through which legislators obtain information and analysis.

This chapter measures client assessment of the overall performance of the policy analysis institution, regardless of the way information is transmitted. In its broadest configuration, this approach allows for broadening the scope of the use of policy analysis to be whatever the client views as important, such as oral or written reports, or both, and to focus on the client rather than the means by which the client uses policy analysis in the policy process. However, this analysis is not simply assessing an amorphous measure of client satisfaction; I also examine other types of use, from influencing policy to instrumental uses such as delay or rationalization.

Using the results of a detailed survey of more than 750 state legislators in nineteen states—described in detail in chapter 5—this work examines legislative attitudes toward research generally and legislators' views of the usefulness of the policy analysis organizations that putatively serve them.[1] Because states share many institutional characteristics, yet vary along important dimensions (such as size, institutional strength of the governor, strength and competitiveness of political parties, and so on), they provide an excellent comparative vehicle for studying the effectiveness of policy analysis organizations and, because of NPRO variation, for studying the effectiveness of policy analysis institutions.

Taken together, the following features are unique to this chapter's analysis:

- a comparative institutional focus;
- an emphasis on institutional effects, not on individual studies or reports;
- multiple definitions of use, including broad measures of overall client satisfaction; and
- evaluating an unambiguous analyst–client relationship between the NPRO and legislators.

MEASURING THE EFFECTS OF POLICY RESEARCH

Legislators use policy research in many ways, as articulated by the review of knowledge utilization studies in chapter 2. In this chapter, I examine two distinct conceptual applications: legislators' assessment of the institutional performance of their NPROs and the ways in which NPROs affect the use of policy research.

Institutional Effectiveness.   The survey measures the institutional effectiveness of NPROs by the assessment of their principal clients: legislators. Based on the survey results, assessment is measured in several ways, which are employed as dependent variables in the subsequent analysis. These include each legislator's assessment (on a four-point scale ranging from "poor" to "excellent") of how well the NPRO in their state:

- gathers and summarizes information;
- conducts short-term policy research and analysis;
- conducts long-term policy research and analysis;
- brings new ideas and fresh perspectives to the legislature;
- provides a critical review of policy proposals;
- communicates and brokers information effectively; and
- performs overall.

Legislators were also asked to evaluate, on a seven-point Likert scale, the extent to which they agree that the NPRO in their state:

- primarily gathers and synthesizes information but does not analyze it;
- is capable of conducting in-depth policy research;
- is well respected in the legislature;
- is truly nonpartisan;
- serves all legislators; and
- is allocated an appropriate level of resources.

Taken together, these measures represent a wide range of institutional performance assessments of policy research organizations.

Effects on Policy Research Utilization.   Carol Weiss noted seven distinct uses of research, from problem solving to enlightenment and political or tactical uses[2] (Weiss 1979). Drawing on her typology and modifying it for the purposes of studying policy research organizations, this study examines several types of research utilization:

1. Policymaking influence: influence of NPROs in policy-making
2. Enlightenment: importance of NPROs as sources for understanding and reaching policy decisions
3. Access to information: importance of NPROs in providing better access to, and satisfying legislative needs for, information
4. Rationalization: importance of NPROs in providing analysis to justify previously held positions
5. Tactical: importance of NPROs in providing analysis to achieve tactical goals, such as delaying decisions

Policymaking influence is measured in two related ways. The first examines legislators' assessments of the absolute influence of NPROs over policymaking in the legislature, measured on a seven-point scale from "no influence" to "dictate policy." As revealed in chapter 5, the mean rating for NPRO influence was well below that of constituents, majority party leaders, committee chairs, the governor, executive branch agencies, and most other stakeholders. The issue addressed here is different: How do *changes* in the size or type of NPRO affect their perceived influence? The second measure of policymaking influence is relative: legislators' individual assessments of NPRO influence in relation to their assessment of the most influential among the other twelve possible sources of influence. For example, if a legislator rated NPRO influence as a 4, and her highest influence rating (e.g., the governor) was a 6, I assume this implies a greater relative ranking of influence than if the legislator rated the NPRO a 1 compared with the highest ranking of 5. The difference between these scores is rescaled so that larger numbers imply greater influence.

Enlightenment is measured by legislators' responses to two questions concerning the use of information in policymaking. The first is the extent to which legislators agree that NPROs serve as information sources and help them understand and reach policy decisions. The second question was the extent to which legislators agree with the statement, "I often use policy analysis to understand how a policy works."

Information access is measured in four ways, using legislators' responses (measured on the seven-point scale from "strongly disagree" to "strongly agree") to the following statements:

- "If I need good nonpartisan analysis of a policy issue important to me, I can get it."
- "Legislators have all the information and analysis they need to make good public policy decisions."
- "The legislature needs more nonpartisan policy analysis and research."
- "I would use additional policy analysis and research, if it was available."

Increasing values of the first two measures imply greater access to information for legislators, while increasing values of the latter two measures imply less access to information.

One scholar notes, "Members [of Congress] seek information on policy more often to support their positions than to use in developing new positions. Hence information is not valuable in an abstract sense but has value primarily to the extent it supports decisions already made on other grounds" (Bimber 1991, 594). I measured the rationalization and tactical measures of research utilization by legislators' agreement with the following statements (using the same seven-point scale):

Rationalization is expressed by "I usually seek out analysis and research to support a policy position I have already taken."

Tactical is expressed by "As a practical matter, policy analysis and research can be very useful in delaying political decisions."

MEASURING THE TYPES OF NPROs

Two measures are included to classify the research capacity of NPROs. The first is the reported number of policy analysts from the

Table 6.1
Typology of NPROs for Selected States

State	No. of Policy Analysts[a]	NPRO Work Typology[b]
Alabama	2.4	A
Arkansas	0	A
California	54.4	C
Colorado	35	B/C
Connecticut	24.35	B
Delaware	0	A
Georgia	19.25	A/B
Illinois	17.6	B
Indiana	15	A
Kentucky	103	C
Maine	11	B
Maryland	40	C
Massachusetts	0	0
Minnesota	42.25	C
Montana	33.5	C
Nevada	18	B
New Hampshire	4.375	B
Rhode Island	0	A
Vermont	9.5	B

[a] This measure represents the larger of the reported number of policy analysts and an imputed figure calculated by multiplying the time spent on policy analysis by the reported number of professional staff.
[b] Key:
  A = mostly descriptive work, very little or no in-depth analysis
  B = descriptive work, some in-depth analysis normally undertaken during interim sessions
  C = significant ongoing policy analysis capacity
Source: NPRO survey.

written NPRO survey, as shown in table 6.1.[3] Because NPROs vary according to the work they perform as well as their size, the second measure is the type of work performed by the NPROs in a state (last column of table 6.1). Larger scores signify that state NPROs focus more of their efforts on long-term policy analysis than do states with lower scores. (Chapter 3 provides an explanation of the development of this typology.)

This chapter employs these two measures in assessing the impacts on both the institutional performance of the NPROs and their impacts on policy research utilization.[4] Do legislators in states with larger NPROs have more information and do they rate their NPROs more highly than do legislators with smaller and less analytical NPROs? And what impact do NPROs have on different types of knowledge utilization by legislators?

FACTORS EXPLAINING LEGISLATOR SATISFACTION WITH NPROs

That legislators are motivated, at least in part, by the desire to win reelection has a long tradition in political science (Arnold 1979; Fenno 1978; Fiorina 1977; Mayhew 1974). Other literature points to the importance of information in legislatures (Krehbiel 1991). Information can be important to legislators for multiple reasons: It might be symbolic (so the legislator can appear knowledgeable), substantive (so the legislator can be informed about a policy's effects), political (so the legislator can advance electoral or other interests), or some combination of these reasons. Viewed politically, information frequently is seen as instrumental: "[T]he primary object of politics is not the discovery of knowledge, but the instrumental use of knowledge, along with other resources, in the pursuit of various goals" (Bimber 1996, 21). Nonetheless, information may have substantive value beyond purely political goals, such as improving public policy for its own sake. Bimber adds, "Legislators solicit expertise not simply in pursuit of good policy, but because they want control over the policy process" (p. 96).

Legislative satisfaction with the institutional performance of NPROs and the impact of NPROs on legislative research utilization can be conceived as stemming from several sources. The state politics literature finds that policymaking is affected by the state's political-economic environment, which varies considerably among states (Hero and Tolbert 1996; Schneider and Jacoby 1999; Williams and Matheny 1984). A state's political-economic environment includes the relative importance of other political-economic forces in the state, principally the executive branch, interest groups, political parties, and the size of the state economy.[5] The direction of influence is unclear, however. At one level, stronger governors, stronger parties, and stronger interest groups can be expected to lessen the importance of NPROs, because these alternative sources of information or power may supplant the need to rely on NPROs. Several studies find that interest groups and other external sources are important alternative information providers (Mooney 1991b; Ray 1982; Sabatier and Whiteman 1985; Whiteman 1995). Viewed another way, however, we may expect that legislatures, in response to strong external institutional pressures, would create strong NPROs to counteract the information advantage enjoyed by others. The results of chapter 4 suggest that greater external policy analysis capacity also generates more internal capacity.

In addition, scholarship in state politics suggests that political culture is an important determinant of policymaking (Morgan and Watson 1991; Mead 2002). Although political culture is less a theoretical construct than a typology, it captures several salient dimensions of state politics and policy. One scholar states, "Moralistic states tend to show high political participation, competitive parties, strong merit systems, and liberal and innovative programming" (Mead 2002). Another study concludes, "Moralistic states have more interparty competition, higher voter turnout, more policy-relevant parties, and more liberal and innovative policies" (Morgan and Watson 1991, 31). Political culture therefore can be expected to capture several factors relevant to legislative demand for and use of information, and to better isolate the independent effects of state NPROs in affecting information use. In particular, legislators from states with a moralistic political culture—a culture that tends to value progressive notions of information and analysis that informs policymaking—are hypothesized to be more likely to value and use information from NPROs. Legislators from traditionalist and individualistic political cultures are expected to find less value in NPROs.

The second expected source of variation is the legislator's personal ideology, such as party affiliation and degree of political conservatism. Previous studies find that personal values and ideology play a significant role in the use of information and policymaking (Lester 1993; Songer et al. 1985). Because political liberals are more likely to support new government programs or to expand existing ones, they are expected to be heavier users of policy analysis and to place a higher value on the performance of their NPROs. Similarly, Democrats' traditional preference for government that is more activist will likely lead to greater use of policy research to support policy changes. Democrats may be expected to rate NPRO performance higher than do Republicans simply because the former are higher demanders, and accordingly judge the influence and research utilization of NPROs to be more substantial. Chapter 5 showed this to be true in a bivariate model; this chapter assesses this relationship using more complex multivariate models.

Third, legislators' individual characteristics may affect their perception of the importance of the NPRO and its impacts on research utilization. A study of the use of policy analysis by state agency officials found that less-experienced and less well-educated officials were more likely to use policy analysis, while age and gender were unrelated (Lester 1993). We expect to see variation based on a legislator's age, gender, and level of formal education. Younger legislators who have also received more formal education are expected to be more sophisticated with regard to analysis; they therefore rate the performance of their NPROs more critically—expecting them to be more than simply information providers—and to be more disposed to use policy analysis in decision making.

In sum, I hypothesize (1) legislators' assessments of the institutional performance of their nonpartisan policy analysis agency and (2) their assessment of the use of policy research to be a product of four factors: (a) the state's political environment, (b) the legislator's political ideology, (c) the legislator's individual characteristics, and (d) the size or type of the NPRO. This analysis incorporates each of these factors into a model operationalized using the following indicators (see appendix 6.1 for detailed variable definitions):

State Political-Economic Environment

- State party competition (Ranney measure)
- State interest group impact (ranges from complementary or subordinate to dominant; Thomas and Hrebenar 1999)
- Size of state economy (ln) (gross state product, 2000)

- State political culture (=1 if state has moralistic political culture; 0 otherwise)
- Governor's structural powers (Beyle measure, modified by author; see chapter 4 for details)

Legislator Ideology

- Degree of political conservatism on economic issues (legislator survey)
- Party affiliation (legislator survey) (=1 if Republican; 0 otherwise)

Individual Legislator Characteristics

- Age (legislator survey)
- Gender (legislator survey) (=1 if female, 0 if male)
- Formal education (legislator survey)

Policy Organization

- Number of policy analysts (NPRO surveys)
- Type of work performed by NPRO (NPRO surveys)

RESULTS: LEGISLATORS' VIEWS
OF THE PERFORMANCE OF NPROs

The results show overwhelming support for the impact of the increasing scale and analytical sophistication of NPROs on legislative assessments of their organizational performance, and of legislators' assessments of the adequacy of the information they receive to make policy decisions. In bivariate analyses—shown in the first two columns of results in table 6.2—there is a statistically significant positive association between the strength of the NPRO and legislators' assessments of their abilities to gather and summarize information, perform short- and long-term research, bring new ideas, provide critical reviews, and serve as an effective communicator and information broker. Their overall assessment corroborates this view. In short, compared with legislators in states with smaller or more descriptive NPROs, legislators in states with stronger entities—measured by

Table 6.2
Legislators' Assessment of Their NPROs: NPRO Effects on Various Functions of Policy Analysis

	Bivariate estimates		Type of Work		No. of Policy Analysts		By Chamber[b]	
Dependent Variable	Type of Work	No. of Policy Analysts	Unweighted	Weighted[a]	Unweighted	Weighted[a]	House	Senate
Legislators say their NPRO is good at . . .								
gathering or summarizing information.	***	***	***	***	***	***	***	**
short-term policy analysis.	***	***	***	***	***	***	***	**
long-term policy analysis.	***	***	***	***	***	***	***	***
new ideas or perspectives.	***	***	***	**	***	***	**	
critical review of proposals.	***	***	***	***	***	***	***	**
communication or brokering.	***	***	***	***	***	***	***	**
overall assessment .	***	***	***	***	***	***	***	**

Legislators agree that NPRO . . .								
mostly processes info; it does little analysis.	Minus***	Minus***	Minus***	Minus***	Minus***	Minus***	Minus***	Minus***
is capable of in-depth research.	***	***	***	***	***	***	***	***
is well respected.	***	***	***	***	***	***	***	**
is truly nonpartisan.	***	**						
serves all legislators.								
has the appropriate level of resources.	***	***	***	***	***	***	***	***

Notes: All effects positive unless noted otherwise.

Represents partial coefficients of the effect of the type of NPRO (or number of policy analysts) on various dependent variables, using the same set of independent variables as in the first column in table 6.3.

*Significant at *90 percent; **95 percent; ***99 percent confidence level.

[a]Weighted to correct for response biases in gender, state, political party, and professionalism of state legislature.

[b]Using the type of work as the independent variable of interest. Similar results obtain using the number of policy analysts as the independent variable.

either number of analysts or type of work performed—provide stronger assessments of their NPRO's performance along every dimension. Furthermore, legislators' assessments were positively correlated with large and stronger NPROs when evaluating their capacity for in-depth research, their respect in the legislature, their nonpartisan stance, and the assessment that they had an appropriate level of resources, as shown in the bottom half of table 6.2.

There is, however, a significantly negative association between legislators' evaluations of the strength of their NPRO and their agreement that the NPRO primarily gathers and synthesizes information rather than analyzing it, evidence that NPROs that are perceived to do more analysis rather than simply processing information are rated more highly. The lack of a significant association between the type of NPRO and the perception that it serves all legislators suggests that both weak and strong NPROs are equally likely to serve all members. Those looking for NPROs to serve more legislators may not achieve that result only by expanding the size of the NPROs.

The observed bivariate relationships may be attributable to other intervening factors, such as the legislator's political ideology or educational background, or contextual factors such as state wealth, the level of state party competition, interest group influence, and so forth. Accordingly, the model is estimated, including the nine other independent factors discussed above.[6] The model is estimated using an ordered probit specification; the dependent variables are ordinal and rank-ordered on a four- or seven-point scale.[7]

The remaining columns in table 6.2 show the results of several multivariate models, again using as dependent variables legislators' various assessments of the performance of their state's NPRO. The next two columns of figures (Type of Work: Unweighted; Weighted) present the statistical significance of ordered probit coefficients for the type of work performed by the NPRO, while the subsequent two columns (No. of Policy Analysts: Weighted; Unweighted) do the same for the independent variable measuring the number of policy analysts.[8]

In almost all cases, the same strong positive association exists between legislative assessments of performance and NPRO strength, whether the model is weighted (to correct for survey response bias) or not, and whether it includes the number of analysts or the type of work. Therefore, the strong association noted in the bivariate analyses does not vanish with the inclusion of many other independent influences. The one exception is that legislators' perceptions that strong NPROs were more likely to be truly nonpartisan—evidenced in the bivariate equations—vanishes in the multivariate model. Finally, as with the bivariate model, larger and more analytical NPROs are far less likely to be perceived as simply processing information and performing little analysis. Legislators appear to know what their NPROs do, and while larger NPROs are not perceived to be more (or less) nonpartisan, they are perceived to be more effective in many dimensions of their work.

The last two columns of figures in table 6.2, where the multivariate models were run separately for the House and Senate, show some variation in both the magnitude and statistical significance of the NPRO's effects by chamber. The results generally indicate a positive and significant association between NPRO type and nearly all measures of effectiveness. The only exception is that senators from states with larger NPROs do not believe their NPROs are better at generating new ideas and fresh perspectives (there is no significant effect); otherwise, legislators in both chambers evaluate more favorably NPROs that are larger and conduct more longer-term research.

When the model is run independently for each major political party,[9] there is generally a positive and significant relationship between NPRO type and many measures of success, but the results are larger and more often significant for Democrats than for Republicans. The most striking contrast between Republicans and Democrats is that for Republicans there is no significant association between NPRO type and their assessment of whether the NPRO is well respected, nonpartisan, capable of in-depth research, there to serve all legislators, and so on. Democrats believe strongly that larger and more analytical NPROs are associated with higher ratings for nonpartisanship, capacity to conduct in-depth research, and so on, but Republicans do not share these views: The associations are positive but not statistically significant.

In every model specification, and even controlling for multiple independent economic, political, and individual characteristics, there is a strong and statistically significant association between legislators' assessments of their NPROs and their access to information and the size and type of the NPRO. There is also a strong and significant association between legislators' assessment of their NPRO and whether they are frequent users of policy analysis. I report other associations, across various model specifications and with multiple dependent variables, below. In sum, the positive association between legislators' perceptions of their access to information and the performance of their NPROs is robust across many different model specifications and estimation techniques, i.e., ordered probit, ordered logit, and OLS, and using various measures of the size and type of NPRO. By nearly any measure, larger and more analytical policy research organizations have a significant positive impact on client assessment.

Table 6.3 provides coefficients for all the independent variables used in the model, measuring, as the dependent variable, overall legislative assessment of the performance of their NPROs. In addition to the strong association between NPRO size or type and legislative

Table 6.3
Impacts of NPRO Size or Type on Overall Assessments of Performance (n = 649)

	Ordered Probit		OLS	
Independent Variable	Type of Work	No. of Analysts	Type of Work	No. of Analysts
NPRO Size or Type	0.42***	0.01***	0.31***	0.01***
State Party Competition	0.01**	0.00***	0.00**	0.00***
Interest Group Power	0.08	0.12*	0.07	0.09*
Moralistic Political Culture	−0.21*	0.02	−0.16*	0.01
State GSP (ln)	−0.05	−0.03	−0.03	−0.02
Age	0.26***	0.24***	0.19***	0.17***
Formal Education	−0.07*	−0.06*	−0.05**	−0.04*
Economic Conservatism	0.04	0.03	0.03	0.02
Female	−0.22**	−0.19**	−0.18**	−0.15**
Republican	−0.11	−0.12	−0.07	−0.08
Chi-square (probits) or F-statistic (OLS)	71.93***	57.60***	7.74***	6.08***

Note: Dependent variable measures legislators' assessments of their NPRO's performance in serving the legislature, on a scale of 1 (= poor) to 4 (= excellent).
*Significant at 90 percent; **95 percent; ***99+ percent confidence level.

assessment of performance, the model results indicate that in states with strong party competition, NPROs are rated more highly. Moreover, older legislators, those less formally educated, and males are more likely to give their NPROs higher marks. Legislator ideology (measured by party affiliation and degree of economic conservatism) is unrelated to NPRO performance assessments, and associations with moralistic political cultures and interest group power are weak. Table 6.3 provides both ordered probit and OLS estimates; the sign and significance of the estimates are little changed across model specifications. For the full model, the results indicate a strong association between the type of NPRO and all measures of success, even accounting for other independent variables. Therefore, these results are robust across many model specifications and are not dependent on one particular definition of the NPRO size or type.

As ordered probit coefficients are somewhat difficult to interpret, Figure 6.1 provides four depictions of the marginal estimated impacts of NPRO type on the probability of receiving a poor, average, good, or excellent rating from legislators.[10] As expected, legislators in states where the NPRO conducts longer-term research are far more likely

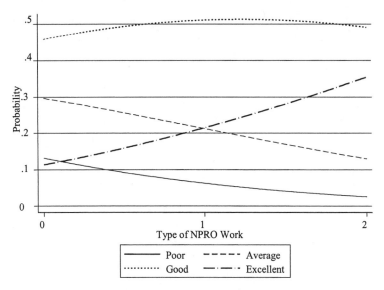

Figure 6.1   Impact of NPRO Type on Overall NPRO Assessment

to rate their NPRO as "excellent" than do legislators in states where NPROs tend to focus on short-term and often descriptive policy research. The probability of being rated "good," the most likely outcome, is not appreciably different in states with different NPRO types. However, in states where the NPRO conducts more longer-term research, there is a much lower probability of being rated "average" or "poor" by legislators.

RESULTS: IMPACTS OF NPROs ON THE UTILIZATION OF POLICY ANALYSIS

The second inquiry concerns the relationship between the size and type of NPROs and the use of policy analysis. "Use" is measured with reference to the five types of utilization discussed above (and their associated measures): policymaking influence, enlightenment, information access, rationalization, and tactics.

To begin to understand the direct relationships between NPRO size or type and various measures of use, table 6.4 shows the results of bivariate and other partial model specifications. The rows of table 6.4 indicate different types of use, while the columns represent different model specifications. Each cell indicates whether the estimated partial coefficient for the NPRO size or type is statistically significant (indicated by increasing statistical significance: *, **, or ***) or not (blank). All coefficients are positive unless noted otherwise.

The first two columns of figures represent the simple bivariate relationships between various measures of use and NPRO type (first column) and size (second). The results indicate that when use is measured as policymaking influence, in either absolute or relative terms, NPRO size and type are not generally a significant statistical explanation. However, when use is measured as enlightenment or, more emphatically, information access, the size and type of NPRO are significantly and positively related to more of these types of use.[11] The statistical relationship is noticeably weaker when use is measured in political (rationalization) or tactical terms.

Several other potential influences of NPROs were investigated and reported in the lower half of table 6.4. The estimates suggest that larger or analytical NPROs are associated with the assessment that staff support in the legislature is sufficient (this model specification also controls for the total number of staff per legislator), and that assessments of NPROs are lower when legislators report heavier use of in-depth research studies from universities and think tanks; the latter appear to displace NPROs. There was no relationship between NPRO size or strength and a variety of factors, including the general importance of nonpartisan information to legislators, legislators' assessments of the credibility of partisan research, whether analysis is most useful in presenting just the facts and avoiding political interpretation, and whether staff are used most valuably to gather information or to analyze it.

The remaining columns of table 6.4 report the influence of ideological, political-economic, and individual legislator characteristics over the various measures of use (where the joint statistical significance of these variables is indicated by §), as well as the statistical significance of the type of work the NPRO performs. These results support the finding that larger NPROs have both greater policy-making influence and provide better access to information, even including these additional factors. The influence of the other factors is mixed. Clearly, individual legislator characteristics (gender, age, and formal education) are most consistently significant with respect to policymaking influence, information access, and other factors. Legislator ideology and the state's political-economic environment are significant in half as many model specifications, not at all over policymaking influence, and just once for enlightenment. The importance of nonpartisanship in policy analysis is influenced most strongly by the state's political-economic environment.

The results of full model estimations—which include the 10 independent variables identified in table 6.3—are shown in table 6.5. The rows are identical to those in table 6.4 and measure different types of use. The columns represent four different model specifications; all are ordered probit models. The first two use the type of NPRO work as the independent variable (one of ten independent variables included) while the second two use the number of policy analysts as an independent variable. The second and fourth columns represent weighted estimates, with the weights correcting for the survey response biases reported in chapter 5.

Table 6.4

Impacts of Strong NPROs on Various Definitions of "Use"—Partial Model: Statistical Significance of Partial (NPRO) Coefficients[a]:

Dependent Variable	Bivariate Equation		Adding Variable Groups to Bivariate Equations[a]:		
	Type of Work	No. of Policy Analysts	Legislator Ideology	State Political-Economic Environment	Individual Legislator Characteristics
Policymaking influence: absolute measure.		*		**	***§
Policymaking influence: relative measure.				*	*§
Enlightenment: NPRO importance as information source to help understand and reach policy decisions.	***			*	***
Enlightenment: "I often use policy analysis to understand how a policy works."	*	***	***	§	
Information Access: "If I need good nonpartisan analysis, I can get it."	***	***	***	***	***§
Information Access: "Legislators have all the information and analysis they need to make good public policy decisions."	***	***	***§	***§	***§
Information Access: "The legislature needs more nonpartisan policy analysis and research."	Minus***	Minus***	Minus***§	Minus***§	Minus***§
Information Access: "I would use additional policy analysis and research, if it was available."	Minus***	Minus***	Minus***§	Minus***	Minus***§
Rationalization: "I seek policy analysis for a position already taken."	*	**	§		*
Tactical: "Policy analysis useful in delaying decisions."					§

Other Factors

Staff Support: "Overall, staff support in the legislature is sufficient" (including staff per legislator variable).	***	***	***§		***§
Value of Research: "In-depth research studies, such as those performed by universities or think tanks, are often valuable to me."	Minus***	Minus*	Minus***§	Minus***	Minus***§
Partisan Research: "Nonpartisan staff are far more valuable to me than partisan staff."				§	§
Partisan Research: "Information from partisan sources is not credible."					
Information as Facts: "I prefer policy research to present fact and analysis and leave political decisions to me."					§
Information as Facts: "More important for staff to gather and present me with info than to analyze it."				§	§

Notes: All effects positive unless otherwise noted; blank indicates limited statistical significance.

***Coefficient is significant at 99+% level; ** significant at 95% level; * significant at 90% level.

§Indicates that the group of variables, jointly, is significant at the 95+% confidence level.

†The models in the last three columns add groups of variables to the bivariate model, including legislator ideology, the state political-economic environment, and individual legislator characteristics. The coefficients are for the type of work conducted by the NPRO.

Table 6.5
Impacts of Strong NPROs on Various Definitions of "Use"—Full Model: Statistical Significance of Partial NPRO Coefficients

Dependent "Use" Variable	Independent Variable			
	Type of Work	Type of Work[†]	No. of Analysts	No. of Analysts[†]
Policymaking influence: absolute measure.	***	**	**	**
Policymaking influence: relative measure.	**	*	*	*
Enlightenment: NPRO importance as information source to help understand and reach policy decisions.	**	*	*	*
Enlightenment: "I often use policy analysis to understand how a policy works."			*	*
Information Access: "If I need good nonpartisan analysis, I can get it."	***	***	***	***
Information Access: "Legislators have all the information and analysis they need to make good public policy decisions."	***	***	***	***
Information Access: "The legislature needs more nonpartisan policy analysis and research."	Minus***	Minus***	Minus***	Minus***
Information Access: "I would use additional policy analysis and research, if it was available."	Minus***	Minus***	Minus***	Minus***
Rationalization: "I seek policy analysis for a position already taken."				
Tactical: "Policy analysis is useful in delaying decisions."				

Other Factors

Staff Support: "Overall, staff support in the legislature is sufficient" (including staff per legislator variable).	***	***	***	
Value of Research: "In-depth research studies, such as those performed by universities or think tanks, are often valuable to me."	Minus***	Minus***	Minus**	Minus*
Partisan Research: "Nonpartisan staff are far more valuable to me than partisan staff."				
Partisan Research: "Information from partisan sources is not credible."				
Information as Facts: "I prefer policy research to present fact and analysis and leave political decisions to me."				
Information as Facts: "More important for staff to gather and present me with info than to analyze it."				

***Significant at 99% level; **significant at 95% level; *significant at 90% level.

Note: All effects positive unless otherwise noted.

All statistics reflect ordered probit models. The full models include state party competition, interest group strength, an indicator variable for a moralistic political culture, the gross state product, and control variables for the legislator's age, education, conservatism on economic issues, gender, and political party.

†Weights correct for nonrepresentative survey responses in state, legislative professionalism, party, and the respondent's gender.

In contrast to the bivariate estimates, the policymaking influence of the NPROs is statistically associated with both NPRO size and type of work in the multivariate model: legislators in states with strong NPROs perceive them to be more influential than do legislators in states with weaker or smaller ones, controlling for ideological, political-economic, and individual legislator characteristics. This relationship persists whether policymaking influence is measured in absolute or relative terms, although the association is more significant statistically for the absolute measure.

Information access remains, even after the inclusion of many other explanatory factors, the most consistently significant NPRO influence over the legislative use of policy analysis. In every case, using four distinct measures of information access, stronger NPROs are associated with greater legislative access to information. Perhaps most important, legislators in states with larger or more analytical NPROs report a far greater ability to get good nonpartisan information if they need it compared with legislators in states with smaller or more descriptive NPROs. The influence of NPROs over the "enlightenment" function of research utilization is more circumscribed, and is only weakly significant—if at all—in most model specifications. NPRO strength does not affect either rationalization or tactical uses of policy analysis. Therefore, larger or more analytically sophisticated NPROs cannot be expected to assist legislators in rationalizing policies or in delaying political decisions.[12]

For the other factors, the results obtained for the bivariate estimates hold in the multivariate specifications: NPROs are strongly associated with higher ratings for the sufficiency of staff support, even accounting for the number of staff per legislator. In addition, legislators are less likely to view the research of universities and think tanks as valuable in the presence of strong state NPROs, which suggests that legislators look to universities and think tanks for advice only when their NPROs are incapable of providing something comparable. The last four rows of table 6.5 indicate that strong NPROs are not associated with legislators' perceptions concerning partisan research or their preference for staff providing information, analysis, or political judgment.

Figure 6.2 depicts the relationship between legislators' assessments that they have good access to policy analysis and the type of

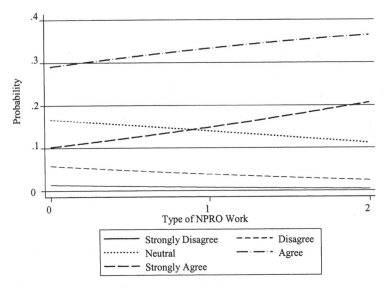

Figure 6.2   Impact of NPRO Type on Access to Policy Information

NPRO.[13] The probability of legislators agreeing or strongly agreeing is measurably improved in states with NPROs that conduct more long-term research. Similarly, the probability of disagreeing with the statement—that legislators have good access to policy information if they need it—declines as the NPRO conducts more long-term research.[14] Nonetheless, the effects are modest. In all cases, changing from a Type A to Type C NPRO—a substantial commitment of resources—affects the probabilities by less than one-tenth.

RESULTS: IMPACTS OF OTHER FACTORS

The results in tables 6.2 and 6.3 indicate a consistently significant association between NPRO type and various measures of success, while tables 6.4 and 6.5 indicate the importance of NPROs in providing better access to information for legislators as well as having influence in the policymaking process. However, associations between legislative assessments of NPROs and other types of hypothesized influences are also of interest, particularly political effects.

Table 6.6 shows the effects of other independent factors that may affect legislators' perceptions of their state NPROs. The most apparent

Table 6.6
Effects of Other Factors on Various Measures of "Success"

Dependent Variable	Party Competition	Interest group power	Moralistic Culture	State GSP	Age	Education	Economic conservatism	Female	Republican
gathering or summarizing information.	++	++			+++	- -			
short-term policy analysis.	+		- -		++	-			
long-term policy analysis.					++	- - -			
new ideas or perspectives.		+			+++	- - -		- -	
critical review of proposals.		+			+	- - -			
communication or brokering.						- - -		- -	-
overall assessment.	++		-		+++	-		- -	

Legislators say their NPRO is good at . . .

	C1	C2	C3	C4	C5	C6	C7	C8
mostly processes info; it does little analysis.	++	+++				++		++
is capable of in-depth research.	+++			+++	– – –		–	–
Legislators agree that NPRO . . . is well respected.	++	+++		+++	– – –	– –	– – –	– –
is truly nonpartisan.	++	+++	++		–		– – –	– –
serves all legislators.	++	+++			–			–
has the appropriate level of resources.	++		+	+++	– – –	++	– – –	–

Note: Equation also includes variable measuring type of NPRO work performed; unweighted equations.
+ is positive and significant at the 90% level; ++ is significant at 95% level; +++ at 99% level.
– is negative and significant at the 90% level; – – is significant at 95% level; – – – at 99% level.
Blank cell denotes no significant effect.

conclusion is that no independent effects are as consistently significant as the NPRO type or size itself, which was significant and positive for every performance measure (except for those suggesting the
NPRO serves all legislators and is nonpartisan). (See table 6.2.) Therefore, the type of NPRO is far more consistently associated with performance than any other independent factor.

Several other influences are noteworthy, however. The first is
that legislators with more formal education provide lower assessments
of their NPROs, while older legislators rate NPROs more highly.
Women and Republican legislators tend to give lower ratings to their
NPROs, while legislators from states with strong interest-group power
give higher ratings to their NPROs, even accounting for NPRO
strength. Economic conservatism has little significance, other than
support for the belief that NPROs have sufficient resources. State
wealth has little consistent impact, although legislators from states
with strong party competition provide an overall higher assessment
of their NPROs than do other legislators.

CONCLUSIONS

In contrast with much of the empirical knowledge utilization literature, which generally finds a modest and usually indirect impact of
policy research, this study finds a consistently significant impact of
state NPROs on both legislators' assessments of the quality and capabilities of their NPROs, and their policymaking influence, defined
in multiple ways. These findings are robust over many different
model specifications, and are true even for institutions embroiled in
highly politicized policy environments. The most consistent finding
is that legislators from states with large or analytical NPROs place
higher value on the work of NPROs than do legislators from states
with smaller NPROs or those whose work product tends to be more
descriptive and short-term. The breadth of strong NPRO influence
is substantial and reaches into almost everything they do, from gathering and summarizing information to providing new ideas and perspectives, from the perception that they are capable of conducting
long-term research to the respect accorded them in the legislature.
NPROs that are larger and able to conduct longer-term research earn

significantly higher ratings across the board. This corroborates earlier research suggesting that proximity and trust are essential in effective communication of information: "The usefulness of information has more to do with the characteristics of the person who possesses it (i.e., an expert) than it does with the substance of the message that is being conveyed" (Rich and Goldsmith 1983, 98). The close physical and institutional proximity of NPROs to the legislatures provides substantial influence.

The impact of NPROs on the process of research utilization is a bit more complicated. Evidence suggests that NPROs have significant influence over policymaking—at least legislators' perceptions of influence—a departure from the findings of the knowledge utilization literature more generally. I conjecture that this difference is due to this study's focus on institutions rather than individual reports, but verifying this requires a research design that compares them directly. At the same time, the impact of NPROs on legislators' assessments of their access to information is very strong. Coupled with the results of chapter 5, this suggests both that while NPROs are not viewed as influential in the policymaking process in absolute terms, larger or analytical operations do enhance NPRO policymaking influence. Furthermore, in every measure, legislators from states with strong or large NPROs judged them to have a positive impact on their access to information for policymaking, as well as overall performance. While the research focus is different, the results of this chapter are consistent with those of scholars who have studied the influence of different information sources on legislative decision making and conclude that trust, proximity, and the type of organization are important to policymaking influence (A. Rich 2001; Weiss 1989).

The institutions entrusted to perform and communicate policy analysis have, at the margin, a substantial impact on information and policymaking in state legislatures. Larger and more analytical NPROs have an appreciable impact on legislators' assessments of their performance and influence. The type of policy analysis institutions clearly affects its influence in multiple ways, despite the conclusion that overall NPROs are not particularly influential compared with other institutions.

NOTES

1. A complicating factor is that the survey asked legislators to evaluate their state's NPRO, yet some states have more than one NPRO. Therefore, while there may be some ambiguity in a legislator's responses (in those states), in that a legislator may have different views of the effectiveness of different NPROs in the state, the data report average results, which we may assume the legislator considers in evaluating a state's policy research capacity. Furthermore, in some states with multiple NPROs, such as California, all are generally similar in that they are all relatively large and analytical compared with those in most other states.

2. These include:
   - Knowledge-driven model (research identifies some problem or opportunity, which then leads to research for practical action, leading to policy adoption or implementation)
   - Problem-solving model (direct application of research to policymaking; research fills a gap in knowledge)
   - Interactive model (multiple information or research constituencies move toward policy responses)
   - Political model (research as rationalization or legitimation, e.g., ammunition for one side of a debate)
   - Tactical (to delay, deflect criticism, increase prestige, and so on)
   - Enlightenment (impact of concepts and perspectives over time)
   - Research as intellectual enterprise

3. This is measured as the larger of (1) the number of "policy analysts" reported by state NPRO directors, and (2) the percentage of time the agency reported spending on policy analysis multiplied by the number of reported professional staff. This is intended to broaden the definition of policy analysis to include both agency personnel and functions. See chapter 3 for further details.

4. I developed these scores independently; nevertheless, they are strongly correlated, with a correlation coefficient of 0.79. Not surprisingly, larger agencies have the wherewithal, in general, to perform more long-term analysis.

5. The importance of governors—indeed, of the executive branch more generally—is significant. One book noted, "If one had to select a single dominant theme characterizing the literature on legislative-executive relations in the United States in recent years, it would be the executive dominance of the legislative branch" (Uslaner and Weber 1977,

106). Interest groups represent another important source of information. One legislator states, "The good lobbyists tell you who they're talking to, and they tell you about what they're hearing on the other side . . . what other people are thinking and saying and where they're coming from and where their bosses are coming from. You can't always trust them, but you also learn which ones you can and can't" (quoted in Whiteman 1995, 45).

6. The measure of gubernatorial power is dropped in this and future model specifications because of strong collinearities with other independent variables.

7. The ordered probit specification treats a rating of 4, for example, as higher than 2 but allows for nonlinearities.

8. The weighted model corrects for response bias by state, gender, party, and chamber.

9. These estimates are not shown but are available from the author on request.

10. This is based on the ordered probit estimates where the dependent variable is their overall assessment of the NPRO. The figure represents the partial coefficient on the type of work performed by the NPRO.

11. Note that the negative coefficient for two types of information access implies greater support for NPRO influence.

12. This conclusion is based on the cross-sectional analysis performed here, not using time-series analysis that would provide more compelling evidence. Cross-sectional results do not imply that changes in NPROs or the political environment within any one state will have effects similar to those observed across states.

13. Specifically, this is the legislative response to the question "If I need good nonpartisan analysis of a policy issue important to me, I can get it."

14. This figure reflects the *partial* coefficients on the type of work performed, i.e., the measured effect, already accounts for other influences such as party competition, the legislator's age, and so on.

Variable Sources and Definitions

Variable	Source
Type of work performed by NPRO	NPRO survey and follow-up interviews
No. of policy analysts	NPRO survey—larger of two measures
Institutional strength of governor (larger numbers denote greater gubernatorial strength)	Measure compiled by Professor Thad Beyle (www.unc.edu/~beyle/gubnewpwr.html), modified to include five of six of his measures that focus on the institutional relationships, i.e., excluding his temporal measure of gubernatorial party control.
State party competition (larger numbers denote greater competitiveness)	Ranney measure, as reported in Morehouse and Jewell 2003, 108–9.
State interest group power	Thomas and Hrebenar 1999 figures, reported in Morehouse and Jewell 2003, p. 79.
Moralistic state political culture (=1; 0=otherwise)	Elazar 1984
Size of state economy (ln)	Gross State Product, 2000; U.S. Census
Degree of political conservatism on economic issues (five-point scale: 1=very liberal; 5=very conservative)	Legislator survey
Party affiliation (1=Republican; 0=Democrat)	Legislator survey
Age (four-point scale of increasing age)	Legislator survey
Sex (0=male; 1=female)	Legislator survey
Formal education (six-point scale of increasing level of formal education)	Legislator survey

CHAPTER 7

Conclusions and Implications:
The Politics of Policy Analysis

The relationship of expertise to power is and will remain controversial. Used inappropriately or undemocratically, expertise risks alienating the very individuals whose welfare it should promote. A noted author and activist, writing about her experience in India, describes this sentiment in language that could have emerged from encounters with expertise almost anywhere:

> I think it's vital to de-professionalize the public debate on matters that vitally affect the lives of ordinary people. It's time to snatch our futures back from the 'experts.' . . . Frankly, however trenchantly, however angrily, however combatively one puts forward one's case, at the end of the day, I'm only a citizen, one of many, who is demanding public information, asking for a public explanation. I have no axe to grind. I have no professional stakes to protect. I'm prepared to be persuaded. I'm prepared to change my mind. But instead of an argument, or an explanation, or a disputing of facts, one gets insults, invective, legal threats, and the Expert's Anthem: "You're too emotional. You don't understand, and it's too complicated to explain." The subtext, of course, is: Don't worry your little head about it. Go and play with your toys. Leave the real world to us. (Roy 2001, 24–25)

Policy analysts—one class of experts—are found in government agencies, legislatures, nonprofit organizations, private interest groups, think tanks, and virtually every other organization that seeks to influence the nature and conduct of public policy. Because these experts are so pervasive within democratic institutions in the United States, it is critical to understand their role and relationship to power and to improve their ability to provide meaningful, accurate, and functional information and analysis to a broad range of current and potential policymaking participants. Equally important is the distribution of expertise. While it is obvious that moneyed interests can afford more expertise than others, the issue remains whether policy analysts in government employ democratize the policymaking process by providing creative solutions and critical perspectives and reviews. Alas, the results here are not encouraging: NPROs are perceived to be decidedly ineffectual in bringing new ideas and perspectives to state policymaking, although stronger NPROs do this better than lesser ones.

Prior research has studied the impact of analysts and their research on the policymaking process, but much remains unstudied and unknown. For one, studies of knowledge utilization neglect the role of policy analysts—in contrast to written policy analysis—as if reports are the only products of policy analysts.[1] Second, despite the growing importance of states in policymaking and implementation, we know almost nothing about policy analysis conducted at the state level. Third, nearly all the literature on knowledge utilization examines the impact of policy research on decision making, while rarely considering the reverse impact of politics on the conduct or institutions of policy analysis. When studied at all, institutions are normally introduced as an independent variable, a potential influence over, as opposed to being influenced by, policymaking. Furthermore, the knowledge utilization literature rarely if ever studies the relationship between policy analysis institutions and client approval. Thus, because we have virtually no information on the institutional impact of policy analysis organizations, only of individual studies, it is likely that scholars are systematically understating this effect. And, finally, there is relatively little investigation of nonpartisan research organizations (NPROs), even at the federal level.[2] This book has examined all of these issues by assessing the survey responses of hundreds of legislators as well as state NPROs in all fifty states. Conclusions and implications are summarized below.

THE IMPORTANCE OF NPROs

NPROs vary substantially from one state to the next in age, size, analytical capacity, and other characteristics, and in ways that are not obviously associated with the size or professionalism of the legislature. Some large, professional legislatures maintain small and largely descriptive NPROs (or none at all), while some small, citizen legislatures maintain relatively large and analytical offices. Yet, there are many common features as well. Most NPROs focus on serving individual legislator requests, providing general service to the entire legislature, and being active in the legislature's day-to-day operations. In addition, many provide staff support for committees and conduct different types of work during interim sessions. They also tend to rely heavily on trust and close contact with legislators to achieve maximum effectiveness.

The fact that politics and institutions affect one another may be obvious to political scientists, but this relationship is little explored in studies of expertise. In this volume, the importance of institutions has manifested itself in two principal ways. First, political institutions affect the nature of policy analysis organizations and, therefore, policy analysis itself. The effects of state party organizations, state political culture, legislative staffing, and, to a lesser extent, think tanks and interest groups are significantly associated with the size and type of institutions created to provide nonpartisan policy advice to the legislature.[3] Furthermore, party competition is associated with larger NPROs, whereas state policy liberalism is linked with more analytical policy research organizations.

Second, policy analysis institutions matter to their chief clients: legislators. Legislators assess more highly and report much better access to information from NPROs that are larger and more analytical. Therefore, NPROs are important information providers in their own right, and larger and more analytical ones are particularly important to policymakers across a wide range of uses. In this fashion, policy analysis in state legislatures appears to fit well the assertion that policy analysis should be, as contemporary understandings suggest, "more a tool of the democratic process than the problem-solving process" (Shulock 1999, 227); the corollary is that the empirical reality fits rather poorly the more traditional conception of policy analysis as disinterested analytical problem solving (Stokey and Zeckhauser 1978). Furthermore, one wonders whether the importance of providing information to policymakers—a role at which NPROs excel—is not underestimated in legislative surveys assessing influence. One suspects that most respondents define influence quite narrowly; therefore, NPRO influence may be understated in the absolute—if not the relative—sense. What is surprising, however, given the findings of the knowledge utilization literature, is the degree to which NPROs, at the margin, also have some influence over policymaking. Legislators do not perceive NPROs to be particularly influential compared with most other political actors, yet they view larger and more analytical NPROs as having greater influence than their smaller and more descriptive counterparts.[4]

IMPLICATIONS FOR STATE NPROs

In a policy world driven by partisan debate and advocacy-based policy analysis, the role of NPROs is distinctive. Many policy research and advocacy organizations, such as the Heritage Foundation or the Center on Budget and Policy Priorities, maintain overt political agendas, and state "think tanks" and interest groups have similar priorities. NPROs represent one of the last sources of potentially disinterested, if not unbiased, policy analysis and research for state legislatures. Most research suggests, however, that expertise does not influence policymaking, especially in legislatures (Davidson 1976; Mooney 1991a; Whiteman 1985). A study of expertise in Congress concludes, "If OTA's experience is any guide, circumstances under which legislators make political choices chiefly on the basis of expert claims are indeed rare" (Bimber 1996, 96). What role, then, do NPROs play in this increasingly contested political terrain?

The importance of providing basic information to legislators, the predominant focus of many NPROs, should not be discounted. Rather than sophisticated analysis, sometimes the most important facets of their work are the personal connections and trust they develop with legislators as a result of reliable information provision and the maintenance of nonpartisanship. When asked what he thinks legislators find most useful about the agency's work, the director of a strong NPRO commented, "Stuff that is germane, 'news they can use.' Our responses to legislative inquiries are probably the most important things we do." A director of another NPRO, one that also conducts substantial long-term analysis, still sees their short-term work as most important:

> The keystone, in my view, is direct, face-to-face work inside the daily legislative process. We work, every day, closely with individual members, committees, outside government officials, and representatives of interest groups. We are in the trenches with them, helping them—in committee, on the floor, in conference committee. This close involvement in the nitty-gritty of the legislative process gives [the office] attributes that do not accrue to pure research or drafting offices: hands-on knowledge of what's 'really' going on, how legislators think, what information they need, what information they want, how and why decisions are made, etc. It also gives us day-to-day personal and working relationships with legislators and others involved in the process; they gradually get to know us and come to respect our knowledge and rely on our work.

A study of the former Office of Technology Assessment (OTA) also recognizes the influence of politics over policy research institutions. This study shows that NPROs are known for their political neutrality; similarly, Bimber (1996) argues that institutional structures shape the actions of experts, at least in Congress, resulting in rewards to "experts who provide broadly applicable, politically uncommitted expertise" (p. 7). "What legislators wanted from OTA might be called political propriety. Individually, they wanted expertise that was responsive and relevant, that was framed in ways that illuminated links between technical claims and political interests. But political propriety also involved a counterintuitive demand, namely that expertise do a legislator no harm" (p. 95).

NPROs are far smaller and therefore less able to perform sophisticated analyses than large federal research organizations such as the Congressional Budget Office (CBO) or Congressional Research Service (CRS). Overwhelmingly, state NPROs provide impartial, fact-based information for legislators of both parties, and NPRO directors value highly the nonpartisan nature of their operations as a means to sustain legislative support. NPROs range from information providers with generalist staffs without graduate degrees who conduct little or no research, to organizations with substantial analytical capacity whose staff all have advanced degrees and who routinely conduct longer-term research. Although most provide bill summaries, collect and synthesize information, and provide descriptive assessments, only a small fraction of NPROs are regularly able to conduct sophisticated and longer-term policy analysis. More than just the size of NPROs, the analytical capacity of NPROs influences legislators' perceptions about the value of the NPRO's contribution to the legislature's work. Nonetheless, because larger NPROs represent far greater legislative investments of personnel and funding, recommendations for upgrading NPROs so that they may serve legislators better—whether by expanding size or analytical capacity—should be balanced against the considerable costs of doing so.

One study notes, "Knowledge does not itself necessarily convey power; rather, power frequently lies in the relationship between producers and consumers of knowledge" (Bimber 1996, 5). NPROs, positioned between knowledge and power, have adapted effectively to meet the demands of legislators who want information quickly and with relatively little politicization. The technical sophistication of their analysis is not what matters most to legislators but, rather, the extent to which legislators can trust the information provided, a trust that has developed in large part due to the institutional linkage between legislators and NPROs. Bimber notes, "When legislators talk about expertise, they almost invariably speak in terms of its origins. They do not understand analysis, policy studies, and other forms of expert information in isolation from their understanding of the people who have produced it" (p. 5).

Legislators and NPROs depend on each other. The importance of trust and frequent contact with policymakers is critical to analysts' influential roles as information providers and, to a lesser extent, to their role in influencing policy outcomes. "Close contact between analysts and political players produces a sensitivity not only to timing and number-crafting but also to the kind of evidence needed. Economists in the heat of fire are more likely to recognize the strategic weaknesses of theoretical reasoning and the value of anecdotes, 'three-week studies,' and simplicity of argument" (Robyn 1987, 240). NPROs largely reflect what decision makers want from policy analysis, and it suggests its usefulness is more in providing information and short-term analysis than analytically sophisticated research.

NPROs must continuously adapt to the changing political environments in which they work. Although short-term information provision is important, providing basic information is a necessary but not sufficient role for NPROs. Females, liberals, Democrats, young, and well-educated legislators are more likely to support greater use of policy analysis. In contrast, older legislators, those with less formal education, Republicans, economic conservatives, and males are more likely to believe that the legislature has all the information and analysis it needs to make decisions. Therefore, states considering expansion of their NPRO staff should be attentive both to the costs of expansion and to the types of legislators that would be likely to support or oppose the change. Furthermore, as chapter 6 showed, larger NPROs are not only more effective in performing long-term analysis, they also bring more new ideas and perspectives and critical reviews of policy proposals to their legislatures. Therefore, size matters as much for the qualitative dimensions of what NPROs provide as for the quantitative advantages of having more policy analysts.

NPROs must recognize the changing role of information access and how it affects their role in the legislature. The greater availability of information from alternative sources may push NPROs to consider their value added and bring more analytical resources to policy debates. Otherwise, NPROs that focus their energies on information gathering may find the demand for their services diminished as they become glorified search engines that cannot synthesize or analyze the products of their search. Not only does the received wisdom—that neutral expertise cannot coexist in the political system that compels subservience—appear to be untrue, but state NPROs in some instances have become so neutral as to jeopardize their potential analytical contributions to policymaking. Furthermore, because many NPROs are simply short-term information providers, they fail to promote discussion of the variety of viewpoints missing from those supplied by lobbyists and the legislators themselves, seemingly an essential role of policy analysts paid to represent the public's best interests. Stronger NPROs not only supply more sophisticated analysis but also have the capacity to inform political debate with viewpoints that may not otherwise be represented.

Recent political trends suggest increasing partisanship at both the federal and state levels. A cover report in *National Journal* asks, "The State of Congress: Partisanship, Polarization, and Mistrust Are Transforming the Legislative Process. How Bad Is It?"[5] Most NPRO directors echoed this sentiment, speaking of the increasingly partisan environment in state legislatures. These political developments, coupled with and possibly exacerbated by term limits, have potentially important implications for NPROs, as strong parties are associated with smaller and more descriptive NPROs. Therefore, the more politicized and partisan legislatures become, the less likely are they to support NPROs, especially ones that go beyond simple information gathering and analysis. This tension—between providing legislators what they do not always know that they need and providing basic information—is likely to persist for NPROs in governments everywhere.

The findings detailed previously—that legislators believe that (1) NPROs are important information providers, and larger ones even more so; and that (2) NPROs are not considered to be influential, but stronger and more analytical NPROs are more highly valued and influential in policymaking—raises a related question: Is it true that in some states information is so *unimportant* to state legislative policymaking? In some states, this appears to be the case. In New York, for example, legislative power is highly centralized:

> Partly because of the New York State constitution and partly because of the way the constitution has been exploited, these two men [the Senate Majority Leader and Assembly Speaker] are, in their own spheres, virtually omnipotent. The legislature has an elaborate committee structure, which is supposed to insure that every bill can be debated, in public, by lawmakers who are knowledgeable in the subject area. In reality, if a bill is of any significance it is Bruno and Silver [the two leaders] who determine, independently of the committees, whether or not it will advance.

The same is true once a bill gets to the floor. In Albany, except under total-eclipse-of-the-sun-like circumstances, votes have only one possible result. (Kolbert 2003, 39)

One legislator, who had served in the New York State legislature for eighteen years, told a reporter that, of the approximately 75,000 pieces of legislation that have come to the floor, "in only four instances had there been any uncertainty about the outcome of the vote, and in only one, involving a constitutional amendment to allow casino gambling, had the measure actually failed" (Kolbert 2003, 39). How does this happen in an ostensibly democratic institution? For one, legislative leaders hire the committee staff in New York, and therefore strip the committees of much of their power. But their power does not end there; a legislator added:

How do you get such uniformity of voting from such individual people from different regions of the state, diverse populations, and different income groups? Because everybody's afraid of the leader. And if you don't cooperate you may go back to your office and find that the lights are off and the computers are shut down. Sometimes you go back to your office and the door is locked. (Kolbert 2003, 39)

This book has shown that politics influences policy analysis organizations and that, at the margin, analysis influences policymaking. Information surely is power, yet at the same time NPROs represent important expressions of legislative intent. (Given the account above, it comes as no surprise that New York has little or no nonpartisan research capacity.) Political competition (both party competition and the work of interest groups and think tanks) breeds greater need for information and policy analysis, which can manifest itself in somewhat stronger NPROs than otherwise. Nonetheless, most NPROs focus on legislators' short-term, individual requests. They are there to serve the legislature, and recognize that their very existence depends on their ability to meet mostly short-term requests. This need is particularly acute in term-limited states, where high legislator turnover means that NPROs will have to justify themselves anew more frequently than in the past. With each new electoral cycle will come larger numbers of fresh-faced legislators, and the NPRO will in short order need to make itself useful to them. This will not be through long-term studies—their clients will not be there for the long term—but through providing timely, relevant information to legislators. The electoral cycle applies to policy analysis as well as to politicians, and term limits will impose an even shorter time frame on NPROs that already focus excessively on rapid information dissemination.

There are important parallels between NPROs and similar institutions at the federal level. Like their state counterparts, federal legislators place value on work performed from within the institution, where analysts have developed trust and recognize the pressures and needs of legislators better than most. Representative Jim Holt (D-NJ) said, in comparing the congressional OTA with other information providers, "Some of the independent groups—the National Academies and others—do studies that have a good technical basis, but they aren't written from within the legislative milieu" (Goodman 2000). Although it was a congressional institution, OTA's demise was partly due to the way it fielded requests from legislators. "[OTA] had a bipartisan governing board of senators and representatives and formally responded to requests for study only from committee chairs. As a result, few members of Congress depended on OTA. That—and OTA's small budget—made it expendable" (Goodman 2000). In contrast, nearly all NPROs—at least the NPROs that have survived—have adopted the strategy of addressing individual member needs to the extent there is demand and their resources permit. If the work is done well, this can provide powerful support for the institution. This analysis suggests that policy analysis in politicized settings—such as in state NPROs—tends to be quick, descriptive work and that institutions like OTA, which produce long-term research only at the request of legislative committees, are less likely to be supported within legislatures because they lack the foundation of short-term information provision to individual legislators that almost all NPROs provide. Therefore, NPROs seeking to expand their bailiwick to longer-term research would be well-advised not to abandon short-term information provision to legislators.

While NPROs must adapt to legislative needs to survive and thrive, they must also be sufficiently entrepreneurial to provide what legislators sometimes do not know that they need, such as forecasting important future problems, understanding the implications of policy options, and learning how other states respond to similar problems. Because they are publicly funded, NPROs should also be mindful of promoting greater access to information and perspectives, including that from underrepresented groups, in effect democratizing policy analysis in the legislature. In addition to providing short-term information and analysis—which most NPROs do quite well already—NPROs must become future oriented, identifying and engaging emerging problems, outlining the consequences of policy options, forecasting trends, and generally training some of their attention ahead. The NPRO's home in the legislature provides it with an institutional permanence that allows it to develop a strong relationship with legislators who recognize that the NPRO exists to serve their interests. To thrive, though, they must do more: They must look to the future in a way that individual legislators do not have the luxury to do, to predict (as Kentucky's Long-Term Policy Research Center did) that tobacco quotas would decline or that globalization would bring significant job losses to the state's low-wage manufacturing industries, yet do so without obvious political bias. Earning legislators' trust and providing short-term information is a strong foundation on which to build an effective NPRO, but it is insufficient in the long-term if NPROs seek to distinguish themselves from newer and easily accessible forms of information through technological change. Because larger and more analytical NPROs are better at satisfying legislators' needs for policy information, expanding NPRO capacity could lead, potentially, to significant gains in legislators' access to information yet also, at the margins, to increased policy-making influence.

One of the core issues addressed in *Power, Knowledge, and Politics* is whether and how policy analysis can survive, much less prosper, in the highly politicized environments where legislatures thrive. A number of scholars have described the difficulty of providing neutral competence in political environments (Heclo 1975; Rourke 1992). As is now apparent, the wide proliferation of NPROs in states—and

the perception by their clients that they are truly nonpartisan—
suggest that neutral policy analysis is thriving in the states . . . at least
to some extent. This is not to say that much of the work is sophisticated—for the most part it is not—but it does suggest that nonpartisan information and analysis are valued in small states and large,
in professional and citizen legislatures, and in states wealthy and
poor. Nonpartisan analysis also appears to have survived the deep
budget cuts in state government in the recent past.

TEACHING POLICY ANALYSIS

One of the challenges in understanding policy expertise is that the
feedback mechanism—knowing whether policy advice is correct—
is so weak; it is not simply a matter of knowing whether policymakers
act on the views of experts, but also knowing whether the experts
are right. As President Johnson said, "A President's hardest task is
not to do what is right but to know what is right."[6] Because policy
experts are rarely evaluated for their skill in prediction, there is little
basis for evaluating their skill in telling policymakers "what is right."
This complicates the study of the use of policy analysis and the assessment of what makes a good policy analyst or how to train future
policy analysts.

As is now apparent, the policy analysis supplied to most state
legislatures is a far cry from that taught in many public policy programs. To be sure, some of the work produced by state NPROs is
relatively sophisticated and requires graduate-level training in economic modeling and statistics. However, the vast majority of the
work produced by state policy research organizations is of a more
technically pedestrian type: basic information on how other states
operate programs, descriptions of demographic trends, the costs of
operating existing programs, and so forth. Performing these tasks well
takes skill, to be sure, and several state policy research organizations
routinely hire graduates of public policy and administration programs
to conduct and oversee this work. In some states, highly technical
skills are used in developing budget forecasts, modeling economic
impacts, and so on, but, for the most part, the model state legislative policy analyst is focused primarily on gathering, collating, and

digesting information for policymakers, skills that require little of the technical proficiency taught and valued in public policy and management programs.

Most programs and schools of public policy and administration attract students whose median age is in the mid-20s and who have varied backgrounds and pursue varied careers in the public, non-profit, and private sectors. Therefore, schools focus on how they can best add value to students who are academically proficient and often possess significant work experience prior to arriving on campus.[7] In policy programs, problems (or at least apparent problems) are presented usually through case studies that depict a public leader with a challenging issue that requires some type of decision. Faculty recognize these as somewhat "canned" policy issues, yet students like the "real life" applications and case studies are useful in connecting technical and managerial skills learned in other courses with applications. But policy students also need to be able to *identify* current and future problems, not just provide solutions to hypothetical ones. Kentucky's Long-Term Policy Research Center has been highly effective in this regard; interviews with legislators in other states underscore this need elsewhere. Furthermore, policy analysis is about much more than technical expertise, and policy analysts need interpersonal skills to be effective professionally. Because of the importance of the individual in policy analysis, teaching interpersonal and communication skills is imperative to developing effective policy analysts.[8] Students who believe they will be effective simply by producing the most sophisticated analyses without effective communication will be sorely disappointed.

POLICY ANALYSIS AS TYRANNY?

Scholars have pointed to the potentially pernicious effects of policy analysis on the policymaking process. Suggesting that analysts "speak truth to power" and work to circumvent politics and public participation more generally, these scholars argue that the methods and techniques of policy analysis shut the public out of the discussion altogether and threaten democratic institutions (Banfield 1980; deLeon 1997; Dryzek 1989; Lindblom 1986). Is policy analysis vesting substantial power in an unelected elite, as some have suggested? The answer, at least in state NPROs, is in most respects an emphatic no.[9] If anything, the legislature and the state's political environment have shaped the conduct of policy analysis far more than policy analysis has shaped the conduct of the legislature.[10] Furthermore, the "two-communities" problem that has plagued the application of social science research to political action does not seem to be problematic in most state legislatures, in part because NPRO staff are, of necessity, more a part of the legislative community than of the research community. As a result, the nonpartisan staff is highly responsive to legislative—political—priorities.

The tyranny of analysis is all the more unlikely because of electronic access to, and low cost of disseminating, massive volumes of information. Legislators and their staff have instant access to copious information sources through the Internet, so the advantage of information access that NPROs once enjoyed is now dispersed throughout the legislature. Nonetheless, raw data are not screened and molded to fit policymakers' needs. Also, dissemination is a common property problem: If dissemination costs are low or zero, then policymakers are flooded with information, which makes dissemination a greater problem, not a solution; this is especially true with electronic means of dissemination. Therefore, NPROs must adjust to newer information technologies and focus on filtering, synthesis, and analysis, areas where they should enjoy a comparative advantage.

White was quoted in chapter 1:

> The action-intellectuals have no certain answers for tomorrow. . . .
> To measure something does not mean to understand it. . . . Their
> studies and surveys, however imperfect, are only road maps for the
> future showing the hazy contours of a new landscape. It is vital
> work—*as long as the mapmakers do not confuse themselves as tour
> directors.* (Quoted in Wood 1993, 39; my emphasis)

It is clear from the previous chapters that NPROs cannot in any way be confused with "tour directors." Indeed, they may be more akin to those who assist the tour operators, providing bits of information, sometimes organizing the logistics for the trips, and generally helping to make sure the papers are in order, helping the process run smoothly.

The successful NPROs, to their credit, do not expect or seek recognition for what their legislatures accomplish. As well, the strong political influence on NPROs suggests there is little concern for policy analysis organizations dominating democratic politics. To the contrary, the larger question is whether NPROs can survive and adapt to an increasingly partisan and term-limited political environment.

While much of the literature suggests the increasing politicization of research supporting political institutions (e.g., Heclo 1975), this study concludes that NPROs have been and are likely to continue to be generally cautious and neutral in their assessment of policies and to rely mostly on descriptive information in providing "analysis" to legislators. Therefore, building on the results of Bimber, albeit with a different research design, legislative institutions appear to greatly condition the nature of research and policy advice they receive. Rather than simply trying to find ways in which policy analysis is influential, or to be excessively concerned with tyrannical analysis, future research on knowledge utilization would do well to consider more fully the relationship between policy analysis and the political environment in which it operates.

The problem, rather than analytical tyranny, is the excessive cooptation of analysts by legislators, so that analytical independence—indeed analysis at all—is threatened and reduced to reporting facts. All legislators know they need information and facts, but not all legislators recognize the importance of other forms of policy analysis until they can see its contributions to their work. NPROs therefore need to be entrepreneurial in promoting something more than the provision of basic facts. Furthermore, in serving as reactive information providers rather than proactive analysts, NPROs fail to provide important perspectives and critical reviews that may not reach legislators without sufficient funding by interest groups. NPROs can provide an important check on biased analysis—as when legislators ask their NPROs to verify interest group claims—yet frequently they fail to provide perspectives not represented by well-financed interests.

INFORMATION AND ANALYSIS FOR POLITICS

Clearly, the message of this book for policy analysis is mixed. On the one hand, legislators value policy analysis and policy analysis is even influential at the margins in the policymaking process. On the other hand, much of what constitutes policy analysis in state NPROs is the provision of short-term factual information rather than in-depth studies, and NPROs are not considered to be influential in relation to other political institutions and actors. Additional research is needed to understand more thoroughly how and why policy research is useful to legislators and other decision makers, what factors influence the nature and conduct of policy analysis at the micro level, and what makes some policy research organizations particularly successful. A more nuanced view of how NPROs interact with and take their cues from legislatures can be obtained through detailed case studies examining state legislative policymaking and how policy research organizations—both partisan and nonpartisan—interact and compete with other information providers as well as legislators. Also needed is a better understanding of the research needs of legislators. Despite these caveats, this study indicates that, at least at the state level, policy analysis institutions are important and valued by their legislative clients, that their main function is providing information, and that larger and more analytical policy research organizations are both more highly valued and more influential than smaller, more descriptive institutions. Laurence Lynn argues, "The issue is not whether but how social science-based policy analysis will inform state action in ways that are both constructive and consistent with evolving American political values" (Lynn 2001, 188). While it is certainly true that social science research has important implications for policymaking, little attention is paid to the impact of politics on policy analysis and the institutions that ostensibly sustain it. Study of the reciprocal influence of politics and policy analysis—of power and knowledge—is fruitful research.

Based on empirical results of expertise in other professions and the limited value policymakers seem to place on policy research generally, such as that from universities, policy analysis should guard against strong claims of expertise. Mary Joe Bane, a prominent social welfare researcher and an official in the Department of Health and Human Services in the Clinton administration, suggests to analysts,

> The most important thing we should do, I believe, is to shift our
> perception from seeing ourselves mostly as expert problem solvers

to seeing ourselves mostly as participants in democratic deliberation. . . . We should be more self-conscious, realistic and modest
about what we do: that we are making contributions to public
discussion in which we do not control either the outcomes or the
use of our findings. (Bane 2001, 195)

Academic research is thought generally to have little direct
impact on policymaking, and many are skeptical of how academic
experts engage in the policymaking process (Krugman 1995b; Wilson
1978). Philip Cook, however, argues that appropriate institutional
structures are in place for channeling advice to policymakers; compared with academic disputes, he maintains, "when academic research enters the policy debate, the rules of engagement may be
somewhat different, and arguably for the better" (Cook 2003, 567).
Debating issues with policy implications "raises the stakes" beyond
purely academic disputes and becomes "more overtly adversarial."
Cook argues that "concern for one's academic reputation, and the
heightened possibility of being exposed to attack by other scholars
when working on policy-relevant issues, provides an important check
on [the tendency to make exaggerated claims]" (p. 567).

Regardless of how academics engage in the policymaking process, there is a clear distinction between the guild of scientific expertise and political expertise (e.g., James Carville, Karl Rove, and
other acknowledged "experts" in politics). There are clearly political experts—or at least those who can market themselves as such,
by dint of supporting candidates who win major elections—yet no
external authority sustains or sanctions that role. Political advice is
proffered in private rather than in public; there is not and, it is safe
to say, will never be a "Council of Political Advisers," in contrast
with the public institutional roles for economics (the Council of
Economic Advisers) and the sciences (the National Academies, the
Office of Science and Technology Policy, EPA's Science Advisory
Board, and so on). This is not to say that one form of advice is more
important, but that the type of advice—its intellectual origins and
its value as a public good—has an important effect on how it is used
in the policymaking process. Nonetheless, it is also clear that
external legitimacy does not necessarily confer greater policymaking
influence.

At one level, it would seem that NPROs can play a crucial role in bridging academic research and policymaking. As institutions embedded in the legislature, NPROs have the ear of policymakers and can earn their trust far more easily than can those outside the statehouse. Given the counterfactual of how decision makers make policy in the absence of good data and analysis, policy analysis would seem critical. As one observer put it, "So, one turns again to the pragmatism and incrementalism of the painful progress of science, natural and social, well aware of the uncertainties, false starts, and risks of failure. But the alternatives seem worse: politicians who rule by anecdote, analogy, or metaphor, who misread history, who look back to past solutions no longer appropriate; and government officials who still proceed by the numbers, repeating their experiences and searching for things as they used to be" (Wood 1993, 178). Put in these terms, between the slow, unsteady pace of policy research advances and policymakers' uninformed decisions, there remains ample room for policy analysts to make an impact.

Because the institutional relationship of NPROs to the legislature is so similar across states—virtually all NPROs report directly, and often only, to the legislature—there is no way to test comparatively whether other, more distant relationships would affect the power of NPROs. Nonetheless, evidence from interviews with NPRO directors is telling and, coupled with other research, suggests that trust is an important component to the influence NPROs have in the legislature. One NPRO director stated,

> While this work in the legislative trenches takes much time that could be devoted to more intensive policy research, I think it is this grunt work that, over time, makes our staff especially useful to legislators and instrumental in the decision-making process. We are in the field where the game is played. Over time, we develop deep, specialized knowledge of a subject that is at the same time very practical. We develop relationships with members and other players. We acquire credibility by doing many small things well, so members are more inclined to trust what we may do in the way of larger policy research and analysis. Ultimately, I think all this makes our policy work much more instrumental in the decision-making process than it would be if we were a more "removed" research or drafting office.

As Kingdon (and others) have stated, policy analysts must pick their moments of opportunity, the policy windows. When policy windows are open, good analysis can matter:

> To defeat a client group in a scramble for the public's interest, reformers must appeal heavily to reason. Only a strong case on the merits will attract the attention and support of those institutions that can effectively advocate the interest of the unorganized majority before Congress—namely, the presidency and the press. More directly, a strong showing on the merits is necessary to persuade Congress itself—especially key committee leaders—to terminate an existing special-interest policy. For legislators who are vulnerable to pressure from the client group, no amount of objective evidence may be sufficient. But for those who can afford to be "in doubt," support will hinge on what they find when they "turn on the merits." (Robyn 1987, 57)

Henry Aaron, an economist who served in HEW, notes the lack of theoretical development in the social sciences that thwarts any type of consensus on understanding or policy action. "One can be fairly confident . . . that at any given time there will coexist several theories consistent with any given set of facts that are more or less congenial to persons with differing political or philosophical predispositions" (Aaron 1978, 158). Describing the plight of policymakers, Aaron asks, "What is an ordinary member of the tribe to do when the witch doctors disagree?" (p. 159).

One study concluded that, "Congress is not as hostile an environment for expertise as is sometimes thought" (Bimber 1996, 98). Even in state legislatures, policy analysis institutions—even neutral ones—are held in high regard by their clients and are more influential the larger and more analytical they are. State NPROs have developed an effective form of expertise that state legislators need: attention to individual legislators' needs and a short-term policy focus coupled, in some cases, with additional forward-looking, longer-term analytical research. NPROs are extremely important as information providers, in both absolute and relative terms. Nonetheless, in general they are exceedingly reactive, attentive to short-term legislative requests but often without the inclination and/or the resources to be more forward-thinking and to generate new ideas and critical perspectives for legislators to consider. Like policy analysis organizations more generally, NPROs are well-advised to break the chains of short-term, reactive information provision and both expand and democratize their entry into the policymaking world. How NPROs handle changes in the contemporary political environment, including virtually limitless access to information and an increasingly partisan and term-limited political climate, will determine whether policy research organizations are reduced to basic information providers or challenged to serve as the analytical engines of their legislatures.

NOTES

1. Previous inquiries into the use of policy analysis focused on written policy analysis; while important, this is only a subset—possibly a small one—of what policy analysts produce. In the policy analysis organizations studied here, policy analysts spend a small portion of their time writing anything that policy scholars would consider policy analysis. Instead, much of their time is devoted to attending committee meetings and providing general staff support, briefing legislators and their staffs, providing factual information both written and oral, and other important functions of policy analysts.

2. Bimber's work (1996) on the OTA is an exception, as are studies of think tanks (Abelson 2002; Rich 2002, 2004; Smith 1991).

3. It strains credulity to believe that the causality runs in the opposite direction, i.e., that policy analysis institutions affect political institutions such as party control or state political culture.

4. These findings hinge on the definition of use. Use defined as rationalization or political or tactical is not associated with larger or more analytical NPROs.

5. *National Journal* 2004.

6. State of the Union address, January 4, 1965, cited in Goodwin 1991.

7. There are, to date, very few online programs.

8. Mintrom's recent book is perhaps the only one that addresses this issue squarely with good, practical suggestions for improving personal communication and "people skills" (Mintrom 2003).

9. Similar conclusions have been reached in other studies (Jenkins-Smith 1990; Whiteman 1995).

10. While this is not tested specifically, my conclusion is based on the

strong impact of politics on NPROs as well as the relative lack of influence of NRPOs in relation to other political actors in the state. The importance of basic information provision appears to be corroborated in other arenas. Even in the case of military intelligence, which is widely acknowledged to play a critical role in wartime, recent (albeit somewhat controversial) work suggests that while intelligence is important, its value has been overstated in relation to more fundamental attributes of wartime armies, such as armament, mobility, industrial capacity, tactical skill, and so forth (Keegan 2003). Keegan notes, "Results in war, in the last resort, are an affair of body, not mind; of physical force, not plans or intelligence. Over the longer run, of course, a power of superior intellectual resource will, if its superiority translates into possession of superior industrial, technical and demographic means, ineluctably overcome a power inferior in those qualities. There are no examples in military history of a state weaker in force than its enemy achieving victory in a protracted conflict. Force tells . . . [and] even the possession of the best intelligence does not guarantee victory" (219–20). And in a passage about military intelligence that could have been written about state NPROs, he writes, "Intelligence services have never been busier than they are in the nuclear world and consume more money than has ever before been spent. By far the greater proportion both of effort and funds is devoted, however, to early warning and to listening, continuous processes, intended to sustain security, not to achieve success in specific or short-term circumstances" (Keegan 2003, 296).

Summary of Survey Responses

Due to rounding, percentages may not sum to 100.

The respondent is the:	97% Legislator	3% Staff	0% Other

INFORMATION SOURCES

1. Please check the box indicating the importance of the following sources in helping you to understand and reach public policy decisions:	Never Important 1	2	3	4	5	6	Always Important 7	Mean
a. Legislative leaders	1%	3%	8%	17%	28%	25%	18%	5.1
b. Members (other legislators)	0	1	7	15	34	29	14	5.3
c. Nonpartisan legislative staff (or research office)	1	4	6	15	24	28	21	5.3
d. Partisan legislative staff	8	10	15	22	23	16	6	4.2
e. Legislative special committees or task forces	1	5	10	19	30	25	10	4.9
f. National organizations (e.g., CSG, NCSL)	4	12	15	25	23	16	6	4.2
g. Governor	5	12	18	26	20	12	6	4.1
h. Executive branch agencies	3	7	15	27	27	17	4	4.4
i. Political party organizations	8	18	22	28	16	5	3	3.5
j. Statewide interest groups/lobbyists/associations	1	5	13	28	35	15	3	4.5
k. Independent think tanks	5	9	16	25	27	14	4	4.2
l. University-based research organizations	3	8	16	20	29	17	6	4.4
m. Local grassroots and community organizations	1	2	6	19	31	28	13	5.2
n. Your constituents	0	1	2	8	20	28	40	5.9
o. Print and broadcast media	4	15	21	29	20	8	2	3.8
p. Internet/worldwide web	12	19	22	24	14	8	1	3.4

THE LEGISLATURE AND POLICYMAKING

2. Please check the box indicating your level of agreement or disagreement with the following statements:	Strongly Disagree 1	2	3	4	5	6	Strongly Agree 7	Mean
a. The legislature in my state is the most significant participant in public policy decisions.	1%	3%	8%	17%	29%	26%	16%	5.2
b. Most policy decisions in this chamber are made in committees.	3	6	10	16	24	28	13	4.9
c. Decision making in my chamber of the legislature is highly partisan.	2	6	12	18	23	21	18	4.9
d. A small group of people makes most of the legislative decisions.	4	7	11	14	23	26	16	4.9
e. My role is to look out for the needs of my district, more than for the needs of the state as a whole.	6	14	13	26	18	14	9	4.1
f. If there is a conflict, I would tend to vote for what the people in my district want, rather than for my own view of what is right.	11	17	17	16	14	15	10	3.9
g. Most of the policy-related information I need comes from sources inside the Legislature.	3	10	20	26	25	14	2	4.1
h. Overall, staff support in the legislature is sufficient.	12	13	11	11	22	23	8	4.2
i. I spend a lot of time developing public policy expertise.	1	5	14	19	29	22	9	4.7
j. Politics usually can be distinguished from the substance of public policy decisions.	2	8	13	24	27	21	4	4.5
k. I usually can make policy decisions without the need for policy analysis or research.	11	24	23	20	13	7	2	3.3

(continued)

POLICYMAKING INFLUENCE

3. Please check the box indicating your assessment of the relative influence of the following individuals or groups over policymaking for the entire Legislature:	No Influence						Dictate Policy	
	1	2	3	4	5	6	7	Mean
a. Your chamber	1%	1%	4%	24%	37%	27%	6%	5.0
b. Other chamber	2	4	10	29	30	20	4	4.6
c. Majority party leaders	1	3	6	11	28	36	16	5.3
d. Minority party leaders	5	23	30	24	12	4	1	3.3
e. Committee chairs	1	3	9	20	36	25	5	4.8
f. Nonpartisan legislative staff (or research office)	5	12	18	32	20	9	3	3.9
g. Partisan legislative staff	9	15	22	26	18	8	2	3.6
h. Governor	3	7	11	20	25	28	7	4.7
i. Executive branch agencies	1	5	15	31	31	14	2	4.4
j. Statewide interest groups/lobbyists/associations	1	3	12	26	39	16	2	4.6
k. Local grass-roots and community organizations	1	6	16	29	27	17	4	4.4
l. Media	5	18	25	28	18	6	1	3.5
m. Constituents	1	3	9	19	26	28	14	5.1

POLICY ANALYSIS AND RESEARCH

4. Please check the box indicating your level of agreement or disagreement with the following statements:	Strongly Disagree					Strongly Agree	
	1	2	3	4	5	6	7	Mean
a. I often feel overwhelmed by the volume of information related to public policy that is available to me.	4%	10%	11%	15%	24%	22%	15%	4.7
b. I often use policy analysis to understand how a policy works.	1	5	11	24	34	20	5	4.7
c. I usually seek out analysis and research to support a policy position I have already taken.	2	11	16	25	26	14	5	4.3
d. Legislators have all the information and analysis they need to make good public policy decisions.	13	19	21	16	17	11	4	3.5
e. If I need good nonpartisan analysis of a policy issue important to me, I can get it.	1	4	8	14	26	32	15	5.2
f. It is more important for legislative staff to gather and present me with information than to analyze it.	4	10	18	19	23	18	8	4.3
g. The legislature needs more nonpartisan policy analysis and research.	3	8	10	19	21	25	14	4.8
h. I would use additional policy analysis and research, if it were available.	2	6	11	16	23	26	15	4.9
i. In-depth research studies, such as those performed by universities or think tanks, are often valuable to me.	2	6	14	19	28	20	11	4.7
j. Nonpartisan staff are far more valuable to me than partisan staff.	3	7	10	19	19	24	18	4.9
k. As a practical matter, policy analysis and research can be very useful in delaying political decisions.	2	7	12	28	29	16	6	4.4
l. I prefer policy research and analysis that presents the facts and analysis and leaves the political decisions to me.	0	1	3	8	17	40	31	5.9
m. Information from partisan sources is not credible.	10	19	20	26	13	8	4	3.5

LEGISLATIVE SERVICES OFFICE/STAFF

Please check here if your chamber does *not* have a nonpartisan or bipartisan "Legislative Services Office," and skip to Question 7 below. 63 Respondents

5. Please check the box indicating the performance of your "Legislative Services Office" in the following areas, if applicable:	Excellent	Good	Average	Poor	Mean
a. Gathering and summarizing pertinent information	36	47	12	4	3.2
b. Financial analysis (e.g., projecting budgets or costs)	35	43	15	7	3.1
c. Conducting short-term policy research and analysis	22	44	25	9	2.8
d. Conducting long-term policy research and analysis	17	36	32	14	2.6
e. Evaluating current programs or policies	17	42	29	13	2.6
f. Bringing new ideas and fresh perspectives to the legislature	4	24	46	26	2.1
g. Providing a critical review of policy proposals	10	35	36	19	2.4
h. Communication and information brokering	13	34	38	14	2.5
i. Overall assessment of their performance in serving the legislature	21	49	22	8	2.8

6. Please check the box indicating your level of agreement or disagreement with the following statements:	Strongly Disagree 1	2	3	4	5	Strongly Agree 6	7	Mean
a. The "Legislative Services Office" primarily gathers and synthesizes information related to public policy; it doesn't analyze it.	4%	13%	15%	18%	19%	22%	8%	4.3
b. The "Legislative Services Office" is capable of conducting in-depth policy research.	6	7	11	17	21	26	12	4.9
c. The "Legislative Services Office" staff is well-respected in the legislature.	2	4	5	12	18	33	25	5.4
d. The "Legislative Services Office" is truly nonpartisan.	4	6	7	13	16	29	25	5.2
e. The "Legislative Services Office" is there to serve all legislators.	2	3	2	7	12	29	45	5.9
f. The amount of resources devoted to each of the functions performed by the "Legislative Services Office" is about right.	7	9	13	17	18	25	11	4.5

YOUR SERVICE IN THE LEGISLATURE

7. How many years have you served in the State Legislature?

a. House (or lower chamber) 8 years mean	b. Senate (or upper chamber) 7 years mean

8. Please describe your role in the legislature in 2002: *(please check all that apply)*

Leadership 22%	Committee Chair 27%	Committee Member 67%	Other 9%

The figures sum to more than 100% because some respondents checked more than one item.

9. How would you classify your legislative district?

Safe Democrat 14%	Mostly Democrat 24%	Competitive 29%	Mostly Republican 20%	Safe Republican 13%

10. As a legislator, do you consider yourself to be a:

Generalist 66%	Specialist 38%

The figures sum to more than 100% because some respondents checked more than one item.

(continued)

11. Over the past year, and taking into account all of your election and legislative responsibilities, what proportion of your total work time is legislative?

Less than 30% 6%	30-50% 29%	50-70% 33%	70-90% 24%	More than 90% 8%

12. On economic and fiscal issues (e.g., taxes, spending), your views are best described as:

Very liberal 6%	Fairly liberal 11%	Moderate 34%	Fairly conservative 37%	Very conservative 12%

13. On social issues (e.g., civil rights, immigration, gun control), your views are best described as:

Very liberal 15%	Fairly liberal 22%	Moderate 27%	Fairly conservative 24%	Very conservative 11%

14. Will you be serving in the legislature for the term beginning in 2003?

Yes 85%	Did not seek reelection 6%	Term limited 3%	Lost election 6%	Not sure 0%

ABOUT YOU

15. I am:

Female 30%	Male 70%

16. My current age is:

30 or under 0%	31-50 23%	51-70 64%	Over 70 13%

17. I describe my race/ethnicity as: *(please check all that apply)*

American Indian or Alaska Native 1%	Asian 1%	African American 4%	Hispanic 1%	Hawaiian or Pacific Islander 0%	White 94%

The figures sum to more than 100% because some respondents checked more than one item.

18. My party affiliation is:

Democratic 58%	Republican 42%	Green/Reform 0%	Independent/Other 1%

19. My highest level of formal education is: *(please check one)*

Some high school 0%	College graduate (four-year college) 23%
High school graduate 4%	Postgraduate education 51%
Some college 13%	Other 4%
College graduate (two year college) 4%	

20. My primary occupation is: *(please check one)*

Legislator 46%	Transportation, Communication, or Utilities 2%
Government (besides Legislature) 1%	Farming, Mining, or Construction 4%
Professional Services (law, medicine, finance/insurance, etc.) 21%	Military / Armed Forces 1%
Education 8%	Manufacturing 1%
Wholesale and Retail Trade 3%	Other 12%

21. When the Legislature is in session, I use email:

Daily 74%	Weekly 12%	Less than weekly 6%	Never 7%

References

Aaron, Henry J. 1978. *Politics and the Professors: The Great Society in Perspective*. Washington, D.C.: Brookings Institution.

Abelson, Donald E. 2002. *Do Think Tanks Matter? Assessing the Impact of Public Policy Institutes*. Montreal: McGill-Queen's Univ. Press.

Anderson, Lisa. 2003. *Pursuing Truth, Exercising Power: Social Science and Public Policy in the Twenty-First Century*. New York: Columbia Univ. Press.

Anzai, Yuichiro. 1991. "Learning and Use of Representations for Physics Expertise." In *Toward a General Theory of Expertise: Prospects and Limits*. K. Anders Ericsson and Jacqui Smith, eds. Cambridge: Cambridge Univ. Press, pp. 64–92.

Arnold, R. Douglas. 1979. *Congress and the Bureaucracy: A Theory of Influence*. New Haven, CT: Yale Univ. Press.

Bane, Mary Jo. 2001. "Presidential Address—Expertise, Advocacy, and Deliberation: Lessons from Welfare Reform." *Journal of Policy Analysis and Management* 20(2): 191–97.

Banfield, Edward C. 1980. "Policy Science and Metaphysical Madness." In *Bureaucrats, Policy Analysts and Statesmen*. Robert A. Goldwin, ed. Washington, D.C.: American Enterprise Institute.

Bardach, Eugene. 1977. *Implementation Game: What Happens after a Bill Becomes a Law*. Cambridge: MIT Press.

———. 2000. *A Practical Guide for Policy Analysis: The Eightfold Path to More Effective Problem Solving*. New York: Congressional Quarterly Press.

Barrilleaux, Charles. 1997. "A Test of the Independent Influences of Electoral Competition and Party Strength in a Model of State Policy-Making." *American Journal of Political Science* 41(4): 1462–66.

Berman, Evan M. 2001. *Essential Statistics for Public Managers and Policy Analysts*. Washington, D.C.: Congressional Quarterly Press.

Bibby, John F., and Thomas M. Holbrook. 1999. "Parties and Elections." In *Politics in the American States: A Comparative Analysis*. Virginia Gray, Russell L. Hanson, and Herbert Jacob, eds. Washington, D.C.: Congressional Quarterly Press.

Bimber, Bruce. 1991. "Information as a Factor in Congressional Politics." *Legislative Studies Quarterly* XVI(4): 585–605.

———. 1996. *The Politics of Expertise in Congress: The Rise and Fall of the Office of Technology Assessment*. Albany, NY: State Univ. of New York Press.

Bradley, Robert B. 1980. "Motivations in Legislative Information Use." *Legislative Studies Quarterly* 5(3): 393–406.

Brandl, John E. 1985. "Distilling Frenzy from Academic Scribbling: How Economics Influences Politicians." *Journal of Policy Analysis and Management* 4(3): 344–53.

Bryson, Lyman. 1951. "Notes on a Theory of Advice." *Political Science Quarterly*, 66(3): 321–39.

Burstein, Paul. 2002. "Interest Organizations, Information, and Policy Innovation in the U.S. Congress." Paper presented at the *2002 Annual Meeting of the American Political Science Association*, Aug. 29–Sept. 1.

Camerer, Colin F., and Eric J. Johnson. 1991. "The Process-Performance Paradox in Expert Judgment: How Can Experts Know So Much and Predict So Badly?" In *Toward a General Theory of Expertise: Prospects and Limits*. K. Anders Ericsson and Jacqui Smith, eds. Cambridge: Cambridge Univ. Press.

Caplan, Nathan. 1979. "The Two-Communities Theory and Knowledge Utilization." *American Behavioral Scientist* 22: 459–70.

Caplan, Nathan, Andrea Morrison, and R. Stambaugh. 1975. "The Use of Social Science Knowledge in Policy Decisions at the National Level." Ann Arbor, MI: Institute for Social Research.

Carson, Rachel. 1962. *Silent Spring*. Boston: Houghton-Mifflin.

Charness, Neil. 1991. "Expertise in Chess: The Balance between Knowledge and Search." In *Toward a General Theory of Expertise: Prospects and Limits*. K. Anders Ericsson and Jacqui Smith, eds. Cambridge: Cambridge Univ. Press.

Clucas, Richard A. 2003. "Improving the Harvest of State Legislative Research." *State Politics and Policy Quarterly* 3(4): 387–419.

Cook, Philip J. 2003. "Meeting the Demand for Expert Advice on Drug Policy." *Criminology & Public Policy* 2(3): 565–70.

Council of State Governments. 2000. CSG *State Directory II: Legislative Leadership, Committees & Staff 2000.* Lexington, KY: CSG.

Cox, Gary, and Matthew McCubbins. 1993. *Legislative Leviathan: Party Government in the House.* Berkeley, CA: Univ. of California Press.

Danziger, Sheldon. 2001. "Welfare Reform from Nixon to Clinton: What Role for Social Science?" In *Social Science and Policy-Making: The Search for Relevance in the Twentieth Century.* David L. Featherman and Maris A. Vinovskis, eds. Ann Arbor, MI: Univ. of Michigan Press.

Davidson, Roger H. 1976. "Congressional Committees: The Toughest Customers." *Policy Analysis* 2(2): 299–324.

Dawson, Richard E., and James A. Robinson. 1963. "Inter-Party Competition, Economic Variables, and Welfare Policies in the American States." *Journal of Politics* 25(2): 265–89.

deLeon, Peter. 1997. *Democracy and the Policy Sciences.* Albany, NY: State Univ. of New York Press.

DeMartini, Joseph R., and Les B. Whitbeck. 1986. "Knowledge Use as Knowledge Creation." *Knowledge: Creation, Diffusion, Utilization* 7(4): 383–96.

Derthick, Martha, and Paul J. Quirk. 1985. *The Politics of Deregulation.* Washington, D.C.: The Brookings Institution.

Dillman, Don A. 2000. *Mail and Internet Surveys: The Tailored Design Method,* 2nd ed. New York: John Wiley & Sons.

Dreyfus, Daniel A. 1977. "The Limitations of Policy Research in Congressional Decision Making." In *Using Social Research in Public Policy Making.* Carol H. Weiss, ed. Lexington, MA.: Lexington Books.

Dryzek, John S. 1989. "Policy Sciences of Democracy." *Polity* 22(1): 97–118.

Dunn, William N. 1986. "Improving Social Research for Policymaking." *Knowledge: Creation, Diffusion, Utilization* 7(4): 339–43.

Durning, Dan. 1993. "Participatory Policy Analysis in a Social Service Agency: A Case Study." *Journal of Policy Analysis and Management* 12(2): 231–57.

Elazar, Daniel J. 1984. *American Federalism: A View from the States,* 3rd ed. New York: Harper & Row.

Ericsson, K Anders, and Jacqui Smith. 1991. "Prospects and Limits of the Empirical Study of Expertise: An Introduction." In *Toward a General Theory of Expertise: Prospects and Limits.* K. Anders Ericsson and Jacqui Smith, eds. Cambridge: Cambridge Univ. Press.

Erikson, Robert S., Gerald C. Wright, and John P. McIver. 1993. *Statehouse Democracy: Public Opinion and Policy in the American States.* Cambridge: Cambridge Univ. Press.

Eviatar, Daphne. 2003. "Do Aid Studies Govern Policies or Reflect Them?" *New York Times*, July 26, A17–19.

Farrow, Scott. 1991. "Does Analysis Matter? Economics and Planning in the Department of the Interior." *Review of Economics and Statistics* 73: 172–76.

Featherman, David L. and Maris A. Vinovskis. 2001a. "Growth and Use of Social and Behavioral Science in the Federal Government since World War II." In *Social Science and Policy-Making: A Search for Relevance in the Twentieth Century*, eds. David L. Featherman and Maris A. Vinovskis. Ann Arbor, MI: Univ. of Michigan Press.

———. 2001b. "In Search of Relevance to Social Reform and Policy-Making." In *Social Science and Policy-Making: A Search for Relevance in the Twentieth Century*, eds. David L. Featherman and Maris A. Vinovskis. Ann Arbor, MI: Univ. of Michigan Press.

Feller, Irwin, Michael R. King, Donald C. Menzel, Robert E. O'Connor, Peter A. Wissel, and Thomas Ingersoll. 1979. "Scientific and Technological Information in State Legislatures." *American Behavioral Scientist* 22(3): 417–36.

Fenno, Richard F. 1978. *Home Style: House Members in Their Districts*. Boston: Little, Brown and Co.

Ferejohn, John A. 1974. *Pork Barrel Politics: Rivers and Harbors Legislation, 1947–1968*. Stanford, CA: Stanford Univ. Press.

Fiorina, Morris P. 1977. *Congress: Keystone of the Washington Establishment*. New Haven, CT: Yale Univ. Press.

Fischer, Frank. 1992. "Restructuring Policy Analysis: A Postpositivist Perspective." *Policy Sciences* 333–39.

———. 2000. *Citizens, Experts, and the Environment*. Durham, NC: Duke Univ. Press.

Friedman, Lee S. 1999. "Peanuts Envy?" *Journal of Policy Analysis and Management* 18(2): 211–25.

Goodman, Billy. 2000. "Science Advice in Congress after OTA." *BioScience* 50(6): 486.

Goodwin, Doris Kearns. 1991. *Lyndon Johnson and the American Dream*. New York: St. Martin's Griffin, 215

Gray, Virginia. 1999. "The Socioeconomic and Political Context of States. In *Politics in the American States: A Comparative Analysis*, Virginia Gray, Russell L. Hanson, and Herbert Jacob, eds. Washington, D.C.: Congressional Quarterly Press.

Gray, Virginia, and David Lowery. 2000. "Where Do Policy Ideas Come From? A Study of Minnesota Legislators and Staffers." *Journal of Public Administration Research and Theory* 10(3): 573–97.

Greenberg, David H., and Marvin B. Mandell. 1991. "Research Utilization in Policymaking: A Tale of Two Series (of Social Experiments)." *Journal of Policy Analysis and Management* 10(4): 633–56.

Greenberg, David, Marvin Mandell, and Matthew Onstott. 2000. "The Dissemination and Utilization of Welfare-to-Work Experiments in State Policymaking." *Journal of Policy Analysis and Management* 19(3): 367–82.

Greenberger, Martin. 1983. *Caught Unawares: The Energy Decade in Retrospect.* Cambridge, MA: Ballinger Publishing Co.

Grossback, Lawrence J., and David A. M. Peterson. 2004. "Understanding Institutional Change: Legislative Staff Development and the State Policymaking Environment." *American Politics Research* 32(1): 26–51.

Gueron, Judith. 2002. "Roundtable on TANF," APPAM Conference, November 8, Washington, D.C.

Guston, David H., Megan Jones, and Lewis M. Branscomb. 1997. "The Demand for and Supply of Technical Information and Analysis in State Legislatures." *Policy Studies Journal* 25(3): 451–69.

Halberstam, David. 1983. *The Best and the Brightest.* New York: Penguin Books.

Hamm, Keith E., and Gary F. Moncrief. 1999. "Legislative Politics in the States." In *Politics in the American States: A Comparative Analysis.* Virginia Gray, Russell L. Hanson, and Herbert Jacob, eds. Washington, D.C.: Congressional Quarterly Press.

Harrington, Michael. 1962. *The Other America.* New York: Macmillan.

Haskins, Ron. 1991. "Congress Writes a Law: Research and Welfare Reform." *Journal of Policy Analysis and Management* 10(4): 616–32.

———. 2002. Special Assistant to the President. Roundtable on TANF, APPAM Conference, November 8, Washington, D.C.

Haveman, Robert H. 1976. "Policy Analysis and the Congress: An Economist's View." *Policy Analysis* 2(2): 235–50.

Heclo, Hugh. 1975. "OMB and the Presidency: The Problem of 'Neutral Competence'." *The Public Interest* 38: 80–98.

Hero, Rodney E., and Caroline J. Tolbert. 1996. "A Racial/Ethnic Diversity Interpretation of Politics and Policy in the States of the U.S." *American Journal of Political Science* 40(3): 851–71.

Hill, Elizabeth G. 2003. "California's Legislative Analyst's Office: An Isle of Independence." *Spectrum: The Journal of State Government,* 26–29.

Hird, John A. 1991. "The Political Economy of Pork: Project Selection at the U.S. Army Corps of Engineers." *American Political Science Review* 85(2): 429–56.

226   **REFERENCES**

Jackson-Elmoore, Cynthia, Jack H. Knott, and J. V. Verkuilen. 1998. "An Overview of the State Legislators Survey: Sources of Information and Term Limit Impacts." W. K. Kellogg Foundation.

Jenkins-Smith, Hank C. 1990. *Democratic Politics and Policy Analysis*. Pacific Grove, CA: Brooks/Cole.

Johnson, Charles A. 1976. "Political Culture in American States: Elazar's Formulation Examined." *American Journal of Political Science* 20, 491–509.

Jones, Charles O. 1976. "Why Congress Can't Do Policy Analysis (or Words to That Effect)." *Policy Analysis*, 251–64.

Jones, Megan, David H. Guston, and Lewis M. Branscomb. 1996. *Informed Legislatures: Coping with Science in a Democracy*. Lanham, MD: University Press of America.

Karning, Albert K., and Lee Sigelman. 1975. "State Legislative Reform and Public Policy: Another Look." *Western Political Quarterly* 28, 548–52.

Keegan, John. 2003. *Intelligence in War: Knowledge of the Enemy from Napoleon to Al-Queda*. New York: Knopf.

Kingdon, John W. 1984. *Agendas, Alternatives, and Public Policies*. Boston: Little, Brown & Co.

Kirp, David L. 1992. "The End of Policy Analysis." *Journal of Policy Analysis and Management* 11(4): 693–96.

Klingman, David, and William W. Lammers. 1984. "The 'General Policy Liberalism' Factor in American State Politics." *American Journal of Political Science* 28(3): 598–610.

Knott, Jack, and Aaron Wildavsky. 1980. "If Dissemination Is the Solution, What Is the Problem?" *Knowledge: Creation, Diffusion, Utilization* 1(4): 537–78.

Kolbert, Elizabeth. 2003. "Accountants in the Sky." *The New Yorker*, May 19, 38–43.

Krehbiel, Keith. 1991. *Information and Legislative Organization*. Ann Arbor, MI: Univ. of Michigan Press.

Krugman, Paul. 1995a. "The End Is Not Quite Nigh." *The Economist* April 29

———. 1995b. *Peddling Prosperity: Economic Sense and Nonsense in an Age of Diminished Expectations*. New York: W. W. Norton & Co.

Larsen, Judith K. 1980. "Knowledge Utilization: What Is It?" *Knowledge: Creation, Diffusion, Utilization* 1(3): 421–42.

Lester, James P. 1993. "The Utilization of Policy Analysis by State Agency Officials." *Knowledge: Creation, Diffusion, Utilization* 14(3): 267–90.

Lindblom, Charles E. 1986. "Who Needs What Social Research for Policy-making?" *Knowledge: Creation, Diffusion, Utilization* 7(4): 345–66.

———. 1990. *Inquiry and Change: The Troubled Attempt to Understand & Shape Society.* New Haven, CT: Yale Univ. Press.

Lindblom, Charles E., and David K. Cohen. 1979. *Usable Knowledge: Social Science and Social Problem Solving.* New Haven, CT: Yale Univ. Press.

Lipsky, Michael. 1983. *Street Level Bureaucracy.* New York: Russell Sage Foundation.

Lupia, Arthur, and Mathew D. McCubbins. 1994. "Who Controls? Information and the Structure of Legislative Decision Making." *Legislative Studies Quarterly* XIX(3): 361–84.

———. 1998. *The Democratic Dilemma: Can Citizens Learn What They Need to Know?* Cambridge: Cambridge Univ. Press.

Lynn, Laurence E. 1987. "My Dinner with Andrea." *Journal of Policy Analysis and Management* 6(3): 438–45.

———. 2001. "The Making and Analysis of Public Policy: A Perspective on the Role of Social Science." In *Social Science and Policy-Making: A Search for Relevance in the Twentieth Century,* David L. Featherman and Maris A. Vinovskis, eds. Ann Arbor, MI: Univ. of Michigan Press.

Maass, Arthur. 1951. *Muddy Waters: The Army Corps of Engineers and the Nation's Rivers.* Cambridge, MA: Harvard Univ. Press.

MacRae, Duncan. 1973. "Science and the Formation of Policy in a Democracy." *Minerva* 11: 228–42.

———. 1976. *The Social Function of Social Science.* New Haven: Yale Univ. Press.

Maestas, Cherie, Grant W. Neeley, and Lilliard E. Richardson. 2003. "The State of Surveying Legislators: Dilemmas and Suggestions." *State Politics and Policy Quarterly* 3(1): 90–108.

Mandell, Marvin B., and Vicki L. Sauter. 1984. "Approaches to the Study of Information Utilization in Public Agencies." *Knowledge: Creation, Diffusion, Utilization* 6(2): 145–64.

Mayhew, David R. 1974. *Congress: The Electoral Connection.* New Haven, CT: Yale Univ. Press.

McCubbins, Mathew D., and Talbot Page. 1987. "A Theory of Congressional Delegation." In *Congress: Structure and Policy.* Mathew D. McCubbins and Terry Sullivan, eds. Cambridge: Cambridge Univ. Press, 409–25.

McCubbins, Mathew D., and Thomas Schwartz. 1984. "Congressional Oversight Overlooked: Police Patrols versus Fire Alarms." *American Journal of Political Science* 2(1): 165–79.

Mead, Lawrence M. 2002. "State Governmental Capacity and Welfare Reform." Presented at the Annual Meeting of the American Political Science Association, August 29–September 1.

Meltsner, Arnold J. 1976. *Policy Analysts in the Bureaucracy*. Berkeley: Univ. of California Press.

Mintrom, Michael. 2003. *People Skills for Policy Analysts*. Washington, D.C.: Georgetown Univ. Press.

Moe, Terry M. 1987. "An Assessment of the Postive Theory of 'Congressional Dominance'." *Legislative Studies Quarterly* 12(4): 475–520.

Mooney, Christopher Z. 1991a. "Information Sources in State Legislative Decision Making." *Legislative Studies Quarterly* 16(3): 445–55.

———. 1991b. "Peddling Information in the State Legislature: Closeness Counts." *Western Political Quarterly* 433–44.

Moore, Mark H. 1990. "What Sort of Ideas Become Public Ideas?" In *The Power of Public Ideas*. Robert B. Reich, ed. Cambridge, MA: Harvard Univ. Press, 55–83.

Morehouse, Sarah McCally, and Malcolm E. Jewell. 2003. *State Politics, Parties, & Policy*, 2nd ed. Lanham, MD: Rowman & Littlefield Publishers.

Morgan, David R., and Sheilah S. Watson. 1991. "Political Culture, Political System Characteristics, and Public Policies among the American States." *Publius: The Journal of Federalism*, 31–48.

Nader, Ralph. 1965. *Unsafe at Any Speed: The Designed-In Dangers of the American Automobile*. New York: Grossman.

Nathan, Richard P. 2000. *Social Science in Government: The Role of Policy Researchers*. Albany, NY: Rockefeller Institute Press.

National Conference of State Legislatures. 1999. *Legislative Staff Services*. Denver, CO: NCSL.

National Journal 2004. January 10, cover.

National Science Foundation. 2001. *Survey of Federal Funds for Research and Development: Fiscal Years 1999, 2000, and 2001*, Table A. Arlington, VA.

Nelson, Richard R. 1977. *The Moon and the Ghetto*. New York: W. W. Norton.

———. 1989. "The Office of Policy Analysis in the Department of the Interior." *Journal of Policy Analysis and Management* 8(3): 395–410.

North, Douglass C. 1990. *Institutions, Institutional Change and Economic Performance*. Cambridge: Cambridge Univ. Press.

———. 1993. "Toward a Theory of Institutional Change." In *Political Economy: Institutions, Competition, and Representation*. William A.

Barnett, Melvin J. Hinich, and Norman J. Schofield, eds. Cambridge: Cambridge Univ. Press.

Pack, Janet Rothenberg. 1974. "The Use of Urban Models in Urban Policy Making." Fels Center of Government, Univ. of Pennsylvania, Philadelphia, PA.

Page, Benjamin I., and Robert Y. Shapiro. 1992. *The Rational Public: Fifty Years of Trends in Americans' Policy Preferences*. Chicago: Univ. of Chicago Press.

Page, Benjamin I., Robert Y. Shapiro, and Glenn R. Dempsey. 1987. "What Moves Public Opinion?" *American Political Science Review* 81(1): 23–43.

Patton, Michael Q., Patricia Smith Grimes, Kathryn M. Guthrie, Nancy J. Brennan, Barbara Dickey French, and Dale A. Blyth. 1977. "In Search of Impact: An Analysis of the Utilization of Federal Health Evaluation Research." In *Using Social Research in Public Policy Making*. Carol H. Weiss, ed. Lexington, MA: Lexington Books.

Porter, H. Owen. 1974. "Legislative Experts and Outsiders: The Two-Step Flow of Communication." *Journal of Politics*: 703–30.

Posner, Richard A. 2001. *Public Intellectuals: A Study of Decline*. Cambridge, MA: Harvard Univ. Press.

Pressman, Jeffrey L., and Aaron Wildavsky. 1984. *Implementation*. Berkeley: Univ. of California Press.

Pugliaresi, Lucian, and Diane T. Berliner. 1989. "Policy Analysis at the Department of State: The Policy Planning Staff." *Journal of Policy Analysis and Management* 8(3): 379–94.

Radin, Beryl A. 2000. *Beyond Machiavelli: Policy Analysis Comes of Age*. Washington, D.C.: Georgetown Univ. Press.

Ray, David. 1982. "The Sources of Voting Cues in Three State Legislatures." *Journal of Politics* 44: 1078–87.

Ricci, David M. 1993. *The Transformation of American Politics: The New Washington and the Rise of Think Tanks*. New Haven, CT: Yale Univ. Press.

Rich, Andrew. 2001. "The Politics of Expertise in Congress and the News Media." *Social Science Quarterly* 82(3): 583–601.

———. 2002. "The Characteristics and Influence of State Think Tanks." Public Policy Institute of California, San Francisco, CA.

———. 2004. *Think Tanks, Public Policy, and the Politics of Expertise*. Cambridge: Cambridge Univ. Press.

Rich, Robert F. 2001. *Social Science Information and Public Policy Making*. New Brunswick, NJ: Transaction Publishers.

Rich, Robert F. and Neal M. Goldsmith. 1983. "The Utilization of Policy Research." In *Encyclopedia of Policy Studies*, ed. Stuart S. Nagel. New York: Marcel Dekker, Inc., 93–115.

Robyn, Dorothy. 1987. *Braking the Special Interests: Trucking Deregulation and the Politics of Policy Reform.* Chicago: Univ. of Chicago Press.

Rosenthal, Alan. 1998. *The Decline of Representative Democracy.* Washington, D.C.: Congressional Quarterly Books.

Rourke, Francis E. 1992. "Responsiveness and Neutral Competence in American Bureaucracy." *Public Administration Review*: 539–46.

Roy, Arundhati. 2001. *Power Politics.* Cambridge, MA: South End Press.

Sabatier, Paul, and David Whiteman. 1985. "Legislative Decision Making and Substantive Policy Information: Models of Information Flow." *Legislative Studies Quarterly* 10(3): 395–421.

Sandler, Craig. 1990a. *State House News Service,* online edition. Accessed on January 9 at www.statehousenews.com.

———. 1990b. "Chronology." *State House News Service,* online edition. Accessed on November 14 at www.statehousenews.com.

Sawhill, Isabel. 2002. Roundtable on TANF, APPAM Conference, November 8, Washington, D.C.

Schick, Allen. 1976. "The Supply and Demand for Analysis on Capitol Hill." *Policy Analysis* 2(2): 215–34.

Schneider, Anne Larason, and Helen M. Ingram. 1997. *Policy Design for Democracy.* Lawrence, KS: Univ. of Kansas Press.

Schneider, Saundra K., and William G. Jacoby. 1999. "Variability in State Policy Priorities: 1982–1992." Prepared for delivery at the 1999 Annual Meetings of the American Political Science Association, August, Atlanta, GA.

Schon, Donald A., and Martin Rein. 1994. *Frame Reflection: Toward the Resolution of Intractable Policy Controversies.* New York: Basic Books.

Sharkansky, Ira. 1968. *Spending in American States.* Chicago: Rand McNally.

Sharkansky, Ira, and Richard I. Hofferbert. 1969. "Dimensions of State Politics, Economics, and Public Policy." *American Political Science Review* 63: 867–79.

Shepsle, Kenneth A., and Barry R. Weingast. 1994. "Positive Theories of Congressional Institutions." *Legislative Studies Quarterly* XIX(2): 149–79.

Shulock, Nancy. 1999. "The Paradox of Policy Analysis: If It Is Not Used, Why Do We Produce So Much of It?" *Journal of Policy Analysis and Management* 18(2): 226–44.

Sinclair, Upton. 1905. *The Jungle.* New York: Doubleday.

Smith, Bruce L.R. 1992. *The Advisers: Scientists in the Policy Process.* Washington, D.C.: Brookings Institution.

Smith, James A. 1991. *The Idea Brokers: Think Tanks and the Rise of the New Policy Elite.* New York: Free Press.

Snow, C. P. 1961. *Science and Government*. Cambridge, MA: Harvard Univ. Press.

Songer, Donald R., James M. Underwood, Sonja G. Dillon, Patricia E. Jameson, and Darla W. Kite. 1985. "Voting Cues in Two State Legislatures: A Further Application of the Kingdon Model." *Social Science Quarterly* 983–90.

Steele, Joe L. 1971. *The Use of Econometric Models by Federal Regulatory Agencies*. Lexington, MA: Lexington Books.

Stokey, Edith, and Richard Zeckhauser. 1978. *A Primer on Policy Analysis*. New York: W. W. Norton.

Stone, Deborah A. 1989. "Causal Stories and the Formation of Policy Agendas." *Political Science Quarterly* 104(2): 281–300.

———. 1997. *Policy Paradox: The Art of Political Decision Making*. New York: W. W. Norton.

Stuart, Elaine. 2001. "Taking the Long View." *State Government News*: 10–17.

Szanton, Peter. 1981. *Not Well Advised*. New York: Russell Sage Foundation.

———. 1991. "The Remarkable 'Quango': Knowledge, Politics, and Welfare Reform." *Journal of Policy Analysis and Management* 10(4): 590–602.

Thomas, Clive S., and Ronald J. Hrebenar. 1999. "Interest Groups in the States." In *Politics in the American States: A Comparative Analysis*. Virginia Gray, Russell L. Hanson and Herbert Jacob, eds. Washington, D.C.: Congressional Quarterly Press, 113–43.

U.S. Bureau of the Census. 1975. *Historical Statistics of the United States: Colonial Times to 1970*. Washington, D.C.

———. 2003. *Statistical Abstract of the United States*. Washington, D.C.

U.S. Office of Management and Budget. 2002. *The Budget for Fiscal Year 2003: Historical Tables*, Table 9.7. Washington, D.C.: U.S. Government Printing Office.

Uslaner, Eric M., and Ronald E. Weber. 1977. *Patterns of Decision Making in State Legislatures*. New York: Praeger Publishers.

Weaver, R. Kent, and Paul B. Stares, eds. 2001. *Guidance for Governance: Comparing Alternative Sources of Public Policy Advice*. Tokyo: Japan Center for International Exchange.

Weimer, David Leo, and Aiden R. Vining. 1998. *Policy Analysis: Concepts and Practice, 3rd edition*. Englewood Cliffs, NJ: Prentice Hall.

Weingast, Barry R., and Mark J. Moran. 1983. "Bureaucratic Discretion or Congressional Control? Regulatory Policymaking by the Federal Trade Commission." *Journal of Political Economy*: 765–800.

Weiss, Carol H. 1978. "Improving the Linkage between Social Research and Public Policy." In *Knowledge and Policy: The Uncertain Connection*, ed. Laurence E. Lynn Jr. Washington, D.C.: National Academy of Sciences.

———. 1979. "The Many Meanings of Research Utilization." *Public Administration Review* 5: 426–31.

———. 1980. "Knowledge Creep and Decision Accretion." *Knowledge: Creation, Diffusion, Utilization* 1(3): 381–404.

———, ed. 1982. *Organizations for Policy Analysis: Helping Government Think.* Beverly Hills, CA: Sage Publications.

———. 1989. "Congressional Committees as Users of Analysis." *Journal of Policy Analysis and Management* 8(3): 411–31.

———. 1992. "Helping Government Think: Functions and Consequences of Policy Analysis Organizations." In *Organizations for Policy Analysis: Helping Government Think*, Carol H. Weiss, ed. Newbury Park, CA: Sage Publications.

Weiss, Carol H., and Michael J. Bucuvalas. 1980. *Social Science Research and Decision Making.* New York: Columbia Univ. Press.

Whiteman, David. 1985. "The Fate of Policy Analysis in Congressional Decision Making: Three Types of Use in Committees." *Western Political Quarterly* 38: 294–311.

———. 1995. *Communication and Congress: Members, Staff, and the Search for Information.* Lawrence, KS: Univ. of Kansas Press.

Williams, Bruce A., and Albert R. Matheny. 1984. "Testing Theories of Social Regulation: Hazardous Waste Regulation in the American States." *Journal of Politics* 46: 428–58.

Wilson, James Q. 1978. "Social Science and Public Policy: A Personal Note." In *Knowledge and Policy: The Uncertain Connection.* Laurence E. Lynn, Jr., ed. Washington, D.C.: National Academy of Sciences.

Wittman, Donald. 1995. *The Myth of Democratic Failure: Why Political Institutions Are Efficient.* Chicago: Univ. of Chicago Press.

Wood, Robert C. 1993. *Whatever Possessed the President? Academic Experts and Presidential Policy, 1960–1988.* Amherst, MA: Univ. of Massachusetts Press.

Index